T · H · E
AGGRESSIONS
OF CIVILIZATION

T · H · E
AGGRESSIONS
OF CIVILIZATION

Federal Indian Policy
since the 1880s

Edited by
Sandra L. Cadwalader and Vine Deloria, Jr.

Temple University Press
PHILADELPHIA

Temple University Press, Philadelphia 19122
© 1984 by Temple University. All rights reserved
Published 1984
Printed in the United States of America

Library of Congress Cataloging in Publication Data
Main entry under title:

The Aggressions of civilization.

 Includes bibliographical references and index.
 1. Indians of North America—Government relations—
1869–1934—Addresses, essays, lectures. 2. Indians of
North America—Government relations—1934-   —Addresses,
essays, lectures. 3. Indians of North America—Legal
status, laws, etc.—Addresses, essays, lectures.
I. Cadwalader, Sandra L. II. Deloria, Vine.
E93.A34 1984   323.1′197   84-94
ISBN O-87722-349-1

C O N T R I B U T O R S

SANDRA L. CADWALADER has been executive director of the Indian Rights Association since 1978 and on the Board since 1976. She has published and written for *Indian Truth*, the Association's bi-monthly journal on contemporary Indian affairs.

VINE DELORIA, JR., a Standing Rock Sioux, is author of *Custer Died for Your Sins*, *God is Red*, *Behind the Trail of Broken Treaties*, *The Metaphysics of Modern Existence*, and co-author of *American Indians, American Justice*. A professor of political science at the University of Arizona, Mr. Deloria has directed its graduate program of American Indian Policy Studies. He serves on the Board of the Indian Rights Association.

ROBERT T. COULTER is executive director of the Indian Law Resource Center, a non-profit law firm. An enrolled member of the Citizen Band of Potawatomi, he serves as chairperson of the American Bar Association's Committee on the Problems of the American Indian.

ANN LAQUER ESTIN is a law clerk for the U.S. District Court for the District of Colorado. A former editor of *Indian Truth*, her article "The Federal Plenary Power in Indian Affairs After *Weeks* and *Sioux Nation*," appeared in November 1982 in the *University of Pennsylvania Law Review*, for which she was article editor.

LAURENCE M. HAUPTMAN is an associate professor of history at the State University of New York at New Paltz. He is author of *The Iroquois and the New Deal* and co-editor of *Neighbors and Intruders: An Ethnohistorical Exploration of the Indians of Hudson's River*.

JAMES E. OFFICER is a professor of anthropology at the University of Arizona. He has served as associate commissioner of Indian Affairs and as assistant to Secretary of the Interior Stewart L. Udall, and is author of numerous articles on American Indians and Latin American affairs.

DAVID M. STRAUSFELD, a law student at the University of Pennsylvania, studied Indian reform efforts while a history major at Princeton University; the chapter appearing here is adapted from his thesis.

STEVEN M. TULLBERG is senior staff attorney for the Indian Law Resource Center, where he has worked with his co-author, Mr. Coulter, to bring Indian cases before international forums including the United Nations Working Group on Indigenous Populations.

WILCOMB E. WASHBURN is director of the Office of American Studies at the Smithsonian Institution. He is author of *Red Man's Land, White Man's Law*, and *The Assault on Indian Tribalism: The General Allotment Law of 1887* and editor of *The Indian and the White Man* and *The American Heritage History of the Indian Wars*.

ALVIN J. ZIONTZ, a partner in the Seattle law firm of Ziontz, Pirtle, Morisset, Ernstoff, and Chestnut, is active with the Indian rights committees of the American Civil Liberties Union and the American Bar Association. He has taught and written widely about federal Indian law.

C O N T E N T S

Sandra L. Cadwalader

*M*any of the policies of reform advocated by the humanitarian "Friends of the Indians" of the 1880s are those which, if advocated today, could be fairly labelled reactionary and anti-Indian. In few public policy endeavors has the American liberal instinct been so consistently baffled as it has been in the effort to formulate a truly just approach to the Indians of this country.

Generations of white reformers and politicians have surveyed conditions prevailing among Indians of their time and pronounced them a disgrace. Condemning the insensitivity and inhumanity of their predecessors, each generation formulates "solutions" that reveal more about the non-Indian conscience of the period than the real nature of the Indian "problem." A brief euphoria ensues in which it is believed that the problem, at last understood, will be resolved. Disillusion, however, gradually sets in as the new approach is discovered to bring with it entirely different kinds of debilitating consequences.

That Indian tribes have survived in a society based on values fundamentally antithetical to their own, and one whose policy towards tribalism has swung from extreme to extreme, is an accomplishment of no small order. And if there is a single lesson to be learned from studying the past century of federal Indian policy, it is that the tribes—with their claims to land, water, hunting and fishing rights, to the right to self-government and to cultural preservation—will persist despite the most determined federal efforts to destroy or ignore them.

Most non-Indians, having learned little more than the familiar stories about Indians-at-Thanksgiving, Pocahontas and Sacajawea, are surprised to find modern Indian tribes laying claims to large portions of Eastern states, to one-half of the valuable salmon and steelhead catch in the Pacific Northwest, and to water rights in the parched Southwest. Non-Indians are even more surprised, if not outraged, to find these claims to be legitimate ones that may threaten their property or livelihoods. As the assumption that the Indians are simply

ix

crying over spilt milk gives way to an uneasy recognition that the tribal claims have validity under federal law, they want to know why the unholy mess was not resolved years, decades, or centuries ago.

Nothing, it seems, is as enduring in this country as tribal claims on one hand, and on the other, non-Indian fantasies that the tribes and their claims will disappear if only we wait long enough. After the 1637 massacre of the Pequots in Connecticut at the hands of the Puritans, it was assumed that they were forever destroyed as a people. Yet, in 1983, the Mashantucket Pequots successfully settled an 800-acre land claim and obtained federal acknowledgment of their tribal status by an Act of Congress.

Non-Indian reaction to Indian claims has often been to introduce legislation into Congress to extinguish whatever particular category of claim, treaty or otherwise, is causing the latest uproar. Such legislation is generally supported by non-Indian organizations which call loftily for "equal rights and responsibilities" for Indians. This call for equality conceals a certain exasperation: the feeling that it is time the Indians stopped being different from everyone else—that treaties notwithstanding, they should free themselves from their reservations and join the brotherhood of taxpayers.

To most Indians this kind of thinking has a familiar and ominous ring, recalling the assimilation policy of the nineteenth century and the termination policy of the 1950s and 60s; the last thing they need to hear is more talk about equal rights. For Indians, unlike any other group in this country, equality does not appear as a state of grace, but rather as a threat to their remaining tribal heritage—their land, culture, religion, sovereignty.

A century ago, the assimilationists, including the Indian Rights Association, confidently envisioned a future in which tribes had disappeared from the face of America, to be remembered only as symbols of a by-gone and primitive era. To hasten the day when the individual Indian would take his equal place among non-Indians, the reservations were to be broken up, the Indians educated and Christianized, and encouraged to farm their allotted plots of land as self-sufficient citizens.

Some fifty years later, the Indians were neither equal nor self-sufficient; they had lost approximately two-thirds of their 107 million acres to non-Indian ownership. Assimilationist policies were widely acknowledged to be complete failures. With the Indian Reorganization Act of 1934, federal policy appeared to swing definitively toward supporting tribalism; yet less than twenty years later, in 1953, Congress once again adopted an anti-tribal stance and declared its intention to terminate federal responsibility for Indian tribes. In all essential points, proponents of termination advocated the same ends as had the assimilationists, and again the results were disastrous.

Advocates of assimilation and termination do not receive high grades from Indians for their efforts to assure "equality." It is both fascinating and tragic that so much of the hardship visited on the tribes has been at the hands of politicians and reformers who believed genuinely that they were acting in the Indians' best interest. Indians frequently joke about running like hell the minute a white man shows up offering help, a point of view that is difficult to contradict.

It is often asserted that Indians have lost more in the past century from the assault on their culture and extensive loss of lands than they have gained from the prospect of the American way of life. This volume is an attempt to contribute towards an understanding of the changes that have taken place, and of the complex dynamics underlying the formulation and implementation of federal Indian policy since the 1880s. Understanding the policies, how they worked, and the attitudes that led to them, should help us avoid similar failures in the future.

The Indian Rights Association must admit to its own historical biases. Founded in Philadelphia in 1882, it emerged as the most influential of a number of Indian advocacy organizations then calling for the assimilation of Indians into mainstream American life. Its support for the 1887 Allotment Act was fervent; it believed that breaking up reservations into individual farms would hasten the economic self-sufficiency of a people whose former livelihoods had disappeared. The failure of this policy to achieve its goals has been widely discussed, and as the sole reform organization of that era to survive to this day, the Indians Rights Association carries an acute awareness of the allotment policy as its historic albatross.

Although several of this book's authors have been involved with the IRA, it was never intended to be a book about the organization itself. This was a pragmatic decision. The IRA papers are collected on 136 reels of microfilm, and while an excellent guide to the papers exists,[1] there is no index, the film frames are unnumbered, and there was no likelihood of being able to read all the material, much less to complete the authoritative history, in the time envisioned. Early reviewers, however, encouraged the inclusion of more material about the Association, and we hope to have managed a reasonably objective presentation of its strengths and weaknesses. The two chapters that concentrate specifically on Association activities reveal very different aspects of the organization's character, but together illustrate well the assimilationist mind. In his appraisal of the Association, Vine Deloria, Jr., seeks to balance popular impressions of the organization with an overall survey of its efforts.

When the Indian Rights Association was founded, military action against Indians was still a reality. General Custer's stunning defeat at the hands of the Sioux and Cheyenne had occurred just six years earlier, and the Army's massacre of 300 Indian men, women, and children at Wounded Knee was to shock the public conscience in 1890. To the founders of the Association and other like-minded East Coast reformers, assimilation to the white man's way appeared the most humane and practical solution, especially when the alternatives, in the blunt words of Indian Commissioner Thomas J. Morgan, were extermination or inaction.

The IRA pronounced early on, in language that today makes one cringe, that "the Indian as a savage member of a tribal organization cannot survive, ought not to survive, the aggressions of civilization."[2] Extermination had its proponents, but not among the "Friends of the Indians;" inaction, on the other hand, appeared to doom the Indians to lives of poverty, dependence on federal rations, and perhaps worst of all, to the untrustworthy protection of Congress. Benevolent action appeared the only acceptable course and so the "aggressions" began. Indians no longer had the choice of retreating from Western civilization; in its various guises—Christianity, education, land-in-severalty—civilization would be force-marched onto the reservations.

Herbert Welsh, founder of the IRA, admitted to no doubt about the superiority of Western civilization to "primitive" tribal ways. He also recognized that for most Americans, including Congressmen, Indians represented inconvenient stumbling blocks to white progress. After his first trip to Sioux Territory in 1882, Welsh wrote: "Unfortunately there are but too many who scoff at the elevation of the Indian, not so much because they believe him incapable of improvement, but upon the same principle as, in former years, the slaveholder ridiculed the elevation of the negro, because there is more money to be gained from him when ignorant than when instructed."[3]

It is worth remembering that the assimilationists, who argued that the Indian deserved the rights and protections of American citizenship and that he was capable of learning to live as a white man, were presenting a radical platform for their era. Today we think it preposterous that the Indian's capacity for "civilization" was even debated, but it would have been far more alarming had the conclusion been negative. Nevertheless, Herbert Welsh and the other assimilationists are now deservedly criticized for their disregard of all that was culturally Indian.

There is probably no better example of the Indian Rights Association at its most priggish than its opposition to certain Pueblo dances during the early 1920s. The dance controversy also provides a case study of how the Indian Rights Association and its aging leadership clashed increasingly with the emerging generation of reformers, led by the brilliant and enigmatic John Collier. Welsh, then in his early seventies, came to the controversy armed with numerous sworn affidavits by whites and Christian Indians of activities so obscene and barbaric that he couldn't publish them. These practices, he maintained, had to be prohibited if the Indian was to achieve the civilized lifestyle of the white man.

John Collier, on the other hand, deeply admired the ancient tribal ways. He argued that Western civilization could learn much from the Indians, and above all that the federal government had no right to interfere with the free exercise of Indian religion. These two opposed world-views first collided over the Pueblo dance issue. The Indian Rights Association eventually withdrew from this skirmish in discouragement, but the conflict between Collier and the Association was to continue for years. David Strausfeld's chapter traces the rivalry from its beginnings to the passage of the Indian Reorganization Act, and shows how the Indian Rights Association gradually dropped the extreme commitment to assimilation that had been its hallmark for close to fifty years.

A totally different side of the Association's character appears when we review its efforts to assist the Kiowa leader Lone Wolf in preventing the allotment of his Oklahoma reservation. The Association criticized the allotments planned for the Kiowa, Comanche, and Apache reservations as far too small to be workable; more importantly, it denounced the plan to break up the reservation as an abrogation of the Treaty of Medicine Lodge Creek, on the grounds that the requisite consent of three-fourths of the adult males had not been obtained. Ultimately, the Association financed Lone Wolf's appeal to the Supreme Court, which in 1903 ruled against the tribe, articulating the theory of the plenary power of Congress over Indians and upholding Congress's right unilaterally to abrogate Indian treaties. For the IRA, the decision came as a bitter shock. For all their vaunted belief in the moral superiority of the white man's way, the highest legislative and judicial institutions of American society would not honor their legal commitments to Indian tribes.

The passage of the Indian Reorganization Act in 1934 brought the Assimilation Era to an end after a half century. John Collier's radical new views on Indian reform and persistent attacks on the U.S. Bureau of Indian Affairs won him an appointment by President Franklin Roosevelt as Commissioner of Indian Affairs. He was faced with the challenge of implementing his ideas over the opposition of the old guard within the Bureau and a steadfast suspicion by many Indians of anything the government did for or to them.

Collier's reforms constitute the major legislative watershed in Indian affairs of the past century, and it is largely his vision of tribal governments and appreciation for Indian culture and religion that continues to influence Indian policy-making today. Even the Reagan administration, the most conservative in decades and one not noted for its support of minority issues, has pointedly affirmed the federal-tribal relationship as an enduring part of the federal system.

Collier and his reforms have not emerged unscathed, however, and as Laurence Hauptman points out in his chapter on the Indian New Deal, recent appraisals have been increasingly critical. The Indian Reorganization Act is frequently cited as the cause of contemporary factionalism between the elected tribal governments on reservations, which accepted the provisions of the Act, and the traditional leaders. The latter argue that the elected governments are puppets installed at the pleasure of Washington, D.C. to manipulate remaining tribal resources. Other critics charge that Collier's promise of Indian self-rule was always illusory, as it dramatically increased the power of the Secretary of the Interior to regulate aspects of tribal life.

Collier resigned in January 1945. Within a few years a budget-conscious Congress, encouraged perhaps by the anti-colonialist spirit of the post-World War II period, began to discuss the need to "free" Indian tribes from the overbearing and expensive supervision of the federal government. By the mid-sixties, over one hundred tribes and bands had been terminated; most were extremely small, with the exception of the Menominee and the Klamath, but the total population was over 11,000 Indians. The ensuing disaster was swift; within a matter of years, most of the terminated tribes were utterly destitute. The tribes had no means to provide basic services to their members, and the state or county governments were unwilling or unable to step into the vacuum. The legal battle fought by the Menominee of Wisconsin to be restored to federal status eventually persuaded Congress and the Bureau of Indian Affairs that termination was yet one more mistake for which Indians had suffered.

Where does this leave us today? For better or worse, the assimilationists initiated an era in which the majority of reformers and politicians seeking to help Indians have perceived solutions to Indian problems in terms of Anglo-American legal rights and institutions. For the assimilationists, as we have seen, civilization of the Indian was to lead towards American citizenship. For John Collier, continued tribal existence was to be ensured by Western-style elective governments. The Indian Civil Rights Act of 1968 sought to bring tribal governments into greater conformity with federal and state governments by making them subject to most of the guarantees of the Bill of Rights. The Indian Self-Determination and Education Assistance Act of 1975 granted tribes the right to contract with federal agencies to provide the services previously performed by federal bureaucrats; tribal governments burgeoned into extensions of the federal bureaucracy. The Reagan Administration, on the other hand, has taken the position that tribal governments should be patterned more closely on state and local governments, with taxing and revenue-raising powers heretofore not available to them. Thus, while federal policy eventually reversed its efforts to force the assimilation of individual Indians, the means it has employed to strengthen tribal governments have brought those governments increasingly in line with Anglo models—a more subtle form of assimilation.

Is there reason to think that Americans have finally accepted the premise that tribes are here to stay? Indians who remember how quickly a policy of termination succeeded Collier's reforms are not all certain that lightning will not strike again. While it is unlikely that the majority of non-Indians will ever again believe that tribal identity is fundamentally incompatible with American society, it is less certain that Congress can be counted on to preserve the federal-Indian relationship. Services provided to Indians by the federal government are justified in most minds as long as Indians are certifiably worse off than other minority groups in the country. Indians may reasonably fear, however, that once tribes achieve an improved socio-economic level,

Congress will decide, treaty commitments notwithstanding, to withdraw all further trust protections on the grounds that Indians no longer require special consideration.

The century that followed Helen Hunt Jackson's *A Century of Dishonor* is certainly not easy to assess. Congress, the courts, and the Bureau of Indian Affairs all now recognize tribal self-government and tribal sovereignty, but the course has been tempestuous. Indians have attained all the legal and political rights that separated them from whites a century ago, and the tribes have proved that they can survive the most determined efforts to disband them. But beyond such obvious accomplishments, it is difficult to guess how historians and Indian leaders fifty years hence will view the vaunted self-determination era of today. Perhaps the clearest point is that although non-Indians today can play constructive roles in supporting Indian positions, politically and legally, gone forever are the days when non-Indian citizens such as Herbert Welsh or John Collier could presume to speak "on behalf of" Indians.

N O T E S

1. *Indian Rights Association Papers: A Guide to the Microfilm Edition, 1864–1973*, ed. Jack T. Ericson (Glen Rock, N.J.: Microfilming Corp. of America, 1975).
2. Indian Rights Association, *Second Annual Report* (Philadelphia: The Association, 1885), p. 5.
3. Herbert Welsh, *Four Weeks Among Some of the Sioux Tribes of Dakota and Nebraska, Together with a Brief Consideration of The Indian Problem* (Philadelphia: The Association, 1882), p. 7.

T · H · E
AGGRESSIONS
OF CIVILIZATION

THE INDIAN RIGHTS ASSOCIATION: AN APPRAISAL

V I N E   D E L O R I A,   J R.

*I*n 1982 the Indian Rights Association celebrated its centennial anniversary. No other private organization in the field of Indian affairs has rivaled its longevity or record of accomplishments. The Association was founded in 1882 when public attention was shifting from the continuous conflicts on the frontier to new ways of assimilating the surviving members of Indian tribes into American society. It was natural, given this context, that the IRA would begin its corporate life pledging to "secure to our Indian population civil rights and general education, [to] assist the Secretary of the Interior and Commissioner of Indian Affairs in carrying out the wise and just measures recommended by them in their last report, and in time bring[ing] about the complete civilization of the Indians and their admission to citizenship."[1]

This idealistic goal, as it turned out, was a naive gesture by public-spirited citizens who did not believe that the government might willfully and carelessly do harm in its efforts to bring American Indians within the pale of civilization. Once the organization gained experience in Indian matters, however, it abandoned its original strategy. It sought instead to protect the legal rights of Indians and to correct gross abuses of Indians by the various federal agencies which served them.

The times were ripe for such an organization. Thomas Tibbles, an Omaha newspaperman who had assisted the Poncas against the Army, and his wife, Bright Eyes (the daughter of Joseph LaFlesche, the Omaha chief), had recently completed a tour of the eastern cities demanding reform in Indian administration. Helen Hunt Jackson had become a national celebrity with her stunning exposé of Indian policy, *A Century of Dishonor*. Public interest in Indians was climbing toward one of its cyclical peaks. In fact, reform movements were gaining on a number of fronts. Congress had recently established a committee in each House to conduct hearings on women's suffrage. The Chinese Exclusion Bill was being hotly debated in Congress. Before the first year of the IRA had ended, sympathetic whites would be stunned by the announcement of the Supreme Court that the fourteenth amendment did not provide the protections against discrimination which its framers had intended.[2] But reform was in the air, and much energy was being devoted to assisting racial minorities to abandon their cultural traditions and become members of the American melting pot.

The Indian Rights Association could trace some of its roots to colonial times. The Society of Friends had been interested in the welfare of the Indians since the example of William Penn, whose just treatment of Indians was legendary. More recently, William S. Welsh of Philadelphia had been appointed to the Board of Indian Commissioners in 1867 by President Johnson. In the course of fulfilling his duties as a member of this important policy-making board, Welsh had sought the advice of two Episcopal missionary bishops, Henry B. Whipple of Minnesota and William Hobart Hare of Dakota Territory. In the course of their long correspondence, Welsh had learned a great deal about Indians. When Bishop Hare invited him to send Herbert Welsh, his nephew, and Henry Pancoast to Dakota Territory to learn first-hand about Indian problems, Welsh encouraged the two young men to take advantage of Hare's hospitality.

After a summer touring the Great Sioux Reserve and discussing the problems faced by this large tribe, Welsh and Pancoast returned to Philadelphia determined to assist the government in carrying out its Indian policy. On December 15, 1882, a group of about thirty men met to discuss how they might be of assistance. There was little doubt in their minds that the general direction of federal Indian policy was correct. The only apparent alternative was to exterminate the tribes, as many people in the West and certain officers in the Army desired. Or one could establish a set of principles which, if followed in good faith, would lead Indians into realistic accommodation with American society. Being fundamentally humanitarian and loathing violence, the little December group decided to organize a private organization that could work toward full citizenship rights for Indians.

The prospects for succeeding in this venture seemed bright. Many Indians, notably the Five Civilized Tribes of Indian Territory, had already made significant steps toward adopting the white man's institutions. Since their removal from the South in the 1830s, these tribes had adopted written constitutions, created governments that resembled those of the states and nation, established school systems and hospitals, and translated the sacred scriptures into their own languages.

Everyone who knew about the achievements of these Indians believed that other tribes, with encouragement and fair dealing by the government, could accomplish similar feats. Indeed, the tribes of Wisconsin, Michigan, and New York had already made progress in learning the white man's way and seemed well advanced in civilization. Already, provisions were underway by the government to transform old military posts and barracks into boarding schools where Indian children could acquire an education and develop useful employment skills. Complete assimilation seemed but a matter of making existing government programs more efficient.

Popular ethnocentric beliefs also dictated a goal of assimilation. Debates over human progress had been raging since the publication of Charles Darwin's *The Origin of Man*, and cultural evolution, the social application of Darwin's theory, was used to explain a good many American social problems. The civilization of the Anglo-Saxons was considered the apex of human achievement, primarily because of its mastery of technology and creation of formal institutions. Colored races were believed to represent the lower, less advanced stages of human social growth and achievement. The task of people of Western European heritage was to assume this white man's burden and draw the lower races upward. American Indians, just recently reduced from an independent, nomadic hunting and fishing economy to dependence on government largess, were seen as far down the evolutionary ladder, but capable of climbing toward enlightenment if provided with the opportunity.

This analysis of the realities of American social life was naive. For the 1880s, however, it represented the most enlightened scientific and political thinking and seemed unquestionably accurate. We can understand, then, how the founders of the Indian Rights Association believed that a serious government effort to educate and civilize Indians might quickly resolve the problem. It must have appeared to them that American society lacked only the will to undertake this program and see the job through.

The philosophy of the Indian Rights Association reflects changing times. In its early years the organization sought to support the announced programs of the Department of the Interior. This initial optimism did not last long. Field trips to the western reservations convinced the staff and officers of the IRA that much work would be needed to correct the abuses visited upon the Indians by federal employees. A just enforcement of the law seemed the most promising approach, and the organization devoted considerable time to investigating situations in which the Bureau of Indian Affairs had refused to enforce part or all of the law to the detriment of the Indians.

The Association was forced to confront the question of allotment of Indian land in severalty before it had time to consider the subject carefully. Senator Coke of Texas had introduced his allotment bill during the months when the IRA was being organized; Senator Henry L. Dawes had drawn up his Sioux allotment bill before the December meeting, and before the end of the first summer of organizational life the Sioux Commission had failed to gain the tribe's agreement to allotment. But other tribes were already being enticed into subdividing their lands and selling the surplus to the government for homestead entry. Since allotment seemed the irresistible wave of the future, and according to the tenets of cultural evolutionary theory promised a speedy and just solution to the question of Indian property rights, the Association quickly adopted the policy as its own.

Popular interpretations of the Indian Rights Association's support for the Dawes Act attribute more influence to the organization than it deserves. While it is true that the IRA supported allotment, it saw the act in a different context than did the churches and other humanitarian groups that gave unqualified support. The Association advocated allotment as a means of vesting Indians with political rights and of providing them an economic livelihood, rather than as a policy to eliminate all traces of Indian culture. Thus the view of the IRA differed considerably from that of such people as Theodore Roosevelt, who saw allotment as a process of grinding up the tribal mass and producing standardized Indian citizens. Commenting on the Dawes Act in its Fifth Annual Report, the organization noted:

> Legislation can only make a man of the Indian politically, not morally or intellectually; in any other than a political sense it only gives him a chance to be a man. This action of Congress has but forced the "general Indian question" to an issue, and the answer can no longer be delayed. In this critical and dubious interim preceding the time when every legal and political distinction between the red man and the white man shall be wiped out, the important factor will not be legislation. If a general and more systematic education was a great need before the passage of the Land in Severalty Act, it has now become an importunate necessity.[3]

The Indian Rights Association has since had many occasions to regret its support of the allotment policy. This regret cannot possibly rival the organization's chagrin when it discovered, after the passage of the act, that the government did not intend to administer the law impartially—instead, that it perceived the act as an opportunity to substantially reduce tribal land holdings without providing any corresponding benefits. Shortly after the policy became a political reality, the Association found itself opposing the Bureau of Indian Affairs on several occasions when the Bureau tried to force Indians to surrender their lands. When the government proposed to allot the Southern Utes of Colorado, the process threatened to become a complete confiscation. Responding to this possibility, the IRA declared:

> If the government shall determine the establishment of the South-ern Utes on the arable lands they now hold, and lead them to take up allotments there, selling such surplus lands as they do not need, to white settlers, it will mean the carrying out of the Dawes Land in Severalty Law in good faith. If, on the other hand, the Govern-ment shall effect the removal of the Utes, under pressure of selfish interests, it will not only mean an irreparable injury to the Utes, but it will be a very clear intimation to land grabbers elsewhere that the Indian reservations are to be had for the asking, if only they are asked for loud enough and long enough.[4]

In spite of its general agreement with allotment as a means of providing Indians with civil rights comparable to those enjoyed by whites, the Association continued to become embroiled with allot-ment problems. It is difficult to find much correspondence by the organization demanding that the government proceed with allotment, except when Indians themselves requested the Association to assist them in securing good titles to their lands. The correspondence ques-tioning the wisdom of allotting reservations not suited for agriculture, on the other hand, represents a substantial body of material. In the Twelfth Annual Report, the Association reminded everyone that nothing in the allotment policy required its universal application to Indian lands:

> Three safeguards seemed, to those responsible for the provisions of the Severalty Law as enacted and afterward amended, abso-lutely necessary as conditional to the safety of the allottees: (1) That those reservations alone, adapted to agriculture, where the Indians were sufficiently advanced to undertake their cultivation, should be designated by the President for allotment; (2) That leases to whites should be allowed only when, by reason of age or other disability, the allottee was unable to cultivate his land; and (3) that he could not alienate it for twenty-five years, or for a longer period if the President thought it best to extend the time.[5]

The organization's involvement in allotment policy culminated in the famous *Lone Wolf* case,[6] in which it supported the Kiowas against the government on the basis that the Medicine Lodge treaty represented the best efforts of both the government and the Indians to reach a just bargain. The Association maintained that the meeting of the Kiowas and Comanches, which occurred a few weeks after the alleged agreement with the Jerome Commission, effectively cancelled whatever agreement the government thought it had made with the Indians. In the Twentieth Annual Report, the question under litigation in the *Lone Wolf* case was succinctly described:

> If the Supreme Court decides that Congress can with impunity dispose of Indian lands without first securing the consent of the tribes interested, we may look forward to the early confiscation of the reservations now held by Indians in this country, and their settlement by outsiders, the renumeration, if any, being subject to the will of Congress.[7]

This analysis hardly supports the image of the IRA as an organization zealously advocating allotment. If the ideology of allotment appealed to the Association, which it did, proper enforcement of the laws was even more appealing. On balance, there is as much reason to applaud the organization for its efforts to assist tribes resisting allotment, once it became federal policy, as there is to criticize it for helping the law become enacted in the first place. Certainly few other groups which had supported allotment worked to resolve the problems that the policy engendered.

Support of allotment was almost always linked to the necessity of educating the Indians. Much of the Association's work in Washington, D.C. involved securing funds for Indian education, investigating conditions in government schools—particularly where there was evidence of mistreatment of students—and attempting to secure new schools where none existed. During the early reservation days, the government generally allowed education to be handled by missionary societies or by the tribes themselves when funds were adequate. As the federal bureaucracy expanded and missionary efforts began to decline, ways were found to channel funds credited to tribes for educational purposes for missionary school activities. Eventually, religious rivalries took priority over Indian education and the Association was drawn into the conflict between the Protestants and Catholics over the use of Indian monies to support religious education.

In *The Churches and the Indian Schools, 1888–1912*, Francis Paul

Prucha depicts this struggle as a controversy over the rights of Indians to religious instruction of their own choosing.[8] Prucha suggests that anti-Catholic sentiment was plentiful, but notes that the growing political strength of urban Catholics made them something less than helpless victims of the Protestant parry and thrust. Neither Prucha nor the Supreme Court dealt with the larger question of whether Indians should make individual decisions that would bind tribal assets and force them to be distributed on a per capita basis. Unfortunately, the Indian Rights Association never considered this larger question either. Had it done so, the conflict over the use of tribal funds for religious education might not have appeared so starkly sectarian. Nevertheless, the interest of the Association in Indian education was real and continuing. At least part of this concern was evident in the continuous efforts of the Association to extend the Civil Service regulations to the Bureau of Indian Affairs employees, particularly teachers and agents who were in charge of government boarding schools.

Civil Service reform symbolizes only the larger concern of the Association in ensuring that the laws governing Indians were impartially enforced. A survey of its annual reports reveals that a substantial portion of its resources were devoted to investigating the conditions on various reservations and seeking corrective actions by the bureaucracy. At least half of the early annual reports are devoted to a discussion of the problems encountered by the staff during visits of the preceding summers. It seems the organization spent its winters trying to correct the worst abuses they had discovered.

Shortly after the organization was founded, the Bureau proposed to adopt the policy of "home rule" in selecting Indian agents. This policy had little to do with organizing self-government on the reservations; rather, it granted state and territorial officials the privilege of controlling the appointment of people to posts in the Indian Service. Realizing that local interests were often hostile to the Indians, the IRA opposed and reversed this policy before much damage was done. Local politicians, nevertheless, continued to give their supporters, relatives, and friends preference in securing employment in the Bureau of Indian Affairs. This early encounter with the reality of political patronage no doubt spurred the Association to campaign for extension of Civil Service rules over Bureau employees.

The Association always maintained that more honest employees would permit the Bureau of Indian Affairs to administer Indian programs properly. There was rarely any inclination to change the institutional structure of the Bureau. At times, however, the Association felt that the rules were unnecessarily burdensome or were being abused. An incident in 1886 on the Cheyenne River Sioux reservation in Dakota Territory illustrates the kind of small abuses perpetrated on the Indians:

> When information from private sources came to Mr. Painter to the effect that the Indian Agent on the Cheyenne River reservation had issued an order requiring the Indians to trade with the licensed trader at the agency, and not with the merchants at LaBeau, thus forcing those at the upper end of the reservation to travel more than 150 miles in going to and from the agency instead of a very few miles to LaBeau, and to sell their produce for much less than they could get for it near home, while they had to pay much more for what they purchased, the fact was brought to the attention of the Commissioner of Indian Affairs, and also a regulation of the Department allowing Indians to trade elsewhere than with the Government trader, and the agent's order was revoked.[9]

Here we find the Association working for a more sensible administration of the rules, but the incident also illustrates the need for better agents. The Association had to distinguish between the rigid enforcement of rules and deliberate corruption, and often the line separating the two was razor thin.

Some problems could not be resolved through discussions with the Secretary of the Interior or the Commissioner of Indian Affairs. In those instances the Association reluctantly supported litigation to resolve the question. The idea of suing on behalf of Indians was still a novelty in those days. Courts assumed that the federal government was acting in good faith; Indians were thought to lack standing in the courts to sue either private citizens or their federal trustee, and few attorneys knew how to prepare the complaints properly. With the exception of occasional local efforts on behalf of Indians, the Association was the most prominent private presence in early Indian litigation.

The cases supported by the Association divide into two categories. One group involved the defense of Indians accused in state courts of crimes committed on the reservation or in adjacent towns. These cases involved ordinary criminal law aggravated by racial discrimination. Sometimes these seemed distasteful to the Association, but it nevertheless sought to provide the Indians with a competent defense. In 1890 the IRA provided funds for the legal defense of Plenty Horses, who had been accused of killing a Lieutenant Casey during a skirmish between the Sioux and the Army. The Association was not enthusiastic about this case, but found itself on the winning side when the court ruled that a killing committed during hostilities could not properly be described as murder, and Plenty Horses was released.

More spectacular was the role of the Association in securing the release of Spotted Hawk and Little Whirlwind, who were convicted of murder on the false testimony of the man who had actually done the deed. For some reason known only to local officials, the two Indians had been tried separately, and the real killer had appeared as the state's witness against them in exchange for a reduced prison term of ten years. Spotted Hawk was condemned to death, while Little Whirlwind was sentenced to life imprisonment. The time for execution was fast approaching when the IRA became involved.

The case was appealed to the Supreme Court of Montana, where the decision was reversed on the grounds of insufficient evidence. The lawyer representing Spotted Hawk was able to show that the real killer had confessed his crime to three people before he changed his story and implicated Spotted Hawk and Little Whirlwind. During the retrial period the murderer died in prison after making a deathbed confession that resulted in the state dropping charges against Spotted Hawk. The attorney for Little Whirlwind, however, had not made a timely appeal, and he remained in prison when the governor of Montana refused to grant him a pardon.

Fortunately, the incumbent governor had been recently defeated in elections. When the new governor was sworn into office, the Association presented Little Whirlwind's case. The Indian was granted a full pardon, released from prison, and returned home to his family. The Association then conducted a successful campaign to raise money to help Little Whirlwind restock his herd; he expressed amazement that people far away could be so concerned with his welfare.[10]

In 1900, the Association learned that three Laguna Pueblo men had been imprisoned for almost two years in a local jail in New Mexico. One of the men was accused of murder, and the other two were being held as witnesses. The Association wrote a letter to the Department of Justice complaining of the violation of their right to a speedy trial. The Justice Department investigated, made arrangements to release the two witnesses on bond until the trial was held, and pressured local authorities to proceed with the case. When the matter came before a grand jury it dismissed the whole proceeding. The Laguna Pueblo and Spotted Hawk/Little Whirlwind trials were the most successful early criminal cases backed by the Association.

The Association also undertook cases which involved the precise interpretation of federal Indian law. It was less successful in this field, and for good reason. The Association, which rarely initiated litigation, usually found itself supporting the Indian plaintiffs in cases already in litigation. Thus it could not always control the manner in which the case was conducted.

Indian litigation in the early days reveals some interesting patterns. In cases when the government itself sued on behalf of Indians, it was usually successful. *Winters*,[11] *Winans*,[12] and later *Sandoval*[13] were all major cases involving a determination of Indian property rights brought by the United States and successfully pursued. However, *Lone Wolf*, *Quick Bear v. Leupp*,[14] *Barker v. Harvey*[15] (the Warner Ranch case), and *Cherokee Nation v. Hitchcock*[16] were all cases initiated by Indians, with the Association prominently involved in the first three. All four cases were lost. The legal issues had some novelty at the time, because the plaintiffs sought to restrict the power of the federal government over Indians and their property. In addition, the composition of the Supreme Court of that time (1895–1903) was not friendly to the underclass on any front (that court also decided *Plessy v. Ferguson*[17] and *In Re Debs*[18]). It was simply not the right time to litigate complex legal problems dealing with Indians.

Despite work on enforcement and argument of laws, the major activity of the Association during its first quarter century was the publication of information on Indians. Some publications were simply reproductions of newspaper stories dealing with pressing but momentary issues. In general, these stories helped generate letters of support or inquiry to the President or Secretary of the Interior on a particular problem. They were politically effective; they also made the membership feel involved in the activities of the organization, and proved immensely helpful in recruiting new members. Members often felt particularly disposed toward a favorite tribe, or a special relationship to a distant part of the country. These small reports often interested them considerably more than a recitation of the organization's more important activities.

The Association also made large, detailed reports and investigations on specific topics, such as pending policy changes, allotment of reservations, and Bureau practices in timber, mineral exploration, and schools. Titles of three of the larger reports illustrate the scope of the group's activities. *Another Century of Dishonor*, issued in 1904, successfully refuted an effort to interpret the *Lone Wolf* decision as giving Congress complete control of Indian allotments. In 1918 the Association published *Peyote—An Insidious Evil*, a slanted tract supporting Representative Carl Hayden's attempt to prohibit the use of this substance in Indian ceremonies. *Oklahoma's Poor Rich Indians: An Orgy of Graft and Exploitation of the Five Civilized Tribes—Legalized Robbery* was published in 1923. The title alone is intimidating, and the report, written by Matthew Sniffen, Charles H. Fabens, and Gertrude Bonnin, exposed the systematic exploitation of the Osage Indians by county probate courts in Oklahoma.[19]

Prior to 1919, the Association provided the only accurate reports on the conditions of Indians. The Inter-church Movement "borrowed" Matthew Sniffen from the IRA in 1919 to help G. E. E. Lindquist write a report, *The Red Man in the United States*.[20] Thereafter, both private and public groups began to investigate the conditions of Indians, which gradually led to a veritable flood of publications. In 1923, for example, Secretary Hubert Work authorized the Committee of One Hundred to make a detailed report on Indian policy. The American Red Cross investigated Indian health in 1922, but its report was not released for several years. By 1926 the Institute for Government Research, popularly known as the Brookings Institute, had begun several studies on Indian policy. The best known, the Meriam Report, was issued in 1928 and quickly achieved the status of a classic.[21]

In 1928 John Collier convinced the Senate Indian Committee to hold extensive hearings on the conditions of Indians in the United States. These hearings lasted until the Second World War and covered a great variety of topics. They also inspired a number of reports by the Bureau of Indian Affairs on such topics as grazing, irrigation, and tribal courts. It would be comforting to think that the IRA had inspired this flurry of investigations and studies. Certainly the Association's publications had demonstrated that decisions should not be made in Indian matters without careful investigation of their legality and probable consequences. But it was probably more the tenor of the times, the activism of John Collier—who was a genius in ferreting out information embarrassing to the government—and the involvement of an increasing number of citizens, white and Indian, in the field of Indian affairs.

By the beginning of the 1920s, the IRA found it was no longer the only important private organization working to improve the lot of Indians. A variety of women's groups were now working on both local and national problems; a number of churches had assumed active roles; and in 1912 the Indians themselves organized the Society of American Indians. Convening rather symbolically on Columbus Day at Columbus, Ohio, this group was composed of educated Indians who had achieved some measure of success in the white man's world and who recognized the need for a national Indian organization. The SIA lasted more than two decades; it worked on various citizenship measures, and finally split on the issue of Bureau of Indian Affairs supervision over Indians and their property.

John Collier established a new style of political infighting during the struggle over the Bursum bill of 1921, which sought to solve the problem of Pueblo Indian land titles by putting the burden of proof on the Indians instead of the whites who had intruded on their lands. It seems evident that he had informants within the federal establishment willing to give him inside information. His dramatic revelations of government wrongdoing, usually presented in congressional hearings to achieve maximum impact, were entirely different from the gentlemanly stories the Association had printed in the *New York Times* and other eastern newspapers. The IRA had *reported* the news about Indians; Collier *made* news and it always involved Indians. The staid, if respectable performance of the IRA seemed out of date.

The role of the Association changed significantly as more organizations and individuals entered the field of Indian affairs. The IRA was seen by other groups as the elder statesman of Indian reform, and consequently it was often asked to convene meetings on policy, help raise funds, sponsor reports and investigations, and offer its staff as impartial representatives of private Indian interest organizations. The Association also formed a nucleus for many organizations and coalitions particularly under the leadership of Lawrence A. Lindley. In this capacity the IRA helped to found the National Fellowship of Indian Workers, the American Indian Capitol Conference on Poverty, and the Council on Indian Affairs. It was also instrumental in securing financial support from John D. Rockefeller, Jr., for the Meriam Report.

The passage of the Indian Reorganization Act in 1934 wrought many changes in the field of Indian affairs. Its provisions enabled tribes and reservations to represent their members in a formal sense and drastically curtailed the arbitrary authority of the Bureau over the lives of Indian people. Because tribes could now speak for themselves, the nature of work done by the private Indian interest groups also changed. They became less concerned with investigating the conditions on reservations, at least partially because investigations might reveal collusion between Indians and the Bureau of Indian Affairs that could prove embarrassing to the advocates of self-government. Like other groups, the Association chose to work with specific tribes or on specific problems where it could be assured a modicum of Indian support.

The Association was particularly active in the Kinzua Dam controversy, supporting the Senecas against the Army Corps of Engineers. It also did a number of studies, most notably a report on the Fort Hall Reservation and a report on the rehabilitation programs of the Cheyenne River Sioux that recorded their progress in overcoming the dreadful effects of dam construction on the Missouri River. The Association also assisted the Alaska Natives; the IRA had been among the first to support the introduction of reindeer in that state, and its interest continued until the successful passage of claims legislation. Times, however, have changed; the IRA continues to be an influential institution, but it is no longer a dominating presence.

The outstanding characteristic of the Indian Rights Association, and the most important reason for its effectiveness during most of the preceding century, has been its uncanny ability to attract devoted staff. Herbert Welsh, one of its founders, served the organization from 1882 to 1927, a period of 45 years. Matthew Sniffen began his tenure in 1884 at the age of seventeen and worked for the organization until 1939, a period of 56 years. Lawrence Lindley began his work with the Association in 1925 and retired in 1967, a period of 42 years. Long staff tenure has been extremely rare in every other private Indian interest organization, Oliver LaFarge's years with the Association on American Indian Affairs being the sole exception.

The longevity of its staff and officers gave the IRA a corporate memory and experience in dealing with issues unrivaled by any other group. The staff has taken embarrassing stands on some issues—expenditure of tribal funds in sectarian schools, and Pueblo dancing, for example—but on most issues that confronted the organization, the experience of the staff enabled it to avoid obvious pitfalls and carry the fight successfully.

The original goal of the Indian Rights Association was to help Indians achieve American citizenship. Formal citizenship status was achieved in 1924 by act of Congress, but forging a comfortable place in American society, which represents real citizenship, is still not a reality. Yet in the past several decades the tribes have made amazing progress in developing and operating modern institutions. Meanwhile, the old melting pot conception of American society has given way to visions of a pluralistic society in which Indians see themselves as substantial contributors. The original goal of the IRA is now achievable.

N O T E S

1. *Indian Rights Association Papers: A Guide to the Microfilm Edition, 1864–1973*, ed. Jack T. Ericson (Glen Rock, N.J.: Microfilming Corp. of America, 1975), p. 1.
2. *Civil Rights Cases*, 109 U.S. 3 (1883).
3. Indian Rights Association, *Fifth Annual Report* (Philadelphia: The Association, 1888), p. 4.
4. Indian Rights Association, *Tenth Annual Report* (Philadelphia: The Association, 1893), p. 7.
5. Indian Rights Association, *Twelfth Annual Report* (Philadelphia: The Association, 1894), pp. 36–37.
6. *Lone Wolf v. Hitchcock*, 187 U.S. 553 (1903).
7. Indian Rights Association, *Twentieth Annual Report* (Philadelphia: The Association, 1902), p. 40.
8. Francis Paul Pricha, *The Churches and the Indian Schools: 1888–1912* (Lincoln: University of Nebraska Press, 1979).
9. Indian Rights Association, *Fourth Annual Report* (Philadelphia: The Association, 1887), p. 13.
10. IRA, *Twentieth Annual Report*, pp. 67–68.
11. *Winters v. United States*, 207 U.S. 564 (1908).
12. *United States v. Winans*, 198 U.S. 371 (1905).
13. *United States v. Sandoval*, 231 U.S. 28 (1913).
14. *Quick Bear v. Leupp*, 210 U.S. 50 (1908).
15. *Barker v. Harvey*, 181 U.S. 481 (1901).
16. *Cherokee Nation v. Hitchcock*, 187 U.S. 294 (1902).
17. *Plessy v. Ferguson*, 163 U.S. 537 (1896).

18. *In Re Debs*, 158 U.S. 564 (1895).

19. Philip C. Garrett, *Another "Century of Dishonor"*? (Philadelphia: Indian Rights Association, 1904); Herbert Welsh, *Peyote—An Insidious Evil* (Philadelphia: Indian Rights Association, 1918); Gertrude Bonnin, Charles H. Fabens, and Matthew Sniffen, *Oklahoma's Poor Rich Indians: An Orgy of Graft and Exploitation of the Five Civilized Tribes—Legalized Robbery* (Philadelphia: Indian Rights Association, 1923).

20. G. E. E. Lindquist and Matthew Sniffen, *The Red Man in the United States* (New York: George H. Doran Co., 1923).

21. *The Problem of Indian Administration* (Baltimore, Md.: The Johns Hopkins University Press, 1928).

REFORMERS IN
CONFLICT: THE PUEBLO
DANCE CONTROVERSY

D A V I D **M.** S T R A U S F E L D

*T*his essay describes the 1920s controversy over the rights of Pueblo tribal groups to practice their traditional rituals, centering in particular on the confrontation between two of the most active non-Indian participants, John Collier and the Indian Rights Association. It must be emphasized that the focus in this controversy is not the role of Native Americans nor their experience of the policies that were implemented, which certainly merit further study, but the actions of white reformers and their attitudes toward Native peoples.

For centuries, white people have perpetuated two contrasting myths of the Indian. In one myth the Indian is idle, heathen, and deficient in every respect. In the other he is a "Noble Savage" whose natural way of life reveals the deficiencies of Anglo-American society.[1] Like generations of white people before and after them, the IRA, Collier and other non-Indians were often using the language of U.S. Indian policy to argue among themselves—not about Indians, but about their own society.

The Indians Rights Association was one of a number of organizations which sprang up in the last decades of the nineteenth century. This followed the public outcry over the forced removal of the Ponca Indians from their homeland in Dakota to Indian territory in 1877; and the publication of Helen Hunt Jackson's influential book, *A Century of Dishonor*. Organized in Philadelphia on December 15, 1882, by "some thirty or forty gentlemen" who met at the invitation of John Welsh, former minister to England and a wealthy merchant of the West Indian sugar trade, the IRA rapidly became the most influential of these groups.[2] Though the Association claimed to be nonpartisan and interdenominational, its membership was overwhelmingly Republican and its executive board was largely a mixture of Quaker gentry and upper-class Episcopalian Philadelphians.[3]

John Welsh's son, Herbert Welsh, was the guiding force behind the IRA. Born on December 4, 1851, he was educated at the University of Pennsylvania and studied art in Philadelphia and Paris; a trip to the Sioux Reserve in 1882 permanently turned his attention to Indian welfare. Welsh was the acknowledged dean of Indian reformers for close to fifty years, and he was ably seconded by Matthew K. Sniffen, who was associated with IRA even longer, beginning as Welsh's office assistant in 1884 and later serving as IRA Executive Secretary from 1909 to 1939. Together they provided the continuity of leadership which made for the Association's remarkable resistance to change.

Welsh's visit to the mission schools of Episcopal Bishop Hare on the Sioux Reserve in 1882 convinced him of the possibility of civilizing the Indians and inspired him to write *A Month Among the Sioux*, his manifesto for Indian reform. Though his ideas about racial equality were ahead of prevailing American attitudes (in 1896, for example, the Supreme Court upheld racial segregation in *Plessy v. Ferguson*), Welsh fervently denied the equality of cultures. This denial led Welsh and most Indian reformers of his day to conclude that justice to the Indians required, first, a recognition of their humanity, and second, their complete assimilation into Anglo-American society:

> How excellent a thing for the cause of right would it be could intelligent people from the East, see not only evidences of mental training, which these Mission Schools are giving to Indian children, but also observe the practical knowledge of household work which they are rapidly acquiring! . . . Here are children, brought but a few months ago from the ignorance and filth of savage camps, from the closest contact with the barbarity of a nomadic and warlike people, who have already shown qualities of intellect and of heart, and have developed habits of cleanliness and order which reflect credit upon themselves and upon their teachers. . . . [The Indian was not] a wild beast whose extermination is necessary to the safety of a higher order of creation, but a man for whom honor, purity, knowledge and love are not only within the range of possibility, but are qualities which already in numberless instances have been attained. . . . The Indian is a *human being*. . . . He is a man!

Welsh concluded his pamphlet with a plea for organized action on behalf of the Indians similar to that which had led to the abolition of slavery.[4]

Welsh realized that missionary preaching and educational work were not enough. The solution to the Indian question, he argued in *A Month Among the Sioux*, required both vigorous religious and political effort. First, government schools were needed to educate Indian children where mission schools did not exist or were inadequate. Second, Indian tribes should be brought under a "suitable code of laws" based on Anglo-American legal ideas as preparation for eventual citizenship. Third, the rationing system which rewarded indolence and prevented the Indians from making economic progress had to end.[5]

Most important, however, the reservations must be divided into individual plots upon which Native American families could establish Christian homesteads modeled after those of their white neighbors. Welsh and virtually all the reformers of his day endowed the idea of private property with almost magical qualities, and they believed allotment in severalty would destroy the tribal bonds that prevented the Indians from developing into Christian Americans. Allotment also had an immediate practical purpose: the reformers believed that individual ownership was the only way to prevent Indians from being driven off their lands by rapacious Westerners.

The allotment policy was enacted into law in 1887 as the cornerstone of Indian assimilation. Poorly conceived, however, and often corruptly administered, it brought few of the benefits that Welsh and other humanitarians had hoped for. Many Indians lost their lands to unscrupulous Anglos, had them seized for nonpayment of taxes, or sold them and became impoverished. By the turn of the century the IRA actively supported measures to protect the title of Indian allottees, and by the 1920s it was beginning to debate whether the policy needed revision.[6]

Nonetheless, it is striking how little the Association's views changed in the years between its founding in 1882 and its first battles with Collier and other critics of assimilation after the First World War. On the eve of the controversy over Pueblo dances in 1922, the Association was able to look back at its forty years of work with great satisfaction:

> We have seen accomplished in these long years,—and have helped to bring about the happy results,—the creation of the Indian as a man in the eyes of the law and as a citizen, so that thousands today come within that category. . . . We have seen him acquire the right not only theoretically but practically to possess and to cultivate the soil so that he could feel as every man wants to feel that he had ground that would feed him and a permanent home into which he and his family safely could retreat.

The IRA reaffirmed its commitment to

> lift the members of Indian tribes out of a savage stone-age condi-
> tion of human society by the spiritual forces of the Christian
> religion and to develop them intellectually, morally and materi-
> ally through its general influence and to merge them at last com-
> pletely into the best of our own civilization.[7]

It is difficult to imagine an individual more nearly the opposite of
everything the IRA stood for than John Collier. Collier was an influential community organizer in New York City who served as civic secretary of the People's Institute, an educational institution devoted to
promoting community life in immigrant neighborhoods. He regularly
attended Mabel Dodge's weekly salons, which brought together such
radical intellectuals as Max Eastman and John Reed, editors of *The
Masses*, and Emma Goldman, an anarchist, whom Collier himself
introduced to the group. In 1919, disillusioned by the nativist "Amer-
icanization" campaigns of World War I, he left New York for California to assume a position as director of the state adult education
program under the partial sponsorship of the State Immigration Commission. One year later, under surveillance by federal agents because
of his controversial lectures on the virtues of cooperation and the
communist experiment in Russia, and with his program facing drastic
cuts by a hostile legislature, Collier resigned and left with his wife,
three sons, and six dogs for Taos, New Mexico, where he arrived in the
winter of 1920.[8]

Collier's experience in Taos changed his life. He was captivated
by Pueblo communal life and its "ceremonial expressions," which he
described as "a religious creation as powerful and as subtle as Greek
orphic dramatic art could have been; a communal art, remotely imper-
sonal while very passionate and very joyous, exquisite in myriad detail
and as massive-seeming as the Sacred Mountain beyond."[9] Furthermore, his experience among the Pueblos gave him a new vision of
how to regenerate community life in a world that, in his view, was
rapidly being destroyed by materialism and selfish individualism. Collier's work for the People's Institute in New York had attempted to
promote a sense of community in immigrant neighborhoods through
community centers and political forums on issues such as socialism, the
single tax movement, and the popular election of senators. In Taos,
however, he discovered that culture was more important than politics
as a method of providing social cohesion.

Unlike the IRA, which in its annual reports regularly measured Native American advancement in terms of dress, homes, and furnishings, Collier did not believe that material progress necessarily accompanied social or spiritual progress. "What are the tests of superiority?" Collier asked in 1923.

> Does a man's group situation make him more kind, more loyal, more chaste, more temperate; a wiser parent and a happier child . . . does his group experience make him philosophical so that he does not fear and is not restlessly disturbed about personal advantage? Does his group situation encourage him to feel that he is a part of some great and romantic destiny and one with the invisible eternal forces and realities?

Collier asserted that societies like Pueblos' might be materially less advanced but humanly superior to twentieth-century America.[10]

Collier's thought, which was characterized by a romanticization of traditional societies and a concern with the building of personality through social institutions, was influenced by a diverse group of thinkers. Essentially, however, it represents an emotional reaction to a world which he believed subordinated human values, community, and spiritual life to individual aggrandizement.[11] Convinced that the Pueblos offered a model for the redemption of modern society, Collier embarked on a career in Indian affairs. He first gained national prominence leading the fight against the vicious Bursum bill of 1921, which would have confirmed the title of non-Indians to large portions of Pueblo lands.[12] Next he turned his energies to defeating an attempt by the Indian Bureau and its supporters to interfere with Pueblo ceremonial dances.

The IRA's campaign to pressure the Indian Bureau to curtail the practice of objectionable Pueblo dances was prompted by the release of a 1920 report by an Indian Bureau investigator, Rev. E. M. Sweet. Sweet had collected testimonial evidence of immoral practices reportedly associated with some of the ceremonies. These included accounts of public fellatio, simulations of sexual intercourse, exposure by male clowns of their genitals, and children being flogged with yucca leaves as part of their clan initiations.[13]

The IRA had long believed that the Hopi Snake Dance and other Pueblo ceremonials were primitive and degrading, and Rev. Sweet's report provided them with tangible proof. It also offered evidence that young Indian students returning from government schools were "drawn into this vortex through the attending excitement, and otherwise promising lives thus precipitated in vice." Of "so vile a character" were these disclosures (declared the IRA in its 1923 annual report) that they were not permitted to circulate in the mails, although they were "available for reading by any one interested in the welfare of the Indians."[14] In truth, Rev. Sweet's report was based solely on the testimony of whites and Protestant Indians who had repudiated traditional Pueblo ways; not surprisingly, it was tainted with cultural bias.

Nonetheless, with the "evidence" contained in Rev. Sweet's report and the strong support of missionary groups and the Board of Indian Commissioners, the IRA soon succeeded in pressuring the Indian Bureau to take action.[15] On April 26, 1921, Commissioner of Indian Affairs Charles H. Burke, an ardent assimilationist himself, issued a circular (no. 1665) to all superintendents in the Indian Service. It was the policy of the Indian Office to be "somewhat tolerant of pleasure," Burke wrote, but Indian dances "under the most primitive and pagan conditions" were "apt to be harmful." They should be controlled "by educational processes as far as possible but, if necessary, by punitive measures." Burke reminded his superintendents that existing regulations made ceremonials such as the Sun Dance of the Plains Indians, a ceremony involving self-mutilation which had been outlawed since 1910, punishable by fines and imprisonment. These punishments were to apply to any dance which involved "the reckless giving away of property . . . frequent or prolonged periods of celebration . . . in fact, any disorderly or plainly excessive performance that promotes superstitious cruelty, licentiousness, idleness, danger to health, and shiftless indifference to family welfare."[16]

The IRA and its supporters had long viewed Pueblo religious practices as a major obstacle to missionary work. Through the eyes of the IRA's Matthew K. Sniffen and others, the Hopi Snake Dance, a rite to bring rain and bountiful harvests, in which dancers used rattlesnakes as symbols of lightning, grasping them in their arms and mouths, was both primitive and horrifying. The elaborate ceremonials of the Zunis to win the blessings of supernatural powers, especially those concerning fertility, also seemed to them indecent and immoral. Perhaps most alarming, however, was that certain groups of Pueblos performed their ceremonials, or parts of them, in secret, which gave rise to suspicions that even more heinous acts were taking place.[17]

On February 14, 1923, two years after his original order, Burke added a "Supplement" to circular 1665. Endorsing a series of recommendations made at a recent missionary conference, Burke ordered that Indian dances be limited to one each month, in daylight hours, in mid-week, and only at the center of each Indian district. In the planting and harvesting months from March through August most dances would be banned altogether. In addition, no one under fifty years of age would be permitted to witness or take part in ceremonies thought to be particularly objectionable. Burke showed some moderation by instructing his superintendents to use tact and persuasion rather than force in carrying out his directive. Explaining his position in a "Message To All Indians" issued ten days after his order, Burke told the Indians that he would prefer that they give up these "useless and harmful performances" of their own accord, but if at the end of the year it appeared they hadn't, then "some other course" would have to be taken.[18]

Burke's circular of April 26, 1921 had produced little popular reaction, but the heated controversy surrounding the Bursum bill had unified the growing ranks of opponents to the government's assimilation policy, and Burke's "Supplement" met with a storm of opposition. Collier and the new reformers brought their campaign to the public with a barrage of letters and articles in newspapers and magazines around the country. They were aided early in the campaign by major eastern newspapers which launched editorial attacks on the Indian Bureau's policy. Collier also appeared before the House Committee on Indian Affairs to defend Pueblo dances and call for laws to protect Indian religious freedom, but was unsuccessful in moving Congress to take action.[19]

By April the IRA knew it was in for a fight. The Executive Board drew up a resolution supporting Burke's action, and IRA Washington representative Samuel M. Brosius presented a resolution at a Washington meeting of the National Indian Association, a missionary organization, commending Commissioner Burke's action and "urging that the immoral dances be PROHIBITED."[20] In the same month Executive Director Sniffen travelled to New York, visiting the offices of the *Times*, the *Tribune*, and the *World*, newspapers which had editorially opposed the Burke directive. Sniffen presented their editors with copies of documents from Rev. Sweet's report as proof of the dances' immorality and the correctness of Commissioner Burke's actions.[21]

The Association had joined Collier and his supporters in defeating the Bursum bill, but found it difficult to comprehend that these new reformers had a radically different understanding of Indian welfare. In his reply to an editorial in the *Philadelphia Record*, the IRA's Herbert Welsh asserted that many of the "artists, archeologists, newspaper writers and other good people" who had recently criticized the government's position on Indian dances simply had not studied the question enough to realize the potential effect of either their "fierce attacks" or "delicate innuendos." Their interest in Indian affairs had its "good side," he agreed, but their misdirected criticism threatened "the work of Indian civilization for which Catholic and Protestant missionaries, wise thinkers and earnest citizens have long and patiently labored."[22] In an article for *The Southern Workman* during the same month, Sniffen pointed out that the "casual visitor" who witnessed an Indian dance was "interested, and doubtless charmed by its weird picturesqueness, and of course regards it as harmless; but he witnesses only a fractional part of what preceded or follows it." An indication of the true nature of these dances for Sniffen was the fact that the Spanish explorer Bandelier had referred in his letters to their vulgarity and wickedness, and if they were "too indecent for the sensibilities of a Spanish explorer of the sixteenth century one can imagine how vile they must have been."[23]

Yet Welsh, at least, understood the mentality of the new reformers far more clearly than he let on. "I am convinced that at the root of the Indian dance attack," he wrote Secretary of the Interior Hubert Work in early May 1923,

> is the strange wide-spread belief that affects many modern minds, in literature, art, music, religion, philosophy to the effect that primitive man had more that is excellent in all the range of human mentality than the race has gained from the greatest of Christian teachers. "Back to Nature" is their cry. It is to some a captivating theme, but there are dangerous flaws in it.

For proof of these flaws, Welsh suggested a "careful perusal" of Rev. Sweet's report or simply a visit to the "ultra impressionist picture show" at the Pennsylvania Academy of Fine Arts.[24] Welsh evidently did not approve of modern art, but he was quick to perceive a connection between its emergence and the defense of Indian dances. He understood that Collier's movement was but one expression of the revolutionary changes in intellectual and artistic life that were beginning to rock the foundations of everything the IRA then stood for.

Welsh was not about to let this movement gain the upper hand in

Indian affairs. He urged Secretary of the Interior Work to release a statement supporting Commissioner Burke's position on Indian dances. Such a statement would bolster the position of the Indian Bureau and the IRA and its supporters against the "fusilade of attack" levelled upon Burke. The Association barely had time to attend to its usual business, Welsh informed the Secretary, because it was "kept busy answering those silly lucubrations which are coming out almost daily in our most prominent newspapers."[25]

By June 1923, the IRA was engaged in a full-fledged war with the new reformers, and it was feeling the effects. Contributions from the Association's membership had dwindled steadily since the turn of the century, both because of deaths in the ranks of its original supporters and a general decline of interest in Indian affairs. The IRA had hoped that renewed interest generated by the Bursum bill controversy would improve its financial position. But Collier's American Indian Defense Association and other recent reform organizations attracted virtually all the new money available, and the IRA found itself in worse financial shape than ever before. On June 6, 1923, the IRA Executive Board adopted a resolution authorizing the treasurer to borrow on the Association's securities. Six days later Sniffen wrote Welsh that "the reactionary, degenerative, heathenish movement is now being pushed with aggressiveness, and it is not helping us, for the time being."[26]

Most disturbing of all were the letters of criticism that the IRA received from some of its own members. A Philadelphia member named Ralph B. Miller provoked a particularly strong reaction from the Association by questioning its view that certain Indian dances were "contrary to public morals." "What are morals?" Miller asked. "The Mohammedan has a half-dozen wives and is highly moral. The Western European has one wife—and is equally moral. The Mohammedan refrains from alcoholic liquor—and thereby attains a moral status in his community. The Western European drinks considerable quantities of alcoholic liquor—yet retains his moral standing in his community." Morals were simply "a matter of community feeling," Miller wrote, and if white people disapproved of the "so-called immoral practices" of the Pueblo dances, they could "stay away."[27]

Welsh responded to Miller with two long and interesting letters in which he defended the government's assimilation policy and attacked the idea that morality was a relative concept. Welsh was proud of his replies and wanted them published along with Miller's original letter as an IRA leaflet. If IRA members could see the Miller correspondence, Welsh believed, it would have "a very good effect in showing them the true nature of the public agitation to leave Indian dances alone, and will strengthen their support of us."[28]

Welsh first directed Miller's attention to the practical question of helping the Indians survive in America. He contrasted the primitiveness and moral depravity of Indian life with the material and cultural splendor of white civilization, concluding that the Indian would be "stamped out" by civilization if he long remained a "cave dweller," a "rattlesnake worshipper," a "give-away dancer," or a "gypsy-like wanderer doing no honest work but living on dreamy expectations of long vanished hunting grounds upon which now stand the great modern hotels, or theaters, or business sky-touching buildings of the white race." These were modern times, Welsh declared, and in order for the Indian to survive he would have to abandon his "dead, outworn past" and learn the civilized ways of the whites. Most important for Welsh, however, the Indian had to be taught the principles of Christianity, in order to understand the dignity of labor and the evil of war and cruelty.[29]

In his second letter, written one week later, Welsh addressed himself to the question of morality. Although Miller might doubt that morality had any "stable and definite existence," the practical answer to his position was that these Pueblo dances were simply unlawful. Morals were not determined by community feeling, but by the laws of the United States, and

> civilization, as the people of the United States understand the term, is not consistent with a religious dance in which a young Pueblo girl, educated in a Government or missionary school . . . is required to submit her physical body to the loathsome embraces of a heathen Indian man of her tribe . . . who is not her husband, under penalty of punishment by beating, by order of the Cacique [high priest].

Welsh advised Miller to persuade his Indian friends to give up religious practices that did not conform to the "standards of American custom in vogue now among reputable people," and instead of "hankering after the fleshpots of Egypt, the plural marriages of the Mohammedan," to be "content" with the "time-honored ideals of Uncle-Sam."[30]

In February of 1924 the IRA began a new monthly journal, *Indian*

Truth, edited by Matthew K. Sniffen. Aided by this new weapon, the Association attempted to shift the focus of debate on Pueblo religious practices from collective to individual rights. The IRA declared itself in favor of religious liberty "not only for communities but for individuals," and asserted that Christian Pueblo Indians who had abandoned the traditional ways were being persecuted by an "oligarchy of caciques" that forced them to participate in "pagan and revolting customs" at the threat of being expelled from the village or having lands confiscated.[31] Before long the Association abandoned all recognition of community religious rights, maintaining that religious liberty was purely an individual affair. As *Indian Truth* declared on one occasion, religious liberty "means that *every individual* Indian has the right to worship God according to the dictates of his own conscience, whether he belongs to the so-called pagan party or the Christian progressive group among the Pueblos." Any other interpretation of the term "would mean liberty for a ruling minority to tyrannize a majority, in which the right of the individual is ignored."[32]

The IRA's new campaign coincided with events on the Pueblo reservations that increased the tensions between traditional Indians and those eager to assimilate, and that brought the IRA and Collier into more direct conflict than ever before. On April 18, 1924, Commissioner Burke told a meeting of the Taos tribal council that it must immediately return two boys temporarily withdrawn from government schools for training in the tribal priesthood. Openly defiant, seventy-four Indian delegates from fifteen Pueblos attended a meeting of the All Pueblo Council on May 5 and unanimously passed a declaration labelling Burke's order an instrument of religious persecution. They formally stated their position to the Indian Bureau in a May 7 letter (which Collier helped compose), informing Commissioner Burke that they refused to obey his order because their religion taught them "about God and the earth, and about our duty to God, to earth, and to one another" and was "more important to each of us than money, horses, land, or anything else in the world."[33]

A few days earlier, on May 2, thirty Indians from eleven Pueblos had assembled at Santa Ana Pueblo to form the General Council of Progressive Christian Indians. They backed the Indian Bureau's policies and claimed to represent one-fifth of the Pueblo population.[34] In a stab at Collier's participation in the May 5 All Pueblo Council meeting, Sniffen remarked in *Indian Truth* that this "intelligent group," the Council of Progressive Christian Indians, "did not need any prompting from outside influences as to what they want."[35] There is evidence, however, that the Council's first meeting was orchestrated by Nina Otero Warren, a government inspector, and by Sniffen himself.[36]

With the fate of the assimilation policy at stake, the IRA responded with a vigor it had not shown since the turn of the century. In June the Association sent its agent, Clara D. True, with a delegation of seven progressive Pueblo Indians to the biennial convention of the influential Federation of Women's Clubs in Los Angeles. They hoped to defeat a resolution condemning Commissioner Burke's restrictions on Indian dances. Aided by an emotional appeal for the rights of Christian Pueblos, True and her delegation were successful; the convention responded by refusing to take a stand.[37] This publicity stunt, reminiscent of the tactics used by Collier to stir up opposition to the Bursum bill, was uncharacteristic of the dignified IRA, but as *Indian Truth* commented, it "seemed necessary to offset any effort to stampede the Convention into supporting the specious plea of 'religious liberty' for the non-progressives, who really demand religious *tyranny*."[38]

As the IRA's battle went on, Herbert Welsh's attention increasingly focused on John Collier, the new movement's enigmatic leader. He compared Collier to an earlier nemesis, Dr. Thomas A. Bland, the most vocal opponent of the Dawes Land-in-Severalty Act of 1887. As Welsh wrote his son in July 1923,

> Dr. Bland was a long-haired, wild-eyed, tall man, who represented in those days almost precisely the line of thought and method followed by Mr. Collier and his radical associates today. There seems to be the same looseness in the statement of fact, and the same general scheme for keeping the Indian apart from White civilization that we had to content [sic] with then.[39]

Yet something about Collier fascinated Welsh. He confided in Sniffen, "I would really like to know just what his real motives are and what it is that controls him."[40]

Curiously enough, it was Collier's request for a copy of an article about John Woolman that Welsh was distributing which helped him perceive that Collier, like Welsh himself, was guided by deep religious beliefs and genuine social concern. John Woolman was an appropriate medium for this change. An eighteenth-century Quaker leader with leanings towards mysticism, Woolman was one of America's earliest abolitionists; perhaps it is not surprising that his writings, which combine social and humanitarian concern with otherworldly spirituality, attracted both Collier and Welsh.[41] Inspired by a new understanding of Collier's motives, Welsh sent him a copy of the article and made a plea for cooperation:

> Your ideas of what a beautiful religion consists of are strictly opposed to my own, but the fact that you admired John Woolman, the purest of thinkers and actors in life's battle, lead[s] me to think that widely as we are separated there must be something which we hold in common on this great fundamental question. . . . If you care to open out your thought on that subject I shall esteem it a favor. It may lead to intense controversy working out finally into harmony and cooperation. That would be a great thing, would it not?[42]

Welsh's change of heart was sudden. Less than two weeks earlier, in a letter to the *New York Times* published on October 19, he had publicly accused Collier of being at the root of the trouble among the Pueblos. The caciques and their followers "had apparently been so flattered by Mr. Collier's praise of the purity and beauty of their religion," Welsh wrote, that they were "made to feel that unless all these bygone ideas were restored and put in full practice they would be the victims of religious intolerance." He charged that Collier's "extremely skillful propoganda" [sic] had brought about a "revival of ancient pagan ideas of obsolete communal management which if it be not promptly stopped threatens to upset the most fundamental principal [sic] of American free life and intellectual progress [i.e. individual freedom]."[43] Why Welsh chose this moment to extend the hand of friendship to Collier is difficult to understand. Perhaps the seventy-three year old Welsh wished to come to terms with his likely successor as dean of Indian reformers. A dedicated humanitarian who had devoted himself to what he and virtually everyone of his generation believed was best for the Indians, Welsh must have been shocked to find his life's work called into question. John Woolman enabled Welsh to feel that reconciliation with the new generation of reformers was possible.

Before receiving Collier's reply to his appeal, Welsh received another letter from Collier which made him realize that hopes for "harmony and cooperation" were unrealistic. Writing in response to Welsh's October 19 letter to the *New York Times*, Collier denied that there had been a revival of ancient communal practices among the Pueblos, and dismissed Welsh's charge that Christian Indians were being persecuted. He claimed to have read the unpublished affidavits circulated by the IRA, and asserted that even if they were indeed based on fact, they did not call into question the "moral content of Indian creeds and moral quality of their ceremonies." Whatever immorality in the affidavits did exist, he suggested, was due to the breakdown of traditional Pueblo life.[44]

Welsh, who had a much more sweeping view of immorality, had difficulty grasping Collier's meaning. He was puzzled how Collier could blame the breakdown of Pueblo community life for conditions among the Indians which were "deplorable, prejudicial to health, contrary to the principles of religious liberty, law and order and decency," and on November 3 he wrote Collier withdrawing his offer of cooperation.[45] Thanking Collier for his "courteous and admirably expressed letter," Welsh observed that their differences on the Pueblo matter were apparently "too deep to permit hope of any harmony," although he left open the possibility of future cooperation in other areas of Indian affairs. "My own belief," Welsh wrote, "is that your abilities, which are very great in many directions, are being used with fatal effect to bolstering up a set of ideas which are prejudicial to all progress, but you do not think so." Under these circumstances there was no possibility of cooperation. "We will have to go on, each on his own lines," Welsh wrote, "looking to the final verdict of the American people as to where truth and rights rests and what is a correct decision."[46]

Collier also saw the impossibility of closer cooperation between his American Indian Defense Association and the IRA, and before receiving Welsh's second letter he had written to reject his appeal. He agreed that his and Welsh's religious views were probably not "very wide apart," but he did not believe "that the estimate one places on this or that system of religion, or the intensity of his own convictions or feelings in a religious way, can enter into the question of the relationship of the Government to the Indians." What was important to Collier was the principle of religious liberty for "all men and groups." Even if the Indian religions were "less worth while than they are" and Christianity were "all that there is of religious life," he asserted, "it would be improper for the United States Government to coerce the Indians, either directly or indirectly, into forswearing their own creeds or adopting new creeds." Collier avoided the difficult question of reconciling group and individual rights, arguing simply that there could be no reconciliation between his organization and Welsh's because the IRA was dedicated to the forcible Christianization of the Indians. Collier made an effort to carry on a religious dialogue with Welsh, sending him a book with marked passages because his feeling about Christianity was "too intense and intimate to allow a direct statement of it," but there is no evidence that Welsh ever wrote back.[47]

Despite the promise of escalating conflict between the IRA and the new reformers, the IRA had already begun to withdraw from the struggle over Indian religious freedom by the fall of 1924. The Association had grown increasingly disillusioned with what it viewed as the Indian Bureau's weak and vacillating policy. In June of that year, Secretary Work had announced that for the time being the government would not enforce the Bureau's policy prohibiting Indian boys at Taos from being temporarily withdrawn from government schools for religious training; this prompted harsh criticism from the IRA.[48] When the new fall term brought no change in the Bureau's position, but instead a ruling by Commissioner Burke upholding the right of Pueblo tribal officials to confiscate the lands of progressive Indians who refused to perform their share of community work, *Indian Truth* charged angrily that had the Bureau deliberately tried "to break down all the progress that has been made among the Pueblos, it could not go about it in a better way."[49]

Throughout the fall of 1924 and the spring of 1925, the IRA aimed a constant barrage of criticism against the Indian Bureau for backing down from confrontation with the defiant Pueblos, who it claimed were violating the rights of progressive Indians. On one occasion, *Indian Truth* accused the Bureau of responsibility for the whipping of two students, in the presence of members of the Taos tribal council, who had refused to follow "a sacred Taos custom of making leggins out of their trousers and wearing their shirts outside." The Association maintained that the Bureau's "surrender to the Taos Indians in the matter of compulsory education" had "emboldened" reactionary tribal officials in their persecution of progressive Indians.[50] Welsh supplemented Sniffen's highly charged attacks with more soberly expressed criticism of Secretary Work and Commissioner Burke, whom he chided for having "considerably modified" their opposition to the "very un-American and demoralizing state of affairs" on the Pueblo reservations.[51] It was because of the "unaccountable official backing down" of Work and Burke, Welsh reported to the IRA membership, that the Association had been "for months past taxed to the utmost to hold the lines against the tremendous assaults made upon them by those who wished to sweep the old government policy into chaos."[52] Eventually, with the IRA increasingly alienated from the Indian Bureau, and with Commissioner Burke under attack from every side and unable to reassert control on the Pueblo reservations, the campaign to suppress Pueblo ceremonial dances was defeated.

Though the root issues of the conflict over assimilation policy remained unresolved, the years following the Pueblo dance controversy were marked by an easing of tensions between the IRA and its ideological foes. Under the administration of Commissioner Burke's successor, Charles J. Rhoads, a former IRA president, Sniffen and Collier cooperated in formulating a legislative program that was submitted to Congress in Rhoads' name. As late as one year after Collier's appointment as Commissioner of Indian Affairs in 1933, Sniffen was convinced that "anything like 'traditional enmity' belongs to the past."[53] The harmony that existed between the IRA and Collier for close to a decade was not to last, however. Soon new controversy erupted, first over the landmark Indian Reorganization Act, and later over Collier's sometimes strong-armed efforts to implement his policies on the Navajo reservation.

Perhaps one reason for the IRA's eagerness to cooperate with Collier was that he struck a conciliatory tone with the Association and made sure to include it in the process of formulating his administration's policy. On January 7, 1934, Collier held a conference at the Cosmos Club in Washington, D.C. of such groups as the IRA, the American Indian Defense Association, and the National Association on Indian Affairs. He hoped to gain their support for legislation to replace the Dawes Land-in-Severalty Act. This was necessarily a tender subject for the IRA, albeit that for some time it had admitted that allotment, although correct in principle, had failed in practice.[54] The IRA delegation joined the other organizations in recommending that Congress repeal the land allotment law. To replace it they recommended legislation that would consolidate Indian lands presently broken into plots too small for agricultural purposes, promote tribal ownership of grazing and forest lands, and acquire additional lands for landless Indians. In addition, the delegates recommended that the government establish a system of credit that would further Indian economic development and enable organized Indian communities to gradually assume more power over their own affairs.[55]

Collier was delighted by the conference, which he took as a

mandate for a sweeping revision of federal relations with the reservation Indians. The IRA also seemed enthusiastic. *Indian Truth* described the unity as "history-making," and Sniffen, who estimated that 90 percent of the Commissioner's program had been approved, remarked privately that he was surprised and "much pleased" at the delegates' general accord, especially considering the "variety of thought" they represented.[56]

Other IRA officers, however, were more suspicious. After conferring with Jonathan M. Steere, president of the Association since Welsh's retirement, Sniffen instructed the IRA's Washington agent, Richard L. Kennedy (who had expressed confusion about how much leverage the IRA's endorsement of the Cosmos Club platform gave him) that he was free to advance certain legislation—including a proposal to increase participation of the Indians in their own affairs—but he was not to support legislation on the "Land Question" because on this topic there seemed to be some "differences of opinion" within the organization.[57]

Collier's program was introduced jointly by Representative Edgar Howard of Nebraska and Senator Burton K. Wheeler of Montana in mid-February 1934. Major provisions of the Wheeler-Howard bill prohibited future land allotment, extended the trust period on restricted land, and restored existing surplus lands created under the Dawes Act to tribal ownership. It also provided means for tribal communities to assume self-government and incorporate for economic purposes, hence enabling them to exercise broad powers over tribal and individual property, and to borrow money for economic development from a revolving credit fund.[58]

Sniffen was initially favorable to the bill, observing that it had "a good many splendid features." Although it was "at first glance, revolutionary and sweeping," he emphasized that each tribe would elect whether or not to come under its provisions; moreover, Collier had promised not to pressure tribes into accepting the plan.[59] Before long, however, much of Sniffen's initial enthusiasm had faded, perhaps through the influence of more conservative members of the executive board. He began to express concern over provisions of the bill that would essentially abolish inheritance among the Indians by forcing allotted land to revert automatically to the tribe following the death of the owner.[60]

These provisions, central to Collier's plan for regenerating Indian communities, were utterly incompatible with the IRA's assimilationist philosophy. On March 6, Sniffen wrote to Edith M. Dabb, director of the YWCA's Indian Division and a fervent assimilationist, listing the Association's principle objections: (1) the Wheeler-Howard bill proposed to "disregard the vested rights of Indians holding trust patents"; (2) it indicated no "ultimate end to the Indian problem"; (3) it discouraged individualism and encouraged communalism; and (4) it would keep Indian communities tax-exempt indefinitely, "thus putting no responsibility on the Indian."[61]

By early March there was general agreement within the IRA Executive Board that the Association could no longer hold to the agreement reached at the Cosmos Club conference two months earlier. Although the IRA's Law Committee had not yet released its formal report, a statement for that month's *Indian Truth* publicly declared the IRA's opposition to the Wheeler-Howard bill. The statement, which was prepared so carefully that it delayed publication of the March issue, warned that the bill proposed "revolutionary departures" in Indian policy, threatened individual Indian property rights, and sought to perpetuate segregation "under the guise of self-government." At the same time, the IRA gave its approval to cooperative economic activity, as long as it did not involve the reversion of privately-held Indian land to tribal ownership, and also approved a limited degree of self-determination.[62]

Lawrence E. Lindley, IRA financial secretary and later executive director, commented on the statement's ambiguity. He wrote to a friend that it "was a compromise as you may have guessed," and confided that he believed it was too "condemnatory."[63] Two officers of the Association, Charles L. Chandler and Herbert S. Welsh, son of the IRA's founder, shared this view. They approached Sniffen and suggested that a letter be sent to Secretary of the Interior Ickes urging him not to be disturbed by the IRA's attacks on the Commissioner and his program, and to view all criticism as motivated only by a desire to do what was best for the Indians. Chandler and Welsh also argued that there was much of value in the Wheeler-Howard bill, and rather than condemn it, the IRA should cooperate with Collier to amend it. Sniffen resolved to bring up these matters with other IRA officials, but in the end no action was taken.[64] In May, *Indian Truth* published the Law Committee's formal report, which recommended that Titles I and III, the crucial sections concerning self-government and land reform, should be "discarded or entirely rewritten."[65] The conservatives still controlled the organization.

Lawrence Lindley was also critical of the bill, but for different reasons than Sniffen and other members of the executive board. He granted that the attempt to make "individualists" of the Indians had largely failed, that many "unfortunate things" had been done to the Indians in the name of the Christian religion, and that the destruction of tribal governments had damaged Indian pride and initiative. But he argued that the assimilation process had simply gone too far to be reversed. In religion, government, education, and other areas, the Indian had become too much a part of the Anglo-American world to effect a separation. "[T]o try to mold these Indians into old tribal life is just as unwise as what we did before in trying to make white men of them."[66] Lindley, who assumed the reins of the Association from Sniffen in 1939, and served as its executive director through 1967, gradually moved the IRA to moderate its extreme assimilationist stance.[67]

Lindley's argument aside, it has been asserted that Collier's policies did indeed pressure some tribal groups to adopt a way of life (based on the Pueblo model) which was foreign to their traditions or which many tribal members had wholly forgotten. Certainly the IRA believed that this was Collier's intention when he attempted to use his administrative powers to implement his policies among the Navajos, a tribal group which had voted to stay outside the provisions of the Indian Reorganization Act. Opposition to Collier's Navajo program led the IRA to call for his resignation in 1939. Ironically, Collier was now cast as the domineering Indian Commissioner, while the IRA claimed to stand by the principles of Indian self-determination.

As finally passed in June 1934, the Wheeler-Howard Act, also known as the Indian Reorganization Act, was much less objectionable to the IRA than the Bureau's original draft. Congress had diluted the ability of tribes and the Interior Department to acquire allotted lands for the purpose of consolidation, and also denied tribes the power to reclaim land after the death of individual owners. Even in weakened form, however, it represented the most significant Indian legislation since the Dawes Act of 1887. The Act provided for the return of remaining surplus reservation lands to tribal ownership, and for the voluntary exchange of allotments for shares in tribal corporations; in addition, it retained many features of the original draft concerning the process by which a tribe could adopt a constitution, organize a tribal council, and incorporate in order to manage its resources, consolidate tribal lands, and borrow from a revolving ten million dollar credit fund.[68] *Indian Truth* declared that it was "much better than the original bill," although it objected to the provision restricting the revolving loan fund to chartered tribal corporations.[69]

Three years later the IRA actually helped Collier defeat an attempt to repeal the Wheeler-Howard Act. The Association still believed that patient educational work among the Indians would have produced better results than Collier's "fanfare methods," but argued that the Act contained valuable provisions, in particular the extension of trust periods and restrictions against the alienation of tribal land, and that its repeal would only add to the "prevailing confusion."[70] Instead of a complete repeal, the IRA advocated a substitute measure based on the Oklahoma Welfare Act of 1936. Such a reform would allow all tribes, regardless of whether they had voted to accept the provisions of the Act, to borrow from the revolving credit fund. It would also permit cooperative enterprise not organized along tribal lines by authorizing government loans to small cooperative groups and individuals.[71] That the IRA could take such a stand is an indication of the transformation within the organization since the Pueblo dance controversy of the early 1920s.

The running conflict between the IRA and Collier over assimilation policy is interesting as a study of intellectual trends in the formative period after World War I. More important, however, it should warn us of the dangers of allowing ideological agendas to interfere with the right of Native Americans to choose their own values and their own future. Convinced that they knew what was best for native peoples, the IRA and the assimilationists of the late nineteenth and early twentieth centuries attempted to remake the Indian in their own Christian American image. Collier has been accused of a similar ideological arrogance. If concerned white Americans are to play any sort of constructive role in Indian affairs in the decades ahead, it must be with far greater humility and a clearer recognition of the desires and aspirations of Native Americans themselves.

N O T E S

1. See Robert E. Berkhofer, Jr., *The White Man's Indian: Images of the American Indian from Columbus to the Present* (New York: Knopf, 1978).

2.   Constitution and By-laws of the Indian Rights Association, 1884, IRA papers, Historical Society of Pennsylvania, Philadelphia.

3.   Michael Morgan Dorcy, "Friends of the American Indian, 1922–1934: Patterns of Patronage and Philanthropy" (Ph.D. diss., University of Pennsylvania, 1978), p. 225. Dorcy has written the fullest account to date of the history of the IRA, tracing it from its founding into the 1920s. See especially chapter 7. William T. Hagan, a well-known scholar in the field of Indian-white relations, is presently at work on a book about the first twenty years of the IRA.

4.   Herbert Welsh, *Four Weeks Among Some of the Sioux Tribes of Dakota and Nebraska, Together with a Brief Consideration of the Indian Problem* (Philadelphia: H. F. McCann, 1882), pp. 11, 30.

5.   *Ibid.*, p. 29–31.

6.   For example, the IRA lobbied extensively in favor of the Quay bill of 1904 to protect Indian title to allotments. See Office Report, Jan. 6–Feb. 2, 1904, IRA papers; see also the platform adopted at the January 1926 Conference of Friends of the Indian published in *Indian Truth* (Feb. 1926).

7.   Indian Rights Association, *Fortieth Annual Report* (Philadelphia: The Association, 1922), pp. 1–2.

8.   Kenneth R. Philp, *John Collier's Crusade for Indian Reform*, 1920–1954 (Tucson: University of Arizona Press, 1977), pp. 1–25.

9.   John Collier, *From Every Zenith: A Memoir, and some Essays on Life and Thought* (Denver: Sage Books, 1963), pp. 125, 461.

10.   John Collier, "Politicians Pillage the Pueblos," *The Searchlight* 7, no. 8 (Jan. 31, 1923): 15–19.

11.   For discussions of the intellectual sources of Collier's ideas see Philp, *John Collier's Crusade*, pp. 1–25, and Stephen J. Kunitz, "The Social Philosophy of John Collier," *Ethnology* 18 (Summer 1971): 213–229.

12.   The bill, re-introduced by Senator Bursum of New Mexico in July 1922, proposed to resolve the conflicting titles to Pueblo lands which had resulted from overlapping Spanish, Mexican, and American grants. It would have effectively confirmed the claims of non-Indians who had occupied the lands since 1900, whether or not they had title, and provided a loophole that would allow those whose claims did not date back to 1900 to purchase their holdings. See Brian W. Dippie, *The Vanishing American: White Attitudes and U.S. Indian Policy* (Middletown, Ct.: Wesleyan University Press, 1982), pp. 274–279.

13.   Copies of the Sweet report affadavits are still in the Indian Rights Association's files. A number are included in the undated correspondence for the year 1920 in the microfilm collection. See *Indian Rights Association Papers: A Guide to the Microfilm Edition*, ed. Jack T. Ericson (Glen Rock, N.J.: Microfilming Corporation of America, 1975), p. 45.

14. Indian Rights Association, *Forty-First Annual Report* (Philadelphia: The Association, 1923), p. 20.
15. On Oct. 21, 1920, the Board of Indian Commissioners sent a resolution to Commissioner Burke recommending the supervision of all dances and a ban on those that interfered with Indian industrial pursuits. See Philp, *John Collier's Crusade*, p. 81.
16. Quoted in John Collier, "Persecuting the Pueblos," *Sunset* 53, no. 1 (July 1924): 92.
17. See Kenneth R. Philp, "John Collier and the Crusade to Protect Indian Religious Freedom, 1920–1926," *Journal of Ethnic Studies* 1 (Spring 1973): 24.
18. Quoted in Collier, "Persecuting the Pueblos," p. 92. See also Philp, *John Collier's Crusade*, p. 57.
19. Philp, *John Collier's Crusade*, p. 58.
20. Washington Report, April 27, 1923, IRA Papers.
21. Dorcy, "Friends of the American Indian," p. 232.
22. Herbert Welsh to the *Record*, May 3, 1923, IRA Papers.
23. Matthew K. Sniffen, in the monthly magazine *The Southern Workman* (Hampton, Va.: Hampton Institute, May 1923): 209–210.
24. Herbert Welsh to Hubert Work, May 9, 1923, IRA Papers.
25. *Ibid*.
26. Matthew K. Sniffen to Herbert Welsh, June 12, 1923, IRA Papers.
27. Ralph B. Miller to Herbert Welsh, June 5, 1923, IRA Papers.
28. Herbert Welsh to Matthew K. Sniffen, June 14, 1923, IRA Papers; Herbert Welsh to Matthew K. Sniffen June 15, 1923, IRA Papers.
29. Herbert Welsh to Ralph B. Miller, June 13, 1923, IRA Papers.
30. Herbert Welsh to Ralph B. Miller, June 13, 1923, IRA Papers. Welsh's letters to Miller were written a week apart but are dated the same because Welsh, vacationing in New Hampshire, sent them to Philadelphia to be typewritten.
31. *Indian Truth* 1, no. 3 (April 1924): 4.
32. *Indian Truth* 2, no. 5 (May 1925): 2–3.
33. Quoted in Collier, "Persecuting the Pueblos," pp. 92–93; Philp, *John Collier's Crusade*, pp. 60–61.
34. Collier charged that the Council of Progressive Christian Indians represented only fifty out of ten thousand Pueblos and was assisted by whites who wanted to deprive the Indians of their lands. See Philp, *John Collier's Crusade*, p. 63.
35. *Indian Truth* 1, no. 4 (May 1924): 3.
36. See Philp, *John Collier's Crusade*, p. 61.
37. *Ibid*., pp. 61–62.
38. *Indian Truth* 1, no. 5 (June 1924): 6.
39. Herbert Welsh to Herbert S. Welsh, July 5, 1923, IRA Papers; also quoted in Dorcy, "Friends of the American Indian," pp. 239–240.

40. Herbert Welsh to Matthew K. Sniffen, June 30, 1923, IRA Papers; also quoted in Dorcy, "Friends of the American Indian," p. 239.

41. *Dictionary of American Biography*, Vol. 10, ed. Dumas Malone, (New York: Charles Scribner's Sons, 1936): 516–517.

42. Herbert Welsh to John Collier, Oct. 30, 1924, IRA Papers.

43. Herbert Welsh, "The Pueblo Indian Rites," *New York Times* (Oct. 19, 1924), II, 6:8.

44. John Collier to Herbert Welsh, Oct. 28, 1924, IRA Papers.

45. Herbert Welsh to Irving Bacheller, Nov. 5, 1924, IRA Papers.

46. Herbert Welsh to John Collier, Nov. 3, 1924, IRA Papers.

47. John Collier to Herbert Welsh, Nov. 6, 1924, IRA Papers. Like Welsh, Collier apparently gained respect for his adversary through their exchange of letters. In his public response to Welsh's October 19 letter in the *New York Times*, he condemned the IRA for its role in the campaign to suppress Pueblo dances, but noted that the damage caused by the Indian Bureau's policy could not be apparent "in the consciousness of many good people who are helping it along." See John Collier, "The Religion of the Pueblos," *New York Times* (Nov. 16, 1924), IX, 12:4.

48. See *Indian Truth* 1, no. 5 (June 1924): 1–2.

49. *Indian Truth* 1, no. 7 (Aug.–Sept. 1925): 5.

50. *Indian Truth* 2, no. 5 (May 1925): 4.

51. Herbert Welsh, "Pueblo Indian Rites," p. 8.

52. Indian Rights Association, *Forty-Second Annual Report* (Philadelphia: The Association, 1924), pp. 4–5.

53. Matthew K. Sniffen to Louis Ballou, Feb. 19, 1934, IRA Papers.

54. See the platform adopted at the January 1926 Conference of Friends of the Indian published in *Indian Truth* 3, no. 2 (Feb. 1926): 2–3.

55. Philp, *John Collier's Crusade*, pp. 135–136.

56. *Indian Truth* 11, no. 1 (Jan. 1934): 3. Matthew K. Sniffen to Charles Dey Elkus, Esq., Jan. 16, 1933, IRA Papers.

57. Matthew K. Sniffen to Richard L. Kennedy, Jan. 27, 1934, IRA Papers. Richard L. Kennedy, a Princeton University and Harvard Law School graduate, became the IRA's Washington agent in 1933 upon the retirement of Samuel M. Brosius, who had served as Washington agent for thirty-five years. In 1935 Kennedy resigned and was replaced by Lawrence E. Lindley.

58. For a more detailed description of the provisions of the bill, see Graham D. Taylor, *The New Deal and American Indian Tribalism* (Lincoln: University of Nebraska Press, 1980), pp. 20–22.

59. Matthew K. Sniffen to Rev. J. Denton Simms, Feb. 26, 1934, IRA Papers.

60. See Matthew K. Sniffen to Robert Bruce, March 6, 1934, IRA Papers.

61. Matthew K. Sniffen to Edith M. Dabb, March 6, 1934, IRA Papers.

62. *Indian Truth* 11, no. 3 (March 1934): 1–3.
63. Lawrence E. Lindley to Ruthanna M. Simms, March 31, 1934, IRA Papers.
64. See Matthew K. Sniffen to Lawrence E. Lindley, April 4, 1934, IRA Papers.
65. *Indian Truth* 11, no. 6 (May 1934): 8.
66. Lawrence E. Lindley to Dr. Thomas Jesse Jones, Feb. 26, 1934, IRA Papers; Lawrence E. Lindley to Mary Louise Mark, April 2, 1934, IRA Papers. Lindley's criticism of the Wheeler-Howard bill was also based on the belief that protracted ideological debate would delay government action to protect the millions of acres of Indian lands in heirship status that might soon be lost. He felt that Collier should hold off on the controversial aspects of his program and work instead to protect Indian land resources "with as little indication of objectionable 'isms' as possible." See Lawrence E. Lindley to Ruthanna M. Simms, March 31, 1934, IRA Papers.
67. Lindley served as Financial Secretary from 1925 to 1934, as Washington Agent from 1935 to 1939, and as General Secretary (or Executive Director) from 1940 to 1943, and from 1947 to 1967.
68. See Taylor, *The New Deal and American Indian Tribalism*, pp. 27–29.
69. *Indian Truth* 11, no. 7 (Oct. 1934): 1.
70. *Indian Truth* 14, no. 4 (April 1937): 2.
71. The Oklahoma Indians had been exempted from many of the provisions of the Wheeler-Howard Act at the insistence of Senator Elmer Thomas, Democrat from Oklahoma, who believed that these provisions should apply only to reservations in the far West. Philp, *John Collier's Crusade*, p. 176.

INDIAN POLICY
SINCE THE 1880s

W I L C O M B E. W A S H B U R N

*I*n the 1880s, when the Indian
Rights Association was founded, most Americans doubted the continued survival of the native Indians. Their civil rights vis-a-vis white Americans varied from tenuous to nonexistent, and the sanctity of their treaties with the white man was alternately dismissed as irrelevant or a joke. No banker or politician of sound mind would have guaranteed the security of the lands they occupied; it is hard to imagine a more hopeless situation for any group to face.

And yet in 1980, a century later, the Maine Indians established their right to a large portion of Maine because of the State's failure to comply with an act of Congress passed in the eighteenth century. The Indians settled for a reduced portion of land supplemented by a generous monetary award. In 1978, the Supreme Court of the United States declared (in the case of *Martinez v. Santa Clara Pueblo*)[1] that a tribal rule of membership took precedence over a constitutional guarantee to a citizen. Would anyone of that earlier generation have believed that times would change so much—that the Supreme Court, the Congress, and the president would work to protect or enlarge Indian fishing, mineral, and water rights, Indian religious freedom, freedom from state taxation of income earned on reservations, and many other rights derived from treaties and statutes?

All these changes, and many more, were achieved by the combined efforts of whites and Indians operating under laws which linked the conflicting races in the same general legal context. Violation of individual and tribal rights, arbitrary administration of the law, suppression of religious ceremonies, and insensitive attempts to reform and "uplift" the Indians occurred. Documentation for acts of racism, colonialism, and imperialism in Indian-white relations can certainly be found, but it is equally true that many Indian tribes survived and have regained their autonomy and their pride.

In *Our Wild Indians* (1882), Colonel Richard I. Dodge warned that "it is a mere question of time when all the reservations will be over-run."[2] Dodge spoke in light of events in the 1870s: the invasion of the Sioux Black Hills by miners; the defeat of Nez Perce Chief Joseph in his attempt to preserve his Wallowa Valley homeland in Oregon; the overrunning of the Ute homeland in Colorado; the government's clumsy removal of the Ponca Indians from their reservation in the Sioux country, and the government's equally clumsy attempts in 1879 to prevent Chief Standing Bear from leading his band of Poncas back to their original homeland in Nebraska. Dodge's conclusion seemed an accurate assessment of things as they stood in 1882.

Eastern philanthropists were concerned by the increasingly hopeless predicament in which the Indians found themselves. They publicized the outrages being committed against the Indians, organized Indian support organizations, and generally sought a solution to the dilemma. That dilemma was stated succinctly by Commissioner of Indian Affairs Ezra A. Hayt:

> Experience of the Indian Department for the past fifty years goes to show that the government is impotent to protect the Indians on their reservations, especially when held in common, from the encroachment of its own people, whenever a discovery has been made rendering the possession of their lands desirable by the whites.[3]

Hayt urged Congress to pass a severalty bill that would break up the tribal domains and assign each individual Indian a fee simple title (sometimes called "white man's title") to a fixed number of tribal acres. Hayt believed that by the passage of such an act, "the race can be led in a few years to a condition where they may be clothed with citizenship and left to their own resources to maintain themselves as citizens of the republic."[4]

Reformers were initially uncertain how best to protect the Indians. Helen Hunt Jackson, whose famous book, *A Century of Dishonor*, was published in 1881, was skeptical of the early bills promoted by Secretary of the Interior Carl Schurz to allot Indian land in severalty.[5] While government officials often asserted that strong Indian support existed for severalty, these arguments were often more disingenuous than uninformed. Those who knew the Indian best had few illusions about what would happen if tribal lands were divided in severalty. "If I stand alone in the Senate," Senator Henry M. Teller of Colorado asserted in a speech on January 20, 1881,

> I want to put upon the record my prophecy in this matter, that
> when thirty or forty years shall have passed and these Indians shall
> have parted with their title, they will curse the hand that was
> raised professedly in their defense to secure this kind of legisla-
> tion, and if the people who are clamoring for it understood Indian
> character, and Indian laws, and Indian morals, and Indian reli-
> gion, they would not be here clamoring for this at all.[6]

Ethnologist Lewis H. Morgan, whose *Houses and House-Life of the
American Aborigines* was published in 1881, also opposed the severalty legislation, predicting that the result for the Indian "would unquestionably be, that in a very short time he would divest himself of
every foot of land and fall into poverty."[7] Despite the dire warnings
and the sorry record of earlier attempts to allot tribal land, both
political observers and reformers gradually became convinced that it
would be necessary to destroy the tribal governments and allot tribal
land in severalty—even against the wishes of the Indians—to prevent
their destruction. Even the Indian Territory (now the state of Oklahoma), to which many tribes had already been removed, was threatened
by groups of land-hungry neighbors both willing and able to overrun
the Indians and defy the national government.

Allotment was initially understood as a permissive policy to encourage the adoption of white culture, but it gradually evolved into a
coercive measure as Indian resistance to its provisions became apparent. The decision to push for a coercive allotment program was made
at the 1885 meeting of the Lake Mohonk Conference, organized in
1883 by Quaker Albert K. Smiley in behalf of the "Civilization and
Legal Protection of the Indians of the United States."[8] Because of the
intimate network of cooperation between the "Friends of the Indians," as the reformers were usually called, and the national politicians
responsible for enacting Indian legislation, the agreements hammered
out at Lake Mohonk were momentous in their consequences. They
laid the intellectual and political basis for the Dawes Severalty Bill,
introduced into Congress by a frequent participant in the Lake
Mohonk Conferences, Senator Henry L. Dawes of Massachusetts.

One hundred years ago the Indian "problem" was a western
phenomenon. The Indians of the eastern United States were largely
perceived as nonexistent, assimilated or submerged in white (or black)
society, and were generally consigned to the province of literature,
history, and nostalgic reminiscence. A more ruthless America had

long ago pushed the powerful eastern tribes beyond the Mississippi, leaving only pockets of Indians who either hid in the mountains and swamps or huddled in tiny state-administered reservations where they created no obstacle to "progress." These Indian communities had few rights, virtually no relationship to the federal government, and retained their identity only through their profound social and political isolation.

What a change has occurred in the last hundred years! These remnant groups, such as the Eastern Cherokee, Catawba, Passamaquoddy, Penobscot, Pequot, Narragansett, Mashpee, Seminole, Pamunkey, and many others whose names fill the histories of America's earliest centuries, have begun in recent years to take advantage of the changed social and political climate. They have reinstated their claim to tribal status, and occasionally won back some of the lands lost in the course of centuries.

No recovery of land by eastern Indian tribes equals that by the Passamaquoddy and Penobscot Indians of Maine. Under the Maine Indian Land Claims Settlement Act of 1980 (Public Law 96-420), those tribes were authorized to reacquire 300,000 of the 12 million acres taken from them over 160 years earlier in unratified transactions; they were also provided with a $27-million trust fund to support economic development. The success story was a long drawn-out thriller[9] in which the new liberal outlook of the courts surprised both friends and foes of the Indians. While the ultimate solution to the Maine Indian land claims was political, and its cost underwritten by the United States, the steps along the way included a judicial determination that the Indian Trade and Intercourse Act of 1790, which required that all transfers of Indian land be done under the authority of the United States, *did* apply to the Passamaquoddy and Penobscot tribes, even though they were not federally-recognized tribes, and even though their lands probably did not constitute "Indian country" within the meaning of federal statutes.[10]

A number of similar claims are presently being tested in the courts and in negotiations throughout the eastern United States. The ambiguity of the law, the uncertainty of historical reconstruction of events, and the quixotic character of human nature make the outcome of these cases uncertain.

The Mashpee Indians, who sought a declaration of ownership to approximately 13,000 acres in the town of Mashpee, Massachusetts, on Cape Cod, were less successful than the Maine Indians. A jury in the Federal District Court found that the Mashpees did not constitute a tribe in 1870, the year (the Indians charged) their tribal land was allotted by the state of Massachusetts. Nor, in the jury's opinion, did the Mashpees constitute a tribe in 1976, when they filed their lawsuit in Federal District Court seeking all of the town's undeveloped land. They did conclude that the Mashpees had constituted a tribe at certain other times, but not in the years necessary to win their case. Part of the strategy of the town's attorney, James St. Clair, was to quiz the Mashpee Indians on the extent to which they recognized or acknowledged a tribal structure governing their actions. The tactic was successful in allowing the jury to find insufficient tribal authority in the contemporary Mashpee group, while conceding tribal existence at earlier dates. Regardless of success, however, Indian land cases are being conducted in an atmosphere of judicial equality between the parties that was inconceivable a hundred years ago.

Alaska has been an American possession for over one hundred years, but because of its vast territory and the paucity of its population, both native (Inuit, Aleut, and Indian) and non-native, its history has been markedly different from that of the lower forty-eight states. Armed conflicts and aggressive competition for land have been largely absent. Indeed, no specific determination of the aboriginal rights of the natives in U.S. law was made until 1971 with the passage of the Alaska Native Claims Settlement Act.[11]

The Act allocated about 40 million acres of Alaska territory and about $1 billion to the various native communities. In addition, the act created thirteen corporations to manage and develop native-owned wealth. The corporations are to be owned exclusively by the natives for a period of twenty-five years, after which they may sell their interests, which in some cases have already been enormously enriched by the discovery of petroleum.

The Alaska Native Claims Settlement Act has certain similarities to the General Allotment Act of 1887. Because of lack of experience in large-scale business management, and for other reasons, the Alaska natives may lose much of their landed heritage after the twenty-five-year protective period ends, in the same way that many Indians in the western states lost their lands after the expiration of the protective period in the General Allotment Act of 1887. But the Alaska act was more generous than any in the lower states, and the Alaska natives have already shown sophistication in their dealings with American society. Many observers believe they have a good chance of retaining control over their economic future.

One may legitimately ask, in the face of the self-interest of a dominant and expanding white majority, how Indian rights in this country were enlarged rather than diminished, as were aboriginal rights in so many countries. The answer is that however weak the supports of morality and law have been at times, they have provided the basis for a slow but persistent recovery of rights. When the sense of moral outrage among the majority non-Indian population can be aroused, the result is political power capable of overcoming the narrow self-interest of groups opposed to Indian advancement. It is in the cultivation of this moral realm that the Indian Rights Association can take pride. Formed in response to the threatened loss of Indian lands and the repeated violation of their rights, the Association has labored for one hundred years to keep a sense of moral outrage alive. Viewed from today's perspective, the positions it adopted sometimes appear shortsighted, and its founders were often too ready to ignore the Indian point of view. But it was nevertheless this group of benevolent reformers who brought the rights of Indians into the consciousness of the American people when they might otherwise have been ignored.

At the heart of the late-nineteenth-century reform movement lay the cardinal Christian virtue of charity. Combined with this sense of moral obligation to help others was an aggressive conviction of the superiority of Western civilization, particularly as exemplified by white Anglo-Saxon Protestant America. Although often perceived as hypocritical, these values express self-satisfaction more than hypocrisy, a judgment supported by the fact that American Indian policy aimed to both Christianize and civilize the Indian, not destroy him. Debates raged over which should come first, but when the Indian Rights Association was founded there was still agreement that only a combination of Christianity and civilization could make up for assumed deficiencies in the Indian mind and heart. Only a few years earlier, national Indian policy under Ulysses S. Grant had attempted to combine the process by turning the Indian agencies over to different religious orders, but no mix of ministers, soldiers, and bureaucrats seemed able to convert the Indian masses to Christianity and American economic values.

The reform impulse that led to the Indian Rights Association was initially more protective than reformatory. The rapid evolution of technology and demographic change threatened not only the efforts at

Christianization and civilization, but also the very survival of the Indian. The methods chosen to "save" him were not grounded on any absolute principle, and so could evolve in the process of time. At first, persuasion and example were thought sufficient to induce change. But as voluntary methods failed, white reformers turned to practical political measures that often led to coercion. Thus the Sun Dance, the Snake Dance, the Ghost Dance, the Potlatch Ceremony, and the use of peyote for religious purposes were outlawed or administratively discouraged. "Superstition," or "cruelty," "licentiousness," "idleness," "indifference to family welfare," and the like were frequently cited as reasons for suppressing Indian religious ceremonies. However naive these administrators appear to be a hundred years later, one should perhaps judge American policy as a whole by the fact that these ceremonies continue to live after a period of suppression. Indeed, the influence is now in the other direction. Father Paul Steinmetz of the Holy Rosary Mission at Pine Ridge, South Dakota, incorporated the Sacred Pipe of the Lakota into the Catholic liturgy and service of his church. Episcopalian priest Father Peter Powell has accepted the sacred bundles and sacred ceremonies of the Cheyenne as a supernatural reality consistent with Christian belief.

The cycle came full circle with the passage of the American Indian Religious Freedom Act (Public Law 95-341) of August 11, 1978, which reaffirmed the "inherent right of freedom to believe, express, and exercise the traditional religions of the American Indian, Eskimo, Aleut, and Native Hawaiians, including but not limited to access to sites, use and possession of sacred objects, and the freedom to worship through ceremonials and traditional rites." Many past restrictions on Indian religious freedom reflected administrative uncertainty concerning what behavior constituted traditional religious expression. The recent act helps define those terms for administrators.

Uncertainties concerning Indian religious freedom still remain, and probably always will. Current conflicts include attempts (particularly in California) to stop archeologists from disturbing human remains, demands that museums return excavated burial remains to their presumed descendants, and conflicts between regulations of theocratic tribal governments (e.g., the Pueblos of New Mexico) and individual beliefs of tribal members. (This third category accounts for the fact that the Indian Civil Rights Act of 1968 omitted any prohibition against the establishment of religion; the act otherwise guaranteed to Indians most federal constitutional protections vis-a-vis their tribal governments.) It is possible that the Supreme Court will have to clarify the meaning of the Indian Religious Freedom Act, but there is no question that the religious rights of American Indians, after hundreds of years of assault, are more fully protected than ever before.

The hundred years since 1882 have seen a reversal in white attitudes toward Western as well as Indian culture. Nineteenth-century American historians like George Bancroft professed to see the United States as the culmination of civilized evolution.[12] Democratic America—aggressive, expansionist, capitalist, individualistic, Protestant—was the model by which all other civilizations were measured and often found wanting, even within the European community. "Native" or "primitive" peoples around the globe, though regarded as capable of social advancement, were normally consigned to a lower rung on the ladder of evolution. The American Indian was merely another of those stagnant cultures whose primary interest to scientists lay in what they could tell about the evolution of societies. Indeed, Indian tribes and individuals were thought to be vanishing, a concept given credence by the shrinking Indian population in the nineteenth century, a decline reversed about the second decade of the twentieth century.[13]

In the last fifty years, respect for Indian culture and values has grown among both whites and Indians. Indians never wholly abandoned their own traditions, although there is abundant evidence that many, convinced that whites had more powerful "medicine," turned their backs on Indian values. But growing anthropological sophistication has led whites as well as nonwhites to question the primacy of white civilization. The values associated with capitalistic Protestantism have come under particular scrutiny. This self-doubt has not destroyed the white man's belief in the values of his culture; Western achievements in science, economics, music, art, and other fields have been too impressive. But recognition of the limitations of Western values has modified white prejudices toward the achievements of others.

In growing numbers whites have begun to look for guidance outside their own tradition. The influence of the Pueblo Indians upon John Collier (who became Commissioner of Indian Affairs under Franklin D. Roosevelt) is a case in point. Indian policy from the Indian Reorganization Act of 1934 to the present rests partially on the self-doubt that Collier had about his own culture, and on his belief that America needed to learn from those of the Indian.

The engine of Western civilization, which a hundred years ago had been turned on the Indian to the extent of requiring conformity to such external indices as "citizens' dress" and short hair, has now lost its coercive character. In an extraordinary reversal of roles, whites began affecting Indian clothes and hair styles in the 1960s and 1970s. Such works as Vine Deloria's *God is Red* and *Custer Died for Your Sins* were manifestos expressing the Indians' renewed pride in their heritage.[14]

The elimination of cultural barriers is nowhere better seen than in changing attitudes toward Indian art. The term applied to Indians did not exist a hundred years ago. "Curiosities," "ethnographic specimens," "crafts," and in the period following the Indian Reorganization Act of 1934, "arts and crafts," were recognized but not considered art in the Western sense. Today, on the other hand, Indians vie with whites in the art markets of the world, and in many instances attract more attention and command higher prices. Traditional artists like Tony Begay, Al Momaday, and Fred Beaver depict affecting images of the Indian past. Indian artists such as Fritz Scholder, T. C. Cannon, Woody Crumbo, and Fred Kabotie, on the other hand, combine humor and a familiarity with non-Indian art to produce sometimes satirical evocations of what it means to be an Indian in a largely white world. Northwest Coast and Inuit art is particularly prized by collectors and exhibitors on both sides of the Canadian border. Canada can boast powerful artists such as the Ojibwa Norval Morrisseau. So distinctive is the art of Canada's native population that Canadian identity abroad is often expressed through Indian or Eskimo images rather than European-derived Canadian traditions.

Native American art in the United States has had a diverse and controversial development. Interest is particularly well established in the Southwest and Oklahoma, with schools and museums such as the Philbrook Museum of Tulsa, as well as numerous individual collectors and strong tribal organizations. Of course, the Indian as artist faces the same dilemma as that of all Indians in American society: whether to preserve earlier traditions without change, to build new traditions based on distinctive Indian characteristics, or to follow one's individual genius without reference to any tribal tradition. Indian artists have gone in all these directions. What is important is that the Indian may now choose for himself, and he receives increasing encouragement whatever direction he chooses.

Perhaps the relationship of the Sioux with the United States government best reflects the extraordinary political change in Indian affairs that has occurred in the past hundred years. Federal relations with the Sioux one hundred years ago—in the period of military operations including General Custer's defeat at the Little Big Horn in 1876 and the tragedy at Wounded Knee in 1891—were regularly conducted from the barrel of a gun. Though treaties and agreements were negotiated, they were more often disregarded than honored. Force was used not only to subdue, but to control, assimilate, and educate the Sioux. The tribe had no real hopes of regaining its lost land or, until 1920, even of obtaining compensation. At that time, the Sioux were authorized to bring suit claiming compensation for the taking of the Black Hills in South Dakota. Gradually, through the Court of Claims and the Indian Claims Commission, in renewed appeals to the courts, and finally through special legislation authorized by Congress, the Sioux were able to obtain compensation. At first this was a fixed sum, but then interest was allowed on the grounds that it was a Fifth Amendment "taking," making the Sioux eligible for the largest award ever granted to any Indian tribe for the seizure of its land.[15]

These awards, which specialists had doubted would ever be made, have led to the demand by many Sioux for the return of the land itself. Although federal authorities argue that the land was taken over a hundred years ago, and the legal issue now does not concern its return, the persistence of the Sioux, the flexibility of the American legal system, and the radical change in American Indian policy over the past hundred years may indeed make the impossible a reality, as the claims of the Maine Indians became a reality in 1980, by persuading the American people to rewrite or reinterpret their laws once more.

At the heart of the evolving Indian-white relationship, and more fundamental than religion, art, or culture, rests the political relationship between the United States and the only American minority that retains a separate legal status and (more persistently than any other) remains aloof from the American melting pot. Fortunately for the Indian, the dominant white majority, at least since the passage of the Indian Reorganization Act of 1934, has permitted Indians to maintain that separateness. Indeed, the Act allowed Indian nations and tribes to function as autonomous self-governing elements within the larger body politic. That position was underwritten by the trust relationship that the government maintains vis-a-vis the tribes, by the tax-free status of the tribal reservation lands, and by nearly $3 billion annual support from the federal government through the Bureau of Indian Affairs and other federal agencies for over one million Indians. The Supreme Court of the United States has safeguarded the ever-enlarging corpus of tribal rights. Despite many bitter disappointments along the way, Indians and Indian tribes survive and grow in both numbers and power.

N O T E S

1. *Martinez v. Santa Clara Pueblo*, 436 U.S. 49 (1978). The best discussion of the significance of the case is Alvin J. Ziontz, "After Martinez: Civil Rights Under Tribal Government," *University of California Davis Law Review* 12, no. 1 (March 1979): 1–35.

2. Richard I. Dodge, *Our Wild Indians: Thirty-Three Years' Personal Experience among the Red Men of the Great West* (Hartford, Conn.: A. D. Worthington and Co., 1882; reprinted New York: Archer House, 1959), p. 648.

3. Quoted in *Americanizing the American Indians: Writings by the "Friends of the Indian," 1880–1900*, ed. Francis Paul Prucha (Cambridge, Mass.: Harvard University Press, 1973), pp. 80–81.

4. Prucha, *Americanizing the American Indians*, pp. 80–81.

5. Helen Hunt Jackson, *A Century of Dishonor: A Sketch of the United States Government's Dealings with Some of the Indian Tribes* (New York: Harper and Brothers, 1881), pp. 364–366; Wilcomb E. Washburn, *The Assault on Indian Tribalism: The General Allotment Law (Dawes Act) of 1887* (Philadelphia: J. B. Lippincott, 1975), p. 7.

6. Quoted in *The American Indian and the United States: A Documentary History*, ed. Wilcomb E. Washburn (New York: Random House, 1973), III, 1704.

7. Lewis H. Morgan, *Houses and House-Life of the American Aborigines*, ed. Paul Bohannan (Chicago: University of Chicago Press, Phoenix Books, 1965), pp. 80–81.

8. *Second Annual Address to the Public of the Lake Mohonk Conference Held at Lake Mohonk, N.Y., September, 1884, in Behalf of the Civilization and Legal Protection of the Indians of the United States* (Philadelphia: Indian Rights Association, 1884).

9. For an excellent account of the events leading to this litigation see Robert McLaughlin's "Giving It Back to the Indians," *Atlantic Monthly* 239 (Feb. 1977): 70–85. For a more legal analysis, see "Symposium on Indian Law: The Eastern Land Claims," *Maine Law Review* 31, no. 1 (Nov. 1979). Also, Paul Brodeur, "Annals of Law: Restitution," *The New Yorker* (Oct. 1982): 76–155.

10. Robert N. Clinton, "Isolated in Their Own Country: A Defense of Federal Protection of Indian Autonomy and Self-Government," *Stanford Law Review* 33, no. 6 (July 1981): 979–1068. Ftnt. 324 on p. 1043 discusses the current definition of "Indian Country."

11. Wilcomb E. Washburn, "The Indian-White Contact in Alaska," *Actes du LXII Congress International des Américanistes*, Sept. 2–9, 1976, (Paris: Société des Américanistes, 1978), V: 265–269; Wilcomb E. Washburn, *Red Man's Land/White Man's Law: A Study of the Past and Present Status of the American Indian* (New York: Charles Scribner's Sons, 1971), pp.124–133.

12. George Bancroft, *History of the United States of America from the Discovery of the Continent*, 12 vols. (Boston: Little, Brown & Co., 1834–1882).

13. In 1917 the Commissioner of Indian Affairs reported for the first time that more Indians were being born than were dying. Wilcomb E. Washburn, *The Indian in America* (New York: Harper & Row, 1975), p. 272. See also Brian W. Dippie, *The Vanishing American: White Attitudes and U.S. Indian Policy* (Middletown, Conn.: Wesleyan University Press, 1982).

14. Vine Deloria, Jr., *Custer Died for your Sins* (New York: Macmillan, 1969) and *God Is Red* (New York: Grosset and Dunlap, 1973).

15. *United States v. Sioux Nation*, 448 U.S. 371 (1980). See also Wilcomb E. Washburn, "The Supreme Court's Use and Abuse of History," *Organization of American Historians Newsletter* 11, no. 3 (Aug. 1983): 7–9.

THE INDIAN SERVICE
AND ITS EVOLUTION

J A M E S E. O F F I C E R

*I*n 1961, when Philleo Nash and I joined the Bureau of Indian Affairs, most of our anthropologist colleagues turned our pictures to the wall. Mingled with outpourings of sympathy were suggestions that we were traitors to our professions at worst, and naive simpletons at best. "The reactionary old guard will eat you up," one told me; and another remarked that "the Bureau of Indian Affairs has not changed in the last hundred and thirty years. It still has a military mentality left over from the days when it was located in the War Department."

Now, twenty years later as I reflect on those comments, I am inclined to reserve judgment on the hopelessness of the cause; but with respect to the changelessness of the Indian Service, I have no doubt. It is decidedly *not* the same agency that greeted the new-born Indian Rights Association in 1882. It has a different cast, a different scenario, and a different public. In the same theatrical metaphor, Indians today are on the stage, in the audience, and writing part of the script; a hundred years ago, they were standing outside in the rain aware only that the folks inside the theater were up to no good. Not everything has changed, however. The funds that keep the production going today, as a century earlier, come from elsewhere, and from time to time those who represent the investors raise embarrassing questions as to whether they are getting their money's worth.

THE INDIAN BUREAU BEFORE THE TURN OF THE CENTURY

Many of the social service programs of the Bureau of Indian Affairs, as well as most of the resource responsibilities, are creatures of the twentieth century. But even as early as 1882, the BIA was one of the more complex agencies of the federal government. In his annual report for that year, Commissioner Price tells us that his jurisdiction included 59 agencies in 21 midwestern and western states and territories. These field units served nearly 250,000 Indians.[1] The preceding year, the Bureau had either operated or subsidized 106 schools with a combined enrollment of over 4,000 youngsters.[2]

Shortly after Commissioner Price wrote his 1882 report, he established a new position in the agency, that of superintendent of Indian schools. This action led the Bureau in the direction of secular rather than religious education. Moreover, within ten years the directors of Bureau schools were also being called superintendents. As these individuals assumed responsibilities beyond those directly related to education, the term began to replace that of "agent." Well before the beginning of World War I, the heads of local field units of the BIA had become superintendents, although the term "agency" remained in use.

In addition to the growing importance of education, as a Bureau activity, providing law and order on the reservations was of increasing concern during the administration of Price and his immediate successors. The organization of Indian police forces began in the late 1870s, and Congress extended federal jurisdiction to Indian country under the Major Crimes Act of March 3, 1885.[3] Thus the foundation for present-day BIA programs of both public security and education were laid during the same decade that the Indian Rights Association came into being.

The Bureau of Indian Affairs paid relatively little attention to reservation resource development in 1882, except for encouraging Indians to take up farming and stockraising. The BIA staff on most reservations included persons hired to teach Indians the skills needed for these pursuits. The agents were also involved in an effort to persuade Indians to become freighters; Price was able to report that wagon owners received in excess of $150,000 in fiscal 1882 for hauling agency supplies.[4]

John D. C. Atkins, who replaced Price in 1885, was equally dedicated to the idea that "private ownership of land would eventually end tribal relations and develop self-sufficiency, personal independence, and material thrift among the Indians."[5] It was during his administration that Congress passed the legislation known afterward as the Dawes Act, or the General Allotment Act of 1887. This statute led to an increasing emphasis on resource development, beginning first with lands allotted to individual Indians under the act, and later to tribally held lands.

Lobbying groups with a religious orientation, including the Indian Rights Association, had strongly endorsed Atkins's appointment, but by the time he left office they had withdrawn much of their support.[6] His education policies, which emphasized the building and operating of BIA schools and the withdrawal of subsidies from mission schools, although supported by the Indian Rights Association, brought criticism from church organizations. His hesitancy to place key employees of the Bureau under civil service also contributed to the negative reaction.

Those concerned about the decline of the mission schools were even more perturbed at the actions of Thomas Jefferson Morgan, Commissioner of Indian Affairs in the early 1890s. On taking office, he announced plans to discontinue all contracts with sectarian schools. This declaration precipitated an immediate controversy in Congress, where supporters of the missionary groups still enjoyed considerable power. Morgan was unable to gain approval for his plan, but Congress did agree not to increase the federal subsidy for mission schools. The subsidy was finally withdrawn a few years after Morgan's departure.[7]

Morgan was deeply conscious of the need for incorporating the Bureau of Indian Affairs into the civil service system, and in 1891 he succeeded with respect to school personnel, including the school physicians. Agents remained outside the system, however. The Commissioner also lobbied for Congressional authority to place school superintendents in charge of the agencies, and Congress provided that authority early in 1893, just a few weeks after Morgan left office. This action provided the basis for advancing technical and professional personnel in the Bureau's hierarchy, and also encouraged the replacement of "agents" with "superintendents."

Morgan's successor, Daniel M. Browning, was more politician than administrator. He made an effort to undo Morgan's work by having school superintendents exempted from civil service requirements. President Cleveland, well aware of the sensitive civil service issue, did not share Browning's views and helped frustrate the Commissioner's move. By the end of Cleveland's administration in 1897, almost all Indian Bureau employees had been placed under civil service regulations.[8]

The Indian Bureau began the allotment of reservation lands during the 1890s. Special agents for this purpose were assigned to each jurisdiction. They were instructed to reach an understanding with the Indians concerning allotment, and also carry out surveys, issue individual titles, and persuade the tribal members to permit the Bureau to sell at public auction any reservation lands that remained after all eligible Indians had received allotments. Since allottees were of both sexes and all ages, it became quickly apparent that some Indians lacked the ability to make their holding productive. The Bureau sought legislation to permit supervised leasing, an activity that required more and more attention from BIA staff members.

Also of increasing importance was the question of allotment inheritance. The Dawes Act provided that allotments were to remain in a protected trust status for a 25-year period, but Bureau employees had to decide whether to turn estates directly over to heirs in trust status or to pass them along in fee. As with leasing, inheritance responsibilities led to the need for amendments to the Dawes Act. The two decades between 1890 and 1910 produced much legislation relating to both topics.

Morgan and every other commissioner prior to 1933 believed in breaking up the communal status of the reservations as the first step in Indian assimilation. Although opinions varied as to whether unrestricted (fee) titles should be forced on "competent" Indians, the commissioners were convinced that owning land would "civilize" them and improve their lot in life. This belief in the importance of making the Indian a private land owner was the creed by which BIA employees lived for nearly fifty years.

William A. Jones, the first commissioner to serve through two full presidential terms, entered office in 1897 with the conviction that Indian children must be sent away from the reservations to receive the white man's education. Yet by 1903 he had decided that it was better to bring civilization to the child than to try to take the child into civilization.[9] Jones abhorred tribal landholding, however. He left office with the proud declaration that reservations had been broken up under his aegis, and that both surplus and inherited lands had been sold to "sturdy American citizens."[10]

During Jones's administration the Indian Bureau became seriously involved in programs of irrigation, an activity closely related to land allotment. With the creation of the Bureau of Reclamation in

1902, Jones saw fit to recruit a chief engineer for the Indian Bureau, a position later endorsed formally by Congress. The important irrigation branch of the BIA developed from this modest beginning. The year 1902 also saw the first exploitation of oil and gas deposits on reservation lands. Within a few years after Commissioner Jones returned to private life, the Osages of Oklahoma were helping to create a new national stereotype: the oil-rich Indian.

The most significant development of the Indian Bureau as a resource-oriented agency took place largely between 1910 and 1920, but the stage had been set by January 1905 when Jones resigned. Francis Ellington Leupp, who replaced him, was a self-righteous, headstrong individual who has been compared to a later commissioner, John Collier,[11] in temperament and ability. Although an assimilationist, Leupp was more tolerant of Indian culture than his predecessors. Like Collier over a quarter of a century later, however, he was capable of high-handed dealing with Indians, and some of his actions cost him the support of such Indian defense groups as the Indian Rights Association, for whom Leupp had once worked. His former colleagues were particularly upset over the imprisonment of certain Navajos by the arbitrary action of the Commissioner. The Indian Rights Association, who maintained that "the Indian is a person within the meaning of the Constitution and cannot be deprived of his liberty without due process of law,"[12] obtained the Navajos' release in habeas corpus proceedings before the Arizona Supreme Court. Leupp's arrogance appealed to some of his subordinates, however, and during his administration the stereotype of the Indian agent metamorphosed from light-fingered thief to hard-nosed paternalist.

Leupp built on the foundation established by his predecessor and continued the development of the Indian Bureau as a technical services agency. However, his commissionership is probably best remembered for the passage in 1906 of the Burke Act,[13] one of many amendments to the 1887 allotment legislation. Among other things, the bill empowered the Secretary of the Interior to grant Indians unrestricted titles to their allotments prior to the end of the 25-year period of federal trusteeship prescribed in the original act. Although Leupp favored the Burke legislation, he used it only selectively and punitively in the case of alcoholics and parents who would not send their children to school. This behavior further alienated him from his former colleagues in the Indian Rights Association, and their attacks on him doubtless contributed to his resignation in 1909.

THE OMNIBUS ACT OF 1910

Leupp's successor as commissioner of Indian Affairs was Robert G. Valentine, a man who had served Leupp earlier as assistant commissioner. He was commissioner in 1910 when Congress passed the greatest legislative impetus to reservation resource development in the long history of federal Indian administration. Although relatively unknown to persons not connected with the Indian Bureau, the Omnibus Act touched on virtually every aspect of Bureau responsibilities related to Indian lands and resources. J. P. Kinney, in his history of Indian land tenure in America, observed that this legislation "contained so many items of . . . vital importance . . . that the fiscal year beginning July 1, 1910 may appropriately be accepted as the first in a new period of Indian administration."[14] Within ten years after this enactment, the Indian Bureau had acquired a large staff of foresters, irrigation engineers, and real property management specialists; the technical staff joined the educational personnel in the pool from which superintendents were drawn.

It is evident from Commissioner Valentine's last annual report (1912) that he took considerable pride in the resource-related developments during both his administration and that of his predecessor and mentor, Francis E. Leupp. He noted that the annual appropriation for irrigation had risen to nearly $1.5 million by 1911, and that 230,000 acres of reservation land were "under ditch."[15] In the height of the irrigation season, the Bureau was employing 150 engineers, assistants, and field men. Valentine also mentioned that by 1910 the Indian Bureau had established its own forestry program—a development made possible by the Omnibus Act. The 1911 return to Indians from timber sales amounted to over $2 million. Indians were also receiving good profits from oil and gas leases; Osage royalties alone totalled just under $2 million between 1908 and 1911.[16]

Valentine is remembered for attempting some internal reforms that were not well received by critics in the Indian Rights Association and elsewhere. For instance, he tried to transfer the headquarters of the Bureau to Denver so that he might be closer to his Indian constituency. He also made enemies by trying to establish higher grazing fees for cattlemen pasturing their herds on Indian lands, and by prohibiting teachers in federal schools from wearing religious garb. Valentine was lauded, however, for creating the new BIA post of "expert farmer" and incorporating it into the civil service system.[17] In the 1912 report he boasted of the great increase in the number of farmers and stockmen employed by the Bureau, observing that the Navajo reservation staff alone included 250 of the former and 47 of the latter.[18] Valentine also attempted to recruit BIA employees who had experience in settlement house work among immigrant families.

It was in health programs, however, that Valentine made his most important contribution.[19] Between 1910 and 1912, he directed the first major nationwide effort to conquer the dreaded eye disease trachoma, which many Indians suffered from. He was also the first commissioner to implement a program of health education. Before leaving office he succeeded in convincing President Taft of the gravity of the reservation health problem. Taft mentioned the problem in his 1912 message to Congress, which shortly thereafter increased the Bureau appropriation for Indian health.

In spite of many innovations and some positive accomplishments, Valentine was the victim of a prolonged attack from Democratic congressmen prior to the 1912 presidential election. His enemies mounted a major investigation of his conduct in office, and weary of it all, he resigned. He later stated, "If you would have rolled President Taft and Theodore Roosevelt and Mr. Wilson and Mr. Bryan into one, you would not have a big enough man to run the Indian Bureau as it is organized today."[20] Certainly by the time Valentine departed in the fall of 1912, the Bureau of Indian Affairs had become one of the most complicated arms of the federal bureaucracy, a status it has retained ever since.

COMMISSIONER SELLS AND FORCED FEE PATENTS

Cato Sells, who followed Valentine in office, was a Texas politician and banker who knew absolutely nothing about Indian affairs. He became commissioner at a time when morale in the BIA was low and the agency had been without a head for nearly a year. Shortly after being sworn in, he announced that he would eradicate the bootleggers and saloonkeepers who preyed upon the Indians, and would see that reservation lands were put to use to make the Indian self-supporting. He immediately sought the necessary funds from Congress to extend the existing reimbursable loan program—created primarily for financing irrigation projects—to include other types of loans to Indian farmers and stockmen. He was successful in this endeavor and the period between 1912 and 1918 was one of considerable increase in the number of reservation ranchers and farmers. This increase was not enough, however, to eliminate the extensive leasing of reservation lands by non-Indians that had developed earlier. In fact, in some instances Sells found himself encouraging such leasing as a means of preserving Indian water rights.

At the time of Sells' administration, several western states, notably Utah and Wyoming, were threatening to revoke Indian rights to water needed for reservation irrigation projects unless the lands served by these projects were fully utilized. Since Indian farmers and ranchers could not be produced rapidly enough to satisfy this demand, the Bureau began leasing some land to outsiders. A particularly dramatic attempt to solve this problem is presented by Albert H. Kneale in his autobiography, *Indian Agent.*[21] Upon being assigned to head the agency at Fort Duchesne, Utah, Kneale was given four years (1914–1918) to bring 95,000 acres under cultivation. He succeeded, but only by leasing most of the land to Mormon farmers who lived nearby.

The Dawes Act of 1887 had specified that Indian allotments be held in trust, with restrictions against alienation from Indian ownership, for a period of 25 years. For the earliest allotments, the 25-year period began to expire at about the time Sells became commissioner. He firmly believed that lifting the trusteeship would reduce the Indian owner's dependency on the federal government, and he favored removal of restrictions except where the owners were obviously incompetent to manage their own affairs. In 1916, at the urging of Interior Secretary Franklin K. Lane, Sells began utilizing the authority contained in the 1906 Burke Act to confer unrestricted titles on Indians certified as competent. The following year, he announced that all Indians in certain categories would be issued unrestricted (fee) patents to their lands and given control over any funds the Bureau might be managing for them in its individual Indian money (IIM) accounts. He remarked that his competency policy would lead to "a new era in Indian administration" producing a dramatic reduction in federal expenditures.[22]

Between 1916 and his departure from office in 1921, Sells issued more than 20,000 unrestricted titles to Indians judged competent according to the criteria he established. The extent to which this action led to the alienation of reservation land has never been fully determined. However, it is part of the conventional wisdom that Sells's "forced fee patent" policy was a major contributor to the substantial reduction in Indian estate between 1887 and 1933. By the time he resigned, questions were arising about the continuation of the policy, but Sells suffered little of the harassment that Valentine and Leupp had faced. His administration was, in fact, an interlude of tranquility compared with those that preceded and followed it.

THE TROUBLED TWENTIES

President Harding's choice for commissioner was a South Dakota politician and realtor named Charles Henry Burke who had served in Congress from 1899 to 1907 and again from 1909 to 1915. Burke was one of the oldest commissioners ever nominated, and except for John Collier, he stayed in office longer than any other individual. The eight years of Burke's administration constitute one of the stormiest periods in the history of Indian affairs, probably matched only by the decade following 1970. Beginning with the dispute over legislation to settle the issue of squatters on Pueblo lands in New Mexico, continuing with the battle over the leasing of oil lands, and proceeding to the fight over religious freedom, Burke was in constant turmoil with one group of reformers or another. His most persistent attacker was John Collier.

The appropriations that the Indian Bureau was receiving in 1921, when Burke became commissioner, were authorized under many different Congressional acts. Keeping track of all these authorizations had become a problem for the House and Senate committees, as well as for BIA officials. On November 2, 1921, six months after Burke was sworn in, Congress passed a bill to consolidate them into a single piece of legislation. Known since as the Snyder Act, this legislation remains the basic funding authority for the Bureau.[23] More clearly than elsewhere, it defines the scope of federal Indian programs and entrusts the basic administrative responsibility for implementing them to the Bureau of Indian Affairs.

Burke entered office determined to improve the education and health services of the BIA. In both cases, inadequate appropriations frustrated his attempts to recruit quality personnel and construct schools and hospitals. In 1920 Congress had made education compulsory for reservation youngsters, but Burke was not able to enforce the law, and in 1924 found himself obliged to call a temporary halt to the compulsory education program.[24] That same year he orchestrated a second all-out effort to eradicate trachoma. He sponsored the organization of a traveling clinic of trachoma specialists, but the lack of an effective drug made treatment difficult, and recruiting medical personnel proved troublesome. As late as 1927, the entrance salary was $2,100 per year for BIA physicians, and $1,500 for nurses. The annual turnover rate was 56 percent for doctors and 122 percent for nurses.[25]

Indian irrigation proved another area of frustration for Burke. When appropriating money for reservation projects, Congress had insisted that the millions of dollars of construction and maintenance costs be reimbursed; but the Indians had no money with which to repay. In 1924, Burke persuaded Congress to enact legislation deferring the payments, but this was only a temporary solution. Late in his term (1928), he and the commissioner of reclamation joined forces in a survey of Indian irrigation projects. They found that only 3.5 percent of the reimbursable construction costs had been recovered. They also discovered that less than 52 percent of the reclaimed lands were under irrigation, and that only 17 percent of the irrigated land was being farmed by Indians. The two commissioners recommended cancellation of the uncollectable debts, a recommendation Congress accepted some years later.[26]

Frustrated in many other areas, Burke turned his attention to internal reorganization of the Bureau, and with greater success. In 1926 he appointed a general superintendent who had line authority over the administration of schools as well as agricultural and industrial activities. Reporting directly to this individual were nine district superintendents. The commissioner also established the position of chief medical director, and divided Indian country into four medical districts with a director in charge of each. Physicians occupying these posts were commissioned officers in the U.S. Public Health Service.[27]

One of the most important developments in the resource field during Burke's administration was the passage by Congress of a comprehensive statute for oil and gas leasing. The legislation extended full entitlement to mineral revenues to the residents of all reservations.

The battle between Burke and Collier over permitting Indians to continue their native religious practices split the Indian defense groups. In this case, the Indian Rights Association backed the commissioner, whereas the American Indian Defense Association supported Collier. Eventually, Burke agreed to a compromise with Collier and his supporters; among other things, the compromise permitted Indian children certified as candidates for special roles in native religious ceremonies to be excused from school at certain periods of the year. This had been a major issue in a number of traditional Indian communities.[28]

The controversy between Burke and Collier attracted so much national attention that in 1926 Secretary of the Interior Hubert Work contracted with the Institute for Government Research (later known as the Brookings Institute) for a thorough study of Indian affairs. The conclusions of that study, since known as the Meriam Report, were made public in 1928. Collier was not pleased with Work's action and persuaded his friends in Congress to conduct an investigation centering on the personality of Commissioner Burke. The Indian Sub-Committee of the Senate held hearings during 1928. Much of the testimony focused on the single issue of probating Indian estates, where it did reveal the need for reform in the Bureau's approach. The Meriam Report, on the other hand, proved the most searching study of Indian administration ever undertaken. Collier was obliged to admit its worth, calling it "the most important indictment of the Bureau since Helen Hunt Jackson's *A Century of Dishonor*."[29]

Burke's resignation in February 1929 led to the appointment of Charles James Rhoads, a Philadelphia Quaker with close ties to the Indian Rights Association. Although he and Collier had been on opposite sides of some issues during Burke's administration, Collier respected Rhoads and felt he would implement many of the recommendations of the Meriam Report. Unfortunately, the honeymoon did not last long. Early in Rhoads' term Collier realized they had very different opinions on the subject of land allotment. Like his predecessors, Rhoads believed that individualization of Indian land was the most important part of Indian assimilation; overall, he supported the policy set forth in the Act of 1887. The evils of the past, he argued, could be overcome through adapting modern business tools, such as the corporation and the trust, to the administration of Indian property.[30] Collier was willing to accept the notion of corporate control of Indian lands, but opposed further allotment. Corporation for him meant a tribal entity that possessed economic and political powers as well as an exemption from state and local taxation. Rhoads was on record in favor of greater political authority for tribal councils, but he found Collier's proposal far too radical and anti-assimilationist.[31]

The real break between Rhoads and Collier came in 1930 when the commissioner accepted a compromise with the House Appropriations Committee that Collier felt was unnecessary. Through his influence with the Senate Committee on Indian Affairs, Collier succeeded in having the compromise overridden, thus dealing Rhoads an embarrassing defeat. He also used his influence with the committee to force personnel changes in the Bureau that the commissioner and his backers in the Indian Rights Association opposed.[32]

The stock market crash made it impossible for Rhoads to get Congressional action on many of the reforms he had proposed, but his administration was not without accomplishment. He brought in W. Carson Ryan, Jr. to head the Bureau's school program. Ryan was a nationally known spokesman for modern education who had served on the Meriam Report committee. Under his and his successors' aegis, the Bureau developed one of the most innovative education approaches in the country, and continued to provide leadership in this area until the beginning of World War II. Rhoads also established five technical divisions within the Washington office and recruited well-educated young specialists to head them. He initiated the Bureau's first preventive medicine program, giving special emphasis to maternal and infant care.

During most of his four-year administration, Rhoads pressed Congress to enact a bill forgiving the reimbursable charges on Indian irrigation projects. This task was finally accomplished with passage of the Leavitt Act in July 1932.[33] At the beginning of his term, Rhoads had favored transferring Indian irrigation projects to the Bureau of Reclamation, but the more he learned about these projects the more he was convinced that they should remain with the Indian Bureau. In 1930 and 1931 he obtained Congressional support for keeping them.

Following the election of Franklin D. Roosevelt in the fall of 1932, officials of the Indian Rights Association asked the new president to retain Rhoads, but on the advice of Secretary of the Interior Harold Ickes, Roosevelt chose Collier instead. The Indian Bureau's strongest and most persistent critic became its commissioner on April 21, 1933, the day after Rhoads resigned.

JOHN COLLIER AND HIS REVOLUTION

Although supporters of assimilation remained in Congress, in the Indian Bureau, and within the public at large, the ascension of Collier to the commissionership signalled a new direction in federal Indian policy and in the Bureau of Indian Affairs. In an article he wrote for *American Indian Life* shortly before being named commissioner, Collier stated his support for collective and corporate use of Indian property, federal credit programs, replacement of boarding schools with day schools, assistance from the Department of Agriculture for Indian farmers and stockmen, the end of land allotment, and the repeal of laws that adversely affected Indian civil liberties.[34] After taking office, he drafted legislation to realize several of these policies. With many modifications, Congress passed this legislation one year later, in 1934. Known today as the Indian Reorganization Act (IRA), it brought the allotment program to an end, extended indefinitely the period of trusteeship over Indian land, established the basis for democratic tribal governments, and confirmed the right of tribes to greater control over their destinies.[35] Thus the IRA finally reversed a policy established nearly fifty years before.

Collier strongly favored recruiting more Indians for the BIA staff, and insisted that the Indian Reorganization Act contain language assuring Indian preference in federal employment. Congress had occasionally inserted Indian preference clauses in legislation concerned with the internal organization of the Bureau, and while no commissioner had completely ignored these directives, enforcement varied. Collier's dedication to Indian preference produced significant changes in both the number of Indian employees and the positions to which they could aspire. By the time Collier retired in 1945, Haskell Institute at Lawrence, Kansas (an Indian boarding school run by the Bureau) had become a kind of training center for future BIA staff members, and during the 1950s and 1960s many Haskell graduates occupied posts with line responsibilities. The "old school tie" among these individuals led to a belief within the Bureau that getting ahead for Indian employees required membership in the "Haskell clique." Robert L. Bennett, who in 1966 became the first Indian in nearly 100 years to serve as commissioner, was a Haskell graduate, as was John O. Crow, deputy commissioner under Philleo Nash and Louis R. Bruce.

Historian Graham D. Taylor has observed the "deep gulf between the Bureau leadership and the field force in their views of Indians and the purposes of the Indian Reorganization Act."[36] Opposition to Collier's original draft of the bill was widespread among the "old guard," some of whom spoke out so strongly that Secretary Ickes imposed what they referred to as a "gag rule." The Indian Rights

Association also opposed parts of the legislation and aired its views in the journal *Indian Truth*, which was widely circulated among BIA employees in the field.[37]

In his original draft, Collier had included a provision permitting tribal governments "to compel the transfer . . . of many persons employed in the administration of Indian Affairs"—a provision universally opposed by superintendents and other line officers. Although Congress eliminated this provision from the final version, many field employees regarded it as evidence of Collier's antagonism. Furthermore, it encouraged tribal councils to bring actions of various kinds against agency personnel, and the councils began to bypass superintendents on important issues. In 1936 Collier was obliged to reassure superintendents concerning their responsibilities. He also issued a directive to tribal councils that requested them first to submit their comments and complaints to the superintendents, rather than to him.[38]

Much remains to be written about the reservation elections held between 1934 and 1936, when the tribes voted whether or not to come under the Act. During the six years that I supervised the activities of the Indian Bureau's Office of Tribal Operations, I gained first-hand awareness of what a crazy, disorganized effort it was. Since the Bureau lacked field personnel with experience in conducting elections, qualifying voters, and helping to draft organizational documents, Collier turned to anthropologists and lawyers for advice. The former knew a good deal about Indians, but little or nothing about politics and the law. Lawyers, on the other hand, knew little about Indians. Furthermore, BIA personnel in the field, upon whose shoulders the workload fell, were often suspicious of Collier, lawyers, *and* anthropologists. The result was a poorly coordinated, confused operation conducted in an atmosphere of desperate haste.

Some of the biggest headaches for Bureau field personnel lay in areas where the groups were small and the treaties, executive orders, and Congressional statutes establishing reservations were vague concerning which Indians had use and occupancy rights. With few exceptions, such groups had no membership rolls. Without extensive research, often involving records unavailable locally, it was next to impossible to determine which Indians should be eligible to vote on the questions of including the reservation under the Indian Reorganization Act or of approving a constitution. Typical of such an area was the Western Washington Agency, whose constituency included nearly a score of tiny reservations around the perimeter of Puget Sound, on the Olympic Peninsula, and along the Pacific Coast.

A serious situation developed in the case of the Quinault reservation. Established by treaty and statute for a particular class of "fish eating Indians," the reservation lay within the territory of the Quinaults. Persons descended from or closely allied with Quinaults alive at the time the reservation was created, had generally been successful through the years in keeping representatives of other tribes from living on the reservation, even though many of the latter were allotted thereon. With few exceptions the allotments were in heavily timbered and inaccessible areas unsuitable for housing sites. Furthermore, the Indian Bureau had recognized a tribal council representing the resident Indians as authorized to speak for all Indians with interests on the reservation.

When the time came to vote on exclusion from the Indian Reorganization Act, local officials of the Indian Bureau contacted Collier's office for instructions concerning eligible voters. Were only those Indians who lived on or near the reservation, or all Indians living and allotted on the reservation eligible to vote? The Commissioner and his advisers responded that representatives of both groups were eligible, but that non-resident voters must sign an affidavit that they regarded the reservation as their home and intended eventually to settle there. Affidavits were distributed and signed, even though many who signed them had never lived on the reservation and could not have done so had they wished.

When all ballots were in and tabulated, the Bureau became aware that Indians living on or near the reservation had voted heavily for exclusion, whereas allottees living elsewhere had voted *not* to be excluded. However, because the numbers of the latter were greater, the total was against exclusion and the Bureau proclaimed the Quinault reservation to be under the Indian Reorganization Act. The resident population has disputed this position ever since. Furthermore, they refused to develop a constitution under provisions of the Act, since to do so would have obliged them to include non-residents as tribal members. The latter, although allotted on an Indian reservation and of Indian descent, are today looked upon by the Bureau as non-tribal Indians because they are not members of a recognized tribe. They sometimes have difficulty obtaining federal services intended for Indians, while their descendants are characteristically excluded altogether from these benefits.

The resource-oriented activities of the Bureau gained ascendancy during the early years of the Collier administration and were later combined into a branch of land operations that included soil conservation, irrigation, range management, and agricultural extension.[39] The Depression years were marked by increased federal attention to rural areas, and as the Department of Agriculture gained in importance and appropriations, Collier turned to its agencies for help on the reservations.[40] The Soil Conservation Service, transferred in 1935 from the Interior to the Agriculture Department, was particularly important to Collier's program. His emphasis on conservation led to stock reduction projects in the Southwest and made him enemies on such reservations as the Navajo, Hopi, and Papago.

Education was another area of particular importance to Collier. Following Ryan's departure in 1936, the commissioner hired another progressive educator, Willard Beatty, who continued some of Ryan's programs, changed others, and introduced a number of his own. He did not feel that the Bureau should continue educating Indians for non-existent jobs in the cities, and he altered school curricula to help solve rural problems on the reservations. Indian children were taught to plant gardens, care for livestock, and employ modern methods of conservation. The schools became centers of community activity and bilingual methods were employed in a number of areas.

Collier's relations with the House and Senate Indian Committees, which were never strong, continued to weaken after 1936. While promoting the Indian Reorganization Act he had relied on a number of factors, the most important being his close relationship with Senator Burton K. Wheeler, the early honeymoon period of the Roosevelt administration, and his own dedication to a stubborn set of ideals.[41] It is unlikely that Congress had intended to legislate such far-reaching changes in Indian policy as Collier contemplated, and by 1937 even Wheeler concluded that he had been victimized.[42] Had the Indian Rights Association and other defense groups not come to Collier's aid, Wheeler's bill (1937) to repeal the Indian Reorganization Act might have signalled the end of the reform effort.

In 1941, the Bureau of the Budget compelled the removal of the Indian Bureau from Washington to Chicago to make room for war-related activities. Not only was this a blow to Collier's pride, but it weakened his communication with directors of other federal agencies. The war effort also deprived the Bureau of some of its most qualified technical and professional personnel. More than 800 regular employees—doctors, teachers, and linguists among them—left for military service or were transferred to agencies directly devoted to winning the war. By 1944, there were 100 vacancies for doctors and 188 openings for nurses. Collier commented that it had become impossible "to provide Indians even the most essential medical care."[43] Frustrated by personnel and budget problems, continuing attacks from Congress, and loss of support from such tribes as the Navajos, Hopis, and Mohaves, Collier submitted his resignation in January 1945. Although he had tranformed Indian policy, he left the Bureau in a shambles. Its budget in his last year was lower than in 1932 and it was seriously short of technicians and professionals in many critical categories.[44] Earlier gains in school enrollment had been sacrificed to the war effort and many Indian youngsters were not attending classes.

THE POST-COLLIER PERIOD

Collier's choice for his successor was William A. Brophy, an attorney who had worked with the Pueblo tribes during most of Collier's administration and whose wife the commissioner had appointed superintendent of the United Pueblos Agency in 1935 (over the objection of leaders from the Taos and Zuni communities).[45] Because of strong opposition to Collier in Congress, Brophy was interrogated sharply by members of the Senate Interior Committee following his nomination in March 1945. He assured the senators that he did not consider himself obligated to support Collier's program and would have no reservations about following Congressional policy.[46] His confirmation brought a slight improvement in relations between Congress and the Bureau of Indian Affairs. Although Brophy's term technically did not end until June 1948, he was ill for most of the period after 1946, during which the Bureau was run by William Zimmerman, Jr., who had been Collier's assistant commissioner.

During the Brophy-Zimmerman administration there were several developments with heavy impact on the Indian Bureau. In 1946 Congress passed the Indian Claims Act, establishing a special tribunal to decide the validity of land and accounting claims that tribes had long been making against the federal government. An immediate effect of the claims legislation was to involve the Bureau in the approval of the contracts between tribes and their claims attorneys. The act would have a more profound effect later, when the Bureau was called upon to approve compromises between tribes and the government, assist the Indians with developing plans for the use of claims awards, help determine individual beneficiaries, and prepare tribal membership rolls. In the 1960s, as the awards began to come with greater frequency, the BIA was obliged to create special units devoted to claims and enrollment—units that survived the 1978 dissolution of the Indian Claims Commission and subsequent transfer of the remaining cases to the federal Court of Claims.

During the period that Congress was considering the claims legislation, it was also examining proposals for the reorganization of the Bureau of Indian Affairs. One such bill passed both houses and was signed into law by President Truman in August 1946. This legislation authorized the commissioner to set up regional field offices "to facilitate and simplify administration."[47] In response to the reorganization act, Brophy established five geographic districts with headquarters in Minneapolis, Billings, Portland, Phoenix, and Oklahoma City. This administrative change resulted in the delegation of certain powers previously held exclusively by the commissioner to a new class of line officers known as area directors. Tribal leaders began to object almost immediately to the imposition of a new level of bureaucracy; the area office has been a sore point with them ever since. By 1982, there were 12 area offices directed by BIA personnel of Indian descent. The Reagan administration, however, proposed to significantly reduce the number of area offices as an economy measure.

Early in 1947, after Brophy became too ill to serve on a regular basis, the Senate Committee on the Post Office and Civil Service conducted hearings on ways to reduce personnel and expenses of the Bureau of Indian Affairs. Acting Commissioner Zimmerman was summoned to appear at these hearings. He was asked whether the termination of the special relationship between the "more advanced" tribes and the federal government might be one way of reducing expenditures, and to identify any tribes that might be candidates for withdrawal of special government services. Zimmerman provided the Committee with three lists. One included the names of the groups he felt would suffer least from immediate termination of the relationship. The second list contained the names of those that might be ready in ten years. The final list included tribes that would not be prepared for termination in the foreseeable future.

Zimmerman was not a supporter of precipitous withdrawal of

federal services, and did not intend that his lists be used for termination planning without taking account of the caveats he presented along with them. However, they became the basis for later Congressional actions that ignored his cautionary provisos.[48]

The withdrawal policy favored by many Congressmen received a boost from the 1948 report of the Hoover Commission, which strongly urged the federal government to follow a policy of assimilation. The report observed that under the trusteeship of the BIA, Indians had lost the experience inherent in managing their own property.[49] The implied message was that the government should remove itself from the Indian business as rapidly as possible.

John Ralph Nichols, who had served on the Indian Committee of the Hoover Commission, succeeded Brophy as commissioner, but remained in office less than a year. He agreed that the federal government should end its trust relationship with Indians, but cautioned that it should not "walk out before the task is completed." He also chided Congress for being niggardly with funds, pointing out that conversion of the Indians into productive and successful members of society would require an expenditure of at least $150 million.[50]

Replacing Nichols in May 1950 was Dillon S. Myer, who had been director of the War Relocation Authority during World War II. The new commissioner and John Collier had clashed over the placing of Japanese relocation centers on Indian reservations some years before, and Myer had no particular love for either Collier's policies or his friends. He carried out a thorough housecleaning in the Washington office of the Bureau, forcing the departure among others of William Zimmerman, who for all intents and purposes had run the agency during the preceding three years.

Myer, like Jones at the turn of the century, was an able, experienced administrator. He was also a devout believer in termination and established a program unit within the Bureau to prepare proposals for withdrawal of federal services. Under his stimulus, Congress began looking at a variety of termination-related bills. Although none of these became law, several progressed to the hearing stage, and one concerned with transferring legal jurisdiction over California reservations to the state did pass the House of Representatives.[51] Myer organized a cadre of BIA staff members who shared his views regarding termination, and the administrative machinery for a national withdrawal program was largely in place when Myer departed early in 1953. His successor, New Mexico banker Glenn Emmons, thus inherited both a structure and a set of attitudes that were helpful early in his administration as Congress dictated a national withdrawal policy.

THE TERMINATION YEARS

Emmons became commissioner on July 28, 1953, and just four days later Congress approved House Concurrent Resolution 83-108 endorsing termination and naming particular tribes as candidates "at the earliest possible time." Two weeks afterward, Congress enacted Public Law 83-280, directing the transfer of legal jurisdiction over certain Indian reservations to several states and authorizing others to assume such jurisdiction whenever they chose. During Emmons's first two years in office, the withdrawal thrust moved in several directions: to terminate as rapidly as possible those groups considered ready, which meant those on Zimmerman's "first list"; to transfer key functions of the Indian Bureau to other federal departments, to the states, or to the Indian tribes; and to increase efforts in the fields of health, education, resource development, and employment assistance so as to hasten the day when all tribes could be terminated.

Most of the withdrawal legislation affecting particular tribes was enacted by the 83rd Congress during 1954. Among the groups involved were the comparatively large and wealthy Menominee of Wisconsin and the Klamath of Oregon—both owners of large forests. The principal transfer of functions from the Indian Bureau—apart from that contemplated in Public Law 83-280—occurred with the passage of a bill in 1954 to remove health programs from the BIA and place them in the Public Health Service. The Bureau thus lost one of its oldest functions.

Early in his administration, Emmons also began to transfer the agricultural extension responsibilities of the BIA to the extension services of those states in which reservations were located. To do so, he made use of the Johnson-O'Malley Act of 1934, a major legislative enactment of the Collier administration which granted authority to contract with states and their subdivisions for providing services to Indian communities.[52] When he entered office in 1953, Emmons was advised that 20,000 Indian children of school age were not attending classes. He immediately decided to make education his highest priority, and centered much of the effort on the Navajo reservation, where approximately 70 percent of the unenrolled youngsters lived. The Office of Education became an important ally of the Bureau of Indian Affairs during this period; Emmons also used the authority of the Johnson-O'Malley Act to contract with public school districts for the education of Indian children. By 1957, he had achieved a significant improvement in the situation, and by the end of his administration in 1961, a majority of school-age Indians were enrolled in public schools.[53]

When the possibilities for industrial development on the reservations began to surface during the Emmons era, the Bureau established a branch for industrial development. Related to its activities was an attempt to obtain long-term leasing authority for reservations located near urban centers, where the industrial potential appeared highest. Officials of the Emmons administration also perceived opportunities for Indian income through tourism, and began to urge tribes to move in that direction. But despite such activities, the commissioner felt that a significant number of Indians would have to make their living outside the reservations. He placed heavy emphasis on programs of employment assistance, including vocational training for adults and their relocation to urban industrial centers. Not only did Emmons find Congress willing to appropriate large sums to move Indian families from the reservations and sustain them until they could get on their feet, but he was also able to persuade the House and Senate in 1956 to provide authority for a greatly expanded program of adult vocational training. To accommodate the enlarged off-reservation placement effort, Emmons established a network of urban employment offices. The response of individual Indians to this program was often enthusiastic, but tribal leaders viewed it as part of the termination policy and publicly opposed it. Eventually, during the administration of Emmons's successor, tribal leaders were able to shift the emphasis to employment in towns and cities close to the reservations.

Long before Emmons came into office, the Bureau had despaired of keeping track of Indian allottees and their heirs. For many years, the descendants of deceased allottees had been inheriting parcels of land "in common," and as a result some relatively small holdings had dozens of owners. The law required the Bureau to try to obtain the permission of all competent adult owners of allotments before leasing them, but in many cases this was impossible. As a result, the parcels often lay idle. During the late 1950s, the Interior Department and the committees of Congress began collecting information about the heirship snarl. Late in 1960, shortly before Emmons stepped down as commissioner, both the House and the Senate published extensive reports on the situation, and both had prepared legislation when the 87th Congress convened early in 1961.

The termination forces that had enjoyed so much strength at the beginning of Emmons's commissionership quickly ran out of steam. By late 1955, opposition groups began to assert themselves. The National Congress of American Indians, founded a decade before, moved to the forefront among organizations lobbying against termination policy. Friction developed within Congressional ranks over the issue of whether Indian consent should be required before a termination plan could go into effect, or whether "consultation" with a tribe was sufficient.[54] In September 1958, the Secretary of the Interior stated his opposition to any termination proposal that did not involve both consultation *and* consent.[55] When Emmons stepped down as commissioner in January 1961, there was scant likelihood that the new administration would pump air into the deflating termination balloon.

EXPANDING FEDERAL INVOLVEMENT

Seven months elapsed after the resignation of Emmons before President Kennedy nominated Philleo Nash, an anthropologist with broad experience in federal and state politics. During the preceding several months, Nash had served on a four-man task force appointed by Secretary of the Interior Stewart L. Udall to suggest a new direction in Indian administration. The task force report had recommended that termination be abandoned and that the human and natural resources of the reservations be developed instead.

Nash concentrated his efforts on obtaining enlarged appropriations for education and resource development and on involving other federal agencies in raising the living standards of Indian communities. He enjoyed great success in both efforts. Through his instigation the Department of Labor started applying the Manpower Development and Training Act to Indians, and the Department of Commerce began to make its presence felt on the reservations through the Area Redevelopment Act. A major drive to improve Indian housing gained the support and assistance of agencies within the Department of Housing and Urban Development.

To coordinate Bureau activities and keep track of what other agencies were doing on the reservations, Nash set up a division of economic development. He assigned specialists from the division to the area offices, and in some cases, to the lower-level field units. He also greatly strengthened the office of tribal operations, thereby improving its ability to help tribal councils make constitutional changes to enable the tribes to better accommodate business ventures and also plan how to use monies derived from claims awards.

Increased federal involvement not only contributed to reservation development, it also brought to tribal council officials—in many cases for the first time—the experience of making decisions free of domination by the Bureau of Indian Affairs. Although BIA officials were instructed by Nash to be available for consultation, Indian leaders were now expected to make the decisions about tribal economic development. Passage of the Economic Opportunity Act of 1964 greatly increased opportunities for decision-making by Indians, who set up community action programs in many reservations.

Early in Nash's administration, both houses of Congress began considering bills to remedy the complicated heirship problem plaguing the allotted reservations. During late 1961 and all 1962, representatives of the Indians, including tribal attorneys, conferred with Congressional staff members and BIA personnel about amendments to make the legislation more acceptable. The 87th Congress adjourned late in 1962 without action, but a third bill was introduced by Senator Frank Church of Idaho early in the 88th Congress. Church's proposal incorporated many of the suggestions made by Indians and Interior Department officials and was generally lauded at Senate hearings as a good example of compromise legislation.[56] Commissioner Nash delivered a strong statement in support of the measure, and it was also applauded by both the Indian Rights Association and the Association on American Indian Affairs.[57]

In spite of support in some important quarters, the bill enjoyed the backing of neither the National Congress of American Indians nor the National Indian Youth Council, the two most prominent Indian interest groups at that time. Spokesmen for individual tribes were divided in their views, with a majority in opposition. Tribal attorneys were also divided. Many Congressmen, still sensitive to the widespread negative reaction of their Indian constituents to termination legislation passed during the 1950s, were reluctant to support Church's bill. Jealousies between members of the Senate and House Interior committees added to the confusion, and the 88th Congress also adjourned without passing heirship legislation. Frustrated after five years on the heirship project, Senator Church resigned as chairman of the Indian Affairs Subcommittee. George McGovern, his successor, chose not to continue the effort.

Commissioner Nash and his staff were disappointed with the failure of the bill to pass. They had expected it to help them gain control of the enormous record-keeping job. Aware that the situation could only grow worse with time, they decided instead to accelerate computerization of land documents, an effort they had begun shortly before. The defeat of the legislation also made clear to Congress and the Executive Department that the fight against termination had enabled Indians to assemble a strong lobbying force for the first time in their history. Henceforth, consultation with Indian spokesmen would be indispensable for any measures directly affecting the reservations. Bills lacking their support would be doomed to failure.

Bureau employees had regarded Nash with suspicion when he entered office, seeing him as another reformer in the Collier tradition. However, he soon gained their confidence as perhaps no other commissioner ever had. He travelled frequently and came to know area directors, superintendents, and other key field personnel on a one-to-one basis. Already possessed of a considerable knowledge of Indian tribes, he was able to make decisions without extensive briefings concerning the identities and situations of the Lummi, the Tlingit, or the Hupa. He made several trips to Alaska and travelled on the *North Star*, a supply ship maintained by the Indian Bureau.[58] Nash was also successful in establishing a close relationship with Indian leaders. He attended their national meetings, sometimes stayed up all night singing with them, and visited the reservations frequently. The bond between the commissioner and the Indians was clearly demonstrated in 1966 when Nash was asked to resign. Although his proposed successor was an Indian, leaders of several national organizations, including the National Congress of American Indians, rallied to his support.[59]

Nash's replacement was Robert L. Bennett, an Oneida Indian from Nash's home state of Wisconsin. Secretary of the Interior Udall had become acquainted with Bennett while visiting Alaska, where he was area director for the BIA. Udall had always expressed interest in having an Indian as commissioner, and Bennett became the first Native American nominated for the post in nearly a hundred years.

For several months prior to Nash's departure, an Interior Department task force headed by the undersecretary had been working on a legislative measure to accomplish the reforms favored by Udall. Among the proposals was one to allow tribal governing bodies, under certain conditions, to mortgage or sell reservation land in order to raise capital for development ventures. Given the increased sophistication of tribal leaders and the emphasis on economic development in Udall's administration, this provision seemed reasonable.

The task force produced a "working draft" of the proposed bill at about the same time the Senate held hearings on Bennett's nomination. Following the conclusion of the hearings, the Committee on Interior and Insular Affairs released a report highly critical of the Bureau of Indian Affairs. It chastised the Bureau for failing to carry out the mandate for termination contained in House Concurrent Resolution 83-108, and for dragging its feet on other termination legislation. The document came as a surprise to BIA personnel and to the Indians, many of whom had felt the drive for termination was over.

Some Indian leaders now began to see the forced resignation of Nash as part of a plot to revive termination. This feeling grew when they obtained a leaked copy of the task force draft that included the provision concerning mortgage and sale of reservation land. Shortly thereafter, Secretary Udall summoned Bureau officials and some representatives of Congress to a policy meeting in Santa Fe. Convinced that the conclave was an effort to turn the clock back to the mid-1950s, the National Congress of American Indians convened an executive meeting, also in Santa Fe, and demanded admission to the Secretary's conference. At the same time, they released statements to the press accusing the Interior Department of formulating drastic changes in policy without Indian participation.[60] Udall decided against admitting all the Indian leaders to the Interior Department meeting, but did open it to a representative group.

Although Udall's statements at the Santa Fe conference somewhat reduced the fears of the Indians, many remained troubled that the Secretary had permitted legislative drafting to proceed so far without consulting them. As a result, Bennett began his term in a swirl of confusion about what direction Indian affairs were heading. Following the Santa Fe meeting, Bennett initiated a series of discussions with Indian leaders about the kind of legislation needed to promote self-determination. Few of their comments touched on the same issues covered in the department's draft proposal. Nevertheless, Secretary

Udall chose to submit an Omnibus Bill to Congress that included most of the items of the earlier draft. The committees began consideration of the measure in 1967. Although some tribes supported it, most did not, and the bill failed.

Other legislation proposed by the Interior Department was more successful. The guarantees of the Bill of Rights were extended to reservation Indian populations, and Public Law 83-280 was amended to make Indian consent necessary before a state could extend its legal jurisdiction to an Indian reservation. The latter amendment was particularly important to the Indians, since Public Law 83-280 was a basic pillar of the termination policy. Toppling it would provide the first concrete evidence that Congress had abandoned the policy. The departmental proposal was incorporated into a national civil rights act that became law in 1968; it was the most important legislation during Bennett's administration.[61]

When Bennett became commissioner, Congress was considering amendments to the Elementary and Secondary Education Act that would make federal Indian schools eligible for some of its benefits. During the hearings before the Committee on Labor and Public Welfare, several senators became acquainted for the first time with Indian education problems and began to believe that a major national study of the subject was in order. In July 1967, Senator Paul Fannin of Arizona proposed the creation of a special Senate Subcommittee on Indian Education to hold hearings and make recommendations; the Senate approved and named Robert Kennedy its chairman. In June 1968, following Kennedy's assassination, he was replaced by his brother Ted. The final report of the subcommittee was released a year and a half later.[62]

Like his predecessors, Bennett suffered frustrations. One problem came from the solicitor's office, the legal division of the Department of the Interior. The Bureau of Indian Affairs had no lawyers of its own, even though many of the knottiest legal issues of the department concerned Indian matters. Attorneys working on Indian issues in the solicitor's office were frequently unable to persuade their superiors to become aggressive advocates of Indian causes, particularly when Interior Department agencies such as the Bureau of Reclamation, the Bureau of Land Management, or the National Park Service were in opposition. Furthermore, even when the solicitor did decide to take an Indian matter to court, he had to convince the Department of Justice of his reason for doing so, since only attorneys for the latter department are authorized to represent the federal government in court actions.

The Task Force on Indian Affairs appointed by Secretary Udall in 1961 had asked at that time whether the legal work of the BIA could be effectively handled under the existing system,[63] but conflict between Bureau officials and the solicitor's staff had become worse by the time Bennett became commissioner. Tribal leaders were pushing more aggressively for action in long-neglected cases, and new problems had arisen concerning water rights, reservation boundaries, and leasing arrangements. In May 1968, Bennett proposed to Secretary Udall that the Bureau be permitted to develop a legal section of its own; or, as an alternative, that he be allowed to supervise the lawyers handling Indian matters in the solicitor's office.[64] Udall took no action on the proposal, but did direct the solicitor to adopt a stronger policy of Indian advocacy.

During his last three years in office Bennett had to deal with a number of task forces authorized to examine the Indian-federal relationship. The first task force, appointed by President Johnson in 1966, conducted hearings in a highly secretive atmosphere and produced a report containing some dramatic recommendations, including one to transfer Indian affairs to the Department of Health, Education and Welfare. The following year, an inter-agency task force, composed of representatives of the Interior Department, the Bureau of the Budget, and the Office of Economic Opportunity, produced a new set of recommendations, including the creation of a "people-oriented" assistant secretary of the interior for Indian and Territorial Affairs. Johnson rejected this recommendation, but did incorporate other items from the task force report in a special message on Indians delivered to Congress in March 1968. The theme of that message was self-determination, and Johnson highlighted this objective as the basic focus of national Indian policy. Johnson's message also led to the creation of a National Council on Indian Opportunity under the direction of the vice-president. Its basic function was to coordinate the many federal programs for Indians, and its membership included representatives from the cabinet agencies with Indian activities, as well as selected Indian leaders. The Council survived the first administration of President Nixon, but was dissolved when President Ford took office late in 1973.

THE REPUBLICANS TAKE OVER

Nixon was inaugurated in January 1969, and Bennett stepped down in late May, two months before Secretary of the Interior Walter J. Hickel informed the press that the President's choice for a new commissioner was Louis R. Bruce. Born on the Onondaga reservation in New York, Bruce was of Mohawk and Sioux ancestry. His previous experience in the federal government included service with the Federal Housing Administration in the 1960s, when he had worked closely with Commissioner Nash in extending the benefits of public housing to the reservations. Bruce moved quickly to quiet the fears of the Indians regarding termination and to make clear that Indian involvement would be the trademark of his commissionership. During his relatively short term in office, he and his staff initiated changes in the federal-Indian relationship that would make the decade of the 1970s the most notable in the entire history of American Indian administration.

In January 1970, Secretary Hickel announced an "executive realignment" of the top positions in the BIA.[65] The positions of deputy commissioner and assistant commissioner were eliminated; instead of a deputy, two associate commissioners were created to supervise the activities of certain program divisions headed by "directors." This realignment made possible the transfer or retirement of high-ranking officials appointed during the previous Democratic administrations and opened up important jobs for Republican appointees. But nine months elapsed before the carefully chosen newcomers were appointed. On October 18 the Commissioner appointed fifteen Indians to high posts in the Bureau.[66] Only three of these individuals had previously been employed by the BIA. Six had gained governmental experience through association with the Office of Economic Opportunity; of the remaining six, two had been associated with the Office of Education, one had served as a staff member to the Special Senate Subcommittee on Indian Education, two had worked for Indian defense organizations, and one was drawn from private business. Most were not well known to the Washington staff of the Bureau, and several were regarded with suspicion because of their identification with the Office of Economic Opportunity or suspected affiliation with the militant American Indian Movement (AIM).

A month later, the Secretary announced personnel policy changes of great import.[67] The title of superintendent, in use throughout the twentieth century, was replaced by that of "field administrator." Much of the authority delegated previously to the area directors was redelegated to the new positions; and ten of the area directors, along with six heads of field employment assistance (relocation) offices, were reassigned.

Between January 1970 and the announcement of the above administrative changes in November, Bureau personnel assisted the White House staff in preparing a special message to Congress. In July the President sent it to his former colleagues on Congressional Hill. He announced that the policy of his administration would be "self-determination, not termination," and he stated that a number of legislative proposals would soon be laid before the House and the Senate to "break decisively with the past and to create the conditions for a new era in which the Indian future is determined by Indian acts and Indian decisions."[68] He called upon Congress to replace House Concurrent Resolution 83-108 with authority and appropriations to finance reservation development, upgrade the quality of Indian education, and improve the defense of Indian legal rights through an Indian Trust Counsel Authority free of the influence of the departments of Justice and the Interior.

In the period immediately following Nixon's message, Congress took several actions that demonstrated its willingness to reject termination as a Congressional policy objective. The first action repealed termination legislation for the Choctaws. Then the Five Civilized Tribes of Oklahoma, the Choctaw among them, were authorized for the first time since the early 1900s to choose their own leaders. Finally, Congress restored Indian jurisdiction to the Metlakatla reservation in Alaska. The most positive impact, however, was the passage on December 15, 1970 of a bill to restore certain sacred lands to the Pueblo of Taos, New Mexico. The Indian Claims Commission had previously held that these lands were illegally taken from the Indians, setting the stage for a financial award to the Pueblo. But the Indians wanted the land back, an action the Claims Commission had no authority to take. The Indians then sought special legislation to transfer the land from the National Forest Service to the Pueblo. Their success in this endeavor encouraged other Indians to seek the recovery of lost lands held by the federal government.

Late in 1970, the new employees of the Bureau began to move

into action. Their immediate aim was to transfer as much administrative responsibility as possible to the tribes. They sought to convert the BIA from a direct provider of services into a contracting and granting agency. The legislative authority for such transfers was somewhat vague, depending primarily on language contained in acts passed by Congress in 1834 and 1910. As the aggressive newcomers moved ahead, veteran Bureau employees, as well as Congressmen who had considerable experience with Indian matters, raised questions about the legality of the changes. Secretary of the Interior Rogers C. B. Morton, who had replaced Hickel late in 1970, finally stepped in and guided the Bureau toward a more conservative approach. He revived the position of deputy commissioner and filled it with John O. Crow, who had served in the same post during the administration of Commissioner Nash. Morton stated that Crow would be directly responsible for running the internal operations of the agency.[69]

Crow's presence in the Washington office often frustrated the impatient newcomers, some of whom sought support from militant activists in such organizations as the American Indian Movement. Never known for its tight internal security, the Bureau sprung many new leaks during this period and the "moccasin telegraph" began carrying regular reports to Indian leaders everywhere concerning battles behind the scenes in Washington.

As the first session of the 92nd Congress drew to a close in November 1971, Morton called on it to enact the legislation recommended by President Nixon in his 1970 message. He gave special emphasis to the proposal for establishing an Indian Trust Counsel Authority to handle legal matters. He also announced the establishment of a section on water rights within the solicitor's office.[70] A month after the Secretary's action, Congress passed the Alaska Native Claims Settlement Act,[71] probably the most generous piece of Indian legislation in United States history. It demonstrated the strongly pro-Indian sentiment of Congress.

By the end of 1971, when the Alaska legislation was passed, Indian militancy had begun to have important effects on the Bureau of Indian Affairs. For radical organizations such as AIM, the Bureau was the primary target. Some AIM supporters advocated complete elimination of the BIA, while others, especially those with urban backgrounds, criticized the agency for not including off-reservation Indians in its service population. For the most part, elected tribal officials did not participate in the activities of the more militant groups, although some supported them privately and many sympathized with their goals. On the other hand, the elected leaders exerted their own pressures for change, sometimes citing the possibilities of violence by militants as added motivation.

Sensitive to the growing Indian militancy, Bruce began making changes in BIA operations early in his administration. He decided to honor the provisions of the Indian Reorganization Act of 1934 that required Indian participation in the budget process.[72] That legislation stated unequivocally that the Secretary of the Interior was to advise tribes or tribal councils of appropriations estimates "prior to the submission of such estimates to the Bureau of the Budget and Congress." Through the years officials of the Bureau of the Budget had successfully inhibited Interior Department officials from carrying out this directive. Unlike his predecessors, Bruce was able to get White House support for involving Indians in the BIA budget process. Since Bruce's day, the 1934 directive has been honored in the observance rather than the breach.

Bruce cemented his relationship with elected tribal officials in 1971 by helping to form the National Tribal Chairmen's Association, an organization whose power quickly came to rival that of the National Congress of American Indians.[73] Although sometimes referred to as a "puppet of the BIA," the tribal chairmen's group has since its creation exercised important influence in Indian affairs at the Washington level.

As early as September 1971, activists from the American Indian Movement and the National Indian Youth Council had communicated their objection to the Crow appointment by seizing the Bureau's information office in Washington and announcing their intentions of making a citizen's arrest of the deputy commissioner.[74] Slightly over a year later, in November 1972, during a march on Washington proclaimed "The Trail of Broken Treaties," representatives of many tribes occupied the headquarters building of the Bureau and held it for a week. In the process, they inflicted heavy damage on the building and confiscated or destroyed many records. As a result, Secretary Morton asked for the resignations of Commissioner Bruce, Deputy Commissioner Crow, and Assistant Secretary Harrison Loesch. Departing with them early in 1973 were several of the BIA newcomers whose recruitment had been so heralded just two years before.[75]

PICKING UP THE PIECES

In all its stormy history, the Bureau of Indian Affairs had never been in greater disarray than during the first few months of 1973. Headquarters employees were obliged to move to other offices while recovering what remained of their files and furniture. Secretary Morton transferred temporary responsibility for Indian affairs to his assistant secretary for management and budget, who announced that immediate steps would be taken to improve BIA operations. These steps included greater delegations of authority to the field; reductions in the size and responsibility of the Washington office; removal of the Indian Bureau from the jurisdiction of the assistant secretary for public lands; formulation of a legislative proposal to create the position of assistant secretary for Indian affairs; and separation of the Bureau's responsibilities as trustee for the Indians from its responsibilities to deliver services to Indian communities.[76]

Early in February, Morton announced that he had selected a member of the Iowa tribe, Marvin L. Franklin, to serve as his special assistant in the daily direction of the BIA. But within a few weeks the federal government was confronting Indian activists at Wounded Knee, on the Pine Ridge reservation in South Dakota. By the middle of March 1973, the Wounded Knee situation was almost under control. Undersecretary of the Interior John C. Whitaker informed the press that the Nixon administration had resubmitted seven key pieces of proposed legislation to Congress. With some modifications, these were the same bills that Nixon had presented following his message of July 8, 1970. Included in the package were measures to establish the assistant secretary position, create a separate Trust Counsel Authority, provide new guidelines for the Interior Department to contract with tribal councils for administering services, and establish a large-scale financing program to supply tribes with capital for economic development.[77]

In October 1973, nearly a year after the occupation of the BIA headquarters building, Secretary Morton reported that the President was nominating Morris Thompson, an Athapascan Indian from Alaska, to be the new commissioner of Indian Affairs. Thompson had been the Bureau's area director in Juneau. The youngest person ever to be commissioner, he was sworn in early in December. In many respects,

Thompson's administration turned out to be unusual. He took few initiatives of his own with respect to policy, yet his three years in office were marked by some of the most important legislation, judicial decisions, and internal administrative developments recorded by any commissioner.

When Thompson took over, the most important issue facing Bureau personnel was that of Indian employment preference. All commissioners, including Collier, had made sure that Indians were favored at their initial hiring, but had not given them preference thereafter. In his effort to involve Indians in more decision-making, Bruce had urged that Indian preference be expanded. He convinced Secretary Morton, who announced in June 1972 that such a change was in order. Before the Secretary's directive could be implemented, however, several non-Indian employees brought a lawsuit to declare the action illegal and discriminatory.

Late in April 1974, the appeals court decided the case in Morton's favor.[78] This put Commissioner Thompson in a good position to recruit Indians for several high level posts established a year earlier (during realignment of central office functions following the departure of Louis Bruce). He was successful in finding Indians for all but one of these positions.[79] Thompson also sought Indians for numerous other Washington vacancies that had accumulated since early 1973. When he was unable to find qualified Indians, he sometimes reduced the requirements of the positions or simply assigned the responsibilities elsewhere. Such behavior antagonized non-Indian employees and widened the gulf between them and their Indian colleagues. By 1976, the situation had become so critical that officials of the Department of the Interior stepped in and appointed a specialist to investigate the matter and prepare a personnel management plan for the BIA.[80]

Within the Bureau, non-Indian employees began lobbying for legislation that would permit them to retire early with full benefits, or to transfer with preference to other federal agencies. Congress attempted to provide relief in 1976 when it enacted an early retirement bill for non-Indian employees. However, the legislation did not satisfy some of the White House advisors, and the President vetoed it in September of that year.[81]

MAJOR LEGISLATIVE DEVELOPMENTS

Two of the principal champions of the Indians in Congress during the 1970s were Lloyd Meeds of Washington and James Abourezk of South Dakota, chairmen respectively of the House Indian Affairs Subcommittee and its counterpart in the Senate. They worked together efficiently to secure the passage of important legislation in the 93rd and 94th Congresses. The first major legislative development during Thompson's administration came in April 1974 with passage of the Indian Financing Act.[82] A provision of similar nature had been included in the ill-fated Omnibus Bill of 1967, and President Nixon had emphasized the importance of such legislation in his 1970 message to Congress. The 1974 Act provided for the consolidation of the existing BIA loan funds, established a loan guarantee and insurance program, authorized an appropriations increase of $50 million for Bureau credit activities, and authorized non-reimbursable grants to tribes for stimulating economic enterprises.

In the final days of its second session, the 93rd Congress enacted three other bills of importance. The first provided authority for tribal governments to acquire excess federal property from agencies that no longer needed it. The second called for the establishment of an Indian Policy Review Commission to prepare a comprehensive report on the status of the Indians and to make recommendations for improving federal Indian administration.[83] Both these measures became law on January 2, 1975. The third bill, enacted two days later, set up a complex framework for transferring to tribal governments programs traditionally administered by the Indian Bureau and the Indian Health Service. Known as the Indian Self-Determination and Education Assistance Act, it also established a program of assistance to upgrade Indian education, proclaimed the right of Indians to control their own education programs, provided for the training of professional Indian educators, and established an Indian youth intern program.[84]

The American Indian Policy Review Commission, conceived and chaired by Senator Abourezk, included two other Senators, three Representatives, and five Indians. Much of its work was done by a staff headed by Ernie Stevens, one of the OEO-trained Indians placed in a high-level position by Commissioner Bruce in the fall of 1970. The selection of Stevens was not particularly popular with some of the elected tribal officials, who also complained about other Indians chosen to serve on the Commission and its numerous task forces.

Thompson resigned his position in November 1976. A month later President Ford made an interim appointment of Ben Reifel, who at one time had been a career employee of the Bureau, later a South Dakota congressman, and who had excellent credentials for the commissioner's position. However, he remained in office only until January 28, 1977 when President Carter requested his resignation. The brevity of his term made it impossible for him to accomplish much.

THE DEMOCRATS RETURN

Late in February, Cecil D. Andrus, the new Secretary of the Interior, announced that he was calling upon tribal leaders to nominate candidates for a new position, that of assistant secretary for Indian Affairs. Although Congress had not passed legislation to establish such a post, Andrus had discovered that he could abolish one of the existing assistant secretary positions and replace it with the Indian job. While the search for nominees continued, the American Indian Policy Review Commission released its final report in May. Following the pattern of many of its predecessors, the document was full of criticisms of the BIA. Most of those who served on the Commission endorsed a set of wide-ranging legal and philosophical statements concerning Indian sovereignty. Congressman Lloyd Meeds of Washington, however, took exception. In a 100-page dissent, he called the report "one-sided advocacy" seeking to "convert a romantic political notion into a legal doctrine."[85] At the same time he released his comments, Meeds resigned as chairman of the House Subcommittee on Indian Affairs. Shortly thereafter, the subcommittee was abolished and its responsibilities transferred elsewhere.

While these events were taking place, the Senate Committee on Interior and Insular Affairs reached a similar decision with respect to its Indian subcommittee. Senator Abourezk saved the day by garnering sufficient support among his colleagues to obtain the establishment of a Select Committee on Indian Affairs with a two-year life span.

Early in July 1977, Secretary Andrus reported that President Carter's choice to fill the new assistant secretary post was Forrest Gerard, a Blackfoot Indian who had worked with both the Bureau of

Indian Affairs and the Indian Health Service, and who was a staff assistant for Abourezk's now defunct Senate Subcommittee on Indian Affairs. In spite of their previous association, Gerard was not Abourezk's favorite candidate, and the South Dakota senator took his time completing hearings on the appointment.[86] Gerard was finally confirmed and entered office as history's first assistant secretary of the Interior for Indian Affairs.

The last half of 1978 was a productive time for Indian legislation. Senator Abourezk, who had previously announced his retirement, made the most of his final year in Congress. Enactments included bills that restored previously terminated tribes to recognized status, one that settled a water rights issue on an Arizona reservation, and another that declared the Yaqui Indians, immigrants from Mexico earlier in this century, eligible for special federal services. Congress also endorsed a joint resolution on American Indian religious freedom and practices,[87] and passed measures on child welfare and Indian education.[88]

Gerard's administration, which ended with his resignation early in 1980, was relatively tranquil compared with those of his immediate predecessors. Although a group of Indians "marched" on Washington in the summer of 1978 to protest unwanted legislation, there was no repetition of 1972. Gerard concentrated on a management improvement program intended in response to heavy criticism of BIA administration during the Bruce and Thompson years. He also published regulations defining the class of Indians eligible for preference in federal employment.

In December 1979, Congress passed another bill regarding Indian preference in federal employment, and President Carter signed it into law. Shortly thereafter, the Bureau of Indian Affairs received its forty-second and possibly last commissioner. He was William E. Hallett, a Chippewa from Minnesota, who entered office aware that Assistant Secretary Gerard was about to resign. (After Hallett stepped down in early 1981, the Commissioner's position was left unfilled.) Following Gerard's departure in January 1980, however, Secretary Andrus named an acting deputy assistant secretary to guide the Bureau during the first half of the year. In June he recommended Thomas W. Fredericks, a Mandan Indian from North Dakota, to replace Gerard. Although the Senate committee held hearings on Frederick's appointment, it took no action to send the matter to the full body. Andrus then made Fredericks the deputy assistant secretary, and Fredericks ran the BIA from this position for the remainder of 1980. Following adjournment of Congress at the end of the year, President Carter gave Fredericks a "recess" appointment, thus putting him into the record books as the second assistant secretary of the Interior for Indian Affairs.[89]

INDIAN AFFAIRS IN THE REAGAN ADMINISTRATION

Unlike his predecessors Nixon and Carter, President Reagan wasted no time in selecting a nominee to head the Indian Bureau. By late January 1981, Oregon newspapers were circulating reports that the job had been offered to Kenneth C. Smith, a Wasco Indian from the Warm Springs Reservation in that state.[90] More than a month passed before hearings were concluded and the appointment confirmed. Smith was officially sworn in as assistant secretary on May 15.

At the time, the biggest preoccupation of the Indians was the federal budget. During the campaign, Reagan had stated that he opposed termination and supported the concept of tribal sovereignty and strong tribal governments.[91] However, early in March, Interior Secretary Watt reported that the new administration was proposing a 7 percent cut in the budget of the BIA. The notion of *any* budget reductions rang ominously in the ears of tribal leaders. They continued to hear more about cuts, however, through the remainder of 1981. At the end of the year, many were busy conferring with Bureau officials about revising their ranking of tribal priorities to accommodate deeper reductions down the road.[92]

In spite of Reagan's campaign comments about Indian matters, the first year of his administration passed without any news about the President's plans for Indian affairs. In August 1981, he appointed a subcabinet work group, headed by Smith, to develop a policy direction; the members met twice that year and again in January 1982. Represented on the group were the departments of Justice, Agriculture, Education, Labor, Housing and Human Development, and Health and Human Services.[93]

Early in 1982, as if in anticipation of a major policy statement, Assistant Secretary Smith announced a reorganization of the administrative structure of the Bureau of Indian Affairs.[94] Later he reported that the change would provide an annual saving of $16 million and "move the Indian agency a long way toward its goal of making as much of its budget as possible available for . . . programs at the reservation levels." Smith's plan called for consolidating the twelve area offices into five regional service centers and two special program offices, one to cover Alaska, and the other to cover the Navajo reservation. Education field offices were to be similarly reduced.

Announcement of the reorganization was given extensive publicity by Smith's office, which contributed to the general impression that the BIA bureaucrats had already made up their minds and all that remained was implementation. When some Indian leaders objected to such important changes without consulting them or their constituents, Smith and Interior Secretary Watt agreed to permit the National Tribal Chairmen's Association and the National Congress of American Indians to name a seven-member committee to review the reorganization scheme. By May, when he finally passed it to the panel, Smith was referring to the plan as "an option."[95] A year later, in the early summer of 1983, it remained "under consideration."

Late in September 1982—as the National Congress of American Indians prepared to assemble for its annual meeting in Bismarck, North Dakota—Theresa Carmody, press coordinator for the event, told the Associated Press that Secretary Watt would attend and deliver a "major Indian policy statement."[96] It appeared that the long-awaited announcement was at hand. However, as with the reorganization release eight months before, this again turned out to be a false alarm.

In January 1983, two full years after President Reagan's inauguration, the White House finally released a policy pronouncement.[97] The release, intended to coincide with Reagan's signing of the Indian Tribal Governmental Tax Status Act, happened to coincide with publicity surrounding an interview with Secretary Watt that was broadcast on January 19.[98] Comments attributed to the Secretary in an accompanying press release were interpreted as hostile by many tribal leaders, who transferred their hostility to the presidential policy statement. Although Watt almost immediately sought an audience with the National Congress of American Indians to apologize, at least a few Indians in the organization remained skeptical. One commented, "Almost every move Watt has made gives us the idea that we can't take what he and the Administration say at face value."[99]

Although the Administration emphasized that it had sought suggestions from Indian leaders in developing the policy statement, Indian response was lukewarm. Tribal officials interviewed by a *New York Times* reporter applauded a few of its positions, particularly the reassignment of Indian responsibilities within the White House from the Office of Public Liaison to the Office of Intergovernmental Affairs, but they observed that the real issues—new programs for health and rehabilitation, increased funding for tribal programs, and meaningful reform of the Bureau of Indian Affairs—were scarcely addressed in the presidential message.[100] Although not mentioned in the *Times* article, many Indian leaders might have approved Reagan's announced desire to seek the repeal of House Concurrent Resolution 83-108, and to make it possible for tribes to receive federal block-grant funding directly rather than through the states.

As expected, the President strongly endorsed the strengthening of tribal governments and a full-speed move toward Indian self-determination. Overall, it was a conservative policy message with some positive features and no particularly negative ones, but Indians felt it left much unsaid.

A month after the Indian policy statement, Congressional Republicans announced the formation of a special task force "charged with keeping GOP House members informed about Indian affairs." Freshman Congressman John McCain of Arizona, appointed to head the group, told the press that it would be "the primary policy body for Republicans on these [Indian] issues."[101]

CONCLUSION

Perhaps the most significant development in Indian affairs during the past century was the increased involvement of tribal leaders in federal decision-making. By the early 1980s, Indians were participating in decisions about the internal structure of the Bureau of Indian Affairs.

After the mid-1960s, Indian involvement at the policy-making level was accompanied by a significant, if often timid, movement of tribal governments into the administration of social service programs previously run by federal agencies with largely non-Indian staffs. As of 1983, the Indian tribal councils were permitted to determine the extent and pace at which they replaced federal bureaus and departments. No tribe had chosen to take over all the services provided by government, but the Navajos took a step in that direction when they petitioned Secretary Watt to begin negotiations in 1982. However, the tribal chairman who encouraged this discussion was voted out of office late in the year, and the new chairman has not addressed the issue during the first six months of his administration.

As the Indian Rights Association begins its second century, federal and tribal officials have yet to agree on what is meant by "self-determination." Many Indians fear a new round of termination programs; others express concern that tribes might be expected to forgo the financial subsidies to which they had become accustomed. Until agreement is reached on a definition, it seems highly unlikely that Indians would be willing to part company with an agency—however it might vex them—that has been charged with looking after their welfare since 1834. Odds are at least even that the Bureau of Indian Affairs will be around to see the Indian Rights Association celebrate its bicentennial in 2082.

N O T E S

1. Hiram Price, *Annual Report of the Commissioner of Indian Affairs to the Secretary of the Interior* (Washington, D.C.: U.S. Gov't. Printing Office, 1882), p. xiv.
2. Lawrence Schmeckebier, *The Office of Indian Affairs* (Baltimore: The Johns Hopkins University Press, 1927), p. 71.
3. Act of March 3, 1885, 23 Stat. 362, 18 U.S.C. 548.
4. Price, *Annual Report*, p. xiv.
5. Gregory C. Thompson, "John D. C. Atkins, 1885–88," in *The Commissioners of Indian Affairs, 1824–1977*, Robert M. Kvasnicka and Herman J. Viola, eds. (Lincoln, Neb.: Univ. of Nebraska Press, 1979), p. 182.
6. *Ibid.*, p. 187.
7. Schmeckebier, *Office of Indian Affairs*, pp. 84–85.
8. William T. Hagan, *American Indians* (Chicago: University of Chicago Press, 1979), p. 207.
9. W. David Baird, "William A. Jones, 1897–1904," in Kvasnicka and Viola, *The Commissioners*, p. 214.
10. *Ibid.*, pp. 216–217.
11. Donald Parman, "Francis Ellington Leupp, 1905–09," in Kvasnicka and Viola, *The Commissioners*, p. 231.

12. Carl E. Grammer, *Imprisonment Without Trial* (Philadelphia: Indian Rights Association, 1909), pp. 1–2.

13. Act of May 8, 1906, 34 Stat. 182.

14. J. P. Kinney, *A Continent Lost—A Civilization Won* (Baltimore: The Johns Hopkins University Press, 1937), p. 249.

15. Robert G. Valentine, *81st Annual Report of the Commissioner of Indian Affairs, Vol. II: Reports of the Department of the Interior for the Fiscal Year Ended June 30, 1912* (Washington, D.C.: U.S. Gov't. Printing Office, 1912), p. 3.

16. Valentine, *81st Annual Report, Vol. II*, p. 4.

17. Diane T. Putney, "Robert Grosvenor Valentine, 1909–12," in Kvasnicka and Viola, *The Commissioners*, p. 235.

18. Valentine, *81st Annual Report, Vol. II*, pp. 28–29.

19. Putney, "Robert Valentine," p. 235.

20. *Ibid.*, pp. 240–241.

21. Albert H. Kneale, *Indian Agent* (Caldwell, Io.: Caxton Printers, 1950), pp. 294–304.

22. Lawrence C. Kelly, "Cato Sells, 1913–1921," in Kvasnicka and Viola, *The Commissioners*, pp. 247–249.

23. Act of Nov. 2, 1921, 42 Stat. 208.

24. Lawrence C. Kelly, "Charles Henry Burke, 1921–1929," in Kvasnicka and Viola, *The Commissioners*, pp. 254–255.

25. Charles Burke, *Annual Report of the Bureau of Indian Affairs: Annual Report of the Secretary of the Interior* (Washington, D.C.: U.S. Gov't. Printing Office, 1927), p. 2.

26. Kelly, in Kvasnicka and Viola, *The Commissioners*, p. 257.

27. *Ibid.*, p. 255–256.

28. *Ibid.*, p. 259.

29. Kenneth R. Philp, *John Collier's Crusade for Indian Reform, 1920–1954* (Tucson: University of Arizona Press, 1977), p. 90.

30. Lawrence C. Kelly, "Charles James Rhoads, 1929–1933," in Kvasnicka and Viola, *The Commissioners*, p. 266.

31. *Ibid.*, pp. 266–267.

32. *Ibid.*, pp. 268–269; Philp, *John Collier's Crusade*, pp. 98–99, 103–111.

33. Leavitt Act of July 1932, 47 Stat. 564.

34. Philp, *John Collier's Crusade*, p. 113, citing Indian Defense Association, *American Indian Life* (New York: The Association, Jan. 1933), pp. 1–5.

35. Act of June 18, 1934, 48 Stat. 984.

36. Graham D. Taylor, *The New Deal and American Indian Tribalism: The Administration of the Indian Reorganization Act* (Lincoln: University of Nebraska Press, 1980), pp. 113–114.

37. Jonathan M. Steere, "The Collier Bill," *Indian Truth* 11, no. 5 (Philadelphia: Indian Rights Association, May 1934), 1–8.

38. Taylor, *The New Deal*, pp. 114–118.
39. Glenn L. Emmons, "Bureau of Indian Affairs," *Annual Report of the Secretary of the Interior* (Washington, D.C.: U.S. Gov't. Printing Office, 1954), p. 233.
40. Philp, *John Collier's Crusade*, pp. 122–126; Taylor, *The New Deal*, pp. 125–138.
41. Philleo Nash, transcribed speech in *Anthropology and the American Indian* (San Francisco: Indian Historian Press, 1973), p. 28.
42. Philp, *John Collier's Crusade*, pp. 198–199.
43. *Ibid.*, p. 205.
44. *Ibid.*, p. 208.
45. *Ibid.*, p. 194–197.
46. Lyman S. Tyler, "William A. Brophy, 1945–1948," in Kvasnicka and Viola, *The Commissioners*, p. 284.
47. *Ibid.*, p. 285.
48. *Ibid.*, p. 286.
49. William J. Dennehy, "John Ralph Nichols, 1940–1950," in Kvasnicka and Viola, *The Commissioners*, p. 289.
50. *Ibid.*, p. 290.
51. James E. Officer, "The Bureau of Indian Affairs since 1945: An Assessment," in *The Annals of the American Academy of Political and Social Science*, vol. 436 (March 1978), p. 63.
52. Glenn L. Emmons, "Bureau of Indian Affairs," *Annual Report of the Secretary of the Interior* (Washington, D.C.: U.S. Gov't. Printing Office, 1955), p. 233.
53. Patricia K. Ourada, "Glenn L. Emmons, 1953–1961," in Kvasnicka and Viola, *The Commissioners*, p. 301.
54. Officer, "The Bureau of Indian Affairs since 1945," p. 64.
55. *Ibid.*
56. U.S. Senate, *Hearings Before the Subcommittee on Indian Affairs of the Committee on Interior and Insular Affairs, 88th Cong., 1st sess. on S.1049, A Bill Relating to the Indian Heirship Land Problem*, April 29–30, pt. 3 (Washington, D.C.: U.S. Gov't. Printing Office, 1963), pp. 409, 411, 481.
57. *Ibid.*, p. 478, 481.
58. Margaret Connell Szasz, "Philleo Nash, 1961–1966," in Kvasnicka and Viola, *The Commissioners*, pp. 315–316.
59. *Ibid.*, p. 320.
60. Officer, "The Bureau of Indian Affairs since 1945," p. 66.
61. Indian Civil Rights Act of 1968, 82 Stat. 73, 77.
62. U.S. Senate, *Indian Education: A National Tragedy—A National Challenge*, Committee on Labor and Public Welfare, nos. 90–501, 91st Cong., 1st sess. (Washington, D.C.: U.S. Gov't. Printing Office, 1969).

63. Department of Interior, *Report to the Secretary of the Interior by the Task Force on Indian Affairs* (Washington, D.C.: U.S. Gov't. Printing Office, 1961), pp. 58–59.

64. Robert L. Bennett, "Reversing the Trend," Memorandum to the Secretary of the Interior, May 23, 1968; James Officer, "Memorandum for the Secretary," June 1, 1968, personal communication to the Secretary of the Interior (both in possession of the author).

65. Department of Interior, "Executive Realignment Announced for Bureau of Indian Affairs," News Release, Jan. 9, 1970.

66. Department of Interior, "Appointment of 15 Indians to Key BIA Posts Announced," News Release, Oct. 1, 1970.

67. Department of Interior, "Secretary Hickel Unveils Dramatic Changes in BIA," News Release, Nov. 2, 1970.

68. Alvin Josephy, *Red Power: The American Indian's Right to Freedom* (New York: McGraw Hill, 1971), p. 213.

69. Department of Interior, "John O. Crow Appointed Deputy Commissioner of Indian Affairs," News Release, July 23, 1971.

70. Department of Interior, "Morton Cites Conflict of Interests in Indian Trust Responsibility; Urges Passage of Bill to Provide Indians with Independent Aid," News Release, Nov. 22, 1971.

71. The Alaska Native Claims Settlement Act, 85 Stat. 688, Dec. 18, 1971.

72. Bureau of Indian Affairs, "Bruce Policies Receive Vote of Confidence," *Indian Record* (July 1970): 7.

73. Bureau of Indian Affairs, "Tribal Chairmen to Advise BIA," *Indian Record* (June-July 1971): p. 3.

74. Joseph H. Cash, "Louis Rooks Bruce, 1969–1973," in Kvasnicka and Viola, *The Commissioners*, pp. 337–338; James E. Officer, "The Bureau of Indian Affairs since 1945," p. 69.

75. Cash, "Louis Rooks Bruce," in Kvasnicka and Viola, *The Commissioners*.

76. Department of Interior, "Steps Taken to Improve Operations of the Bureau of Indian Affairs," News Release, Jan. 18, 1973.

77. Department of Interior, "Statement of the Honorable John C. Whitaker, Undersecretary of the Interior," Press Conference on Indian Affairs, Washington, D.C., News Release, March 1, 1973.

78. *Morton v. Mancari*, 417 US 535 (1974).

79. Michael T. Smith, "Morris Thompson, 1973–1976," in Kvasnicka and Viola, *The Commissioners*, p. 343.

80. Paul Lorentzen, "Personnel Management Action Plan for BIA," Memorandum to the Commissioner of Indian Affairs, Sept. 7, 1976.

81. Gerald Ford, "Veto of Act Providing Special Retirement Benefits to Certain Non-Indian Employees of the Bureau of Indian Affairs and the Indian Health Service," House Doc. nos. 94–624 (Washington, D.C.: U.S. Gov't. Printing Office, Sept. 27, 1976).

82. Indian Financing Act of 1974, 88 Stat. 77.
83. Act of Jan. 2, 1975, 88 Stat. 1910.
84. Indian Self-Determination and Education Assistance Act, 88 Stat. 2203, Jan. 4, 1975.
85. "U.S. Urged to Recognize Indian Tribal Sovereignty," *Los Angeles Times*, May 15, 1977, p. 1.
86. Officer, "The Bureau of Indian Affairs since 1945," p. 71.
87. American Indian Religious Freedom Act, 92 Stat. 469, Aug. 11, 1978.
88. Indian Child Welfare Act, 92 Stat. 3069, Nov. 8, 1978. Tribally Controlled Community Colleges Assistance Act, 92 Stat. 1325, 1978.
89. "Fredericks Sworn In as Assistant Secretary Under a Recess Appointment," *Indian News Notes* 5, no. 3 (Jan. 15, 1981): 1–2.
90. "Warm Springs Manager Nominated for Top Indian Post, Unofficial Reports Say," *Indian News Notes* 5, no. 5 (Feb. 5, 1981): 1.
91. "Four Indian Organizations Testify, Committee Confirms Watt," *Indian News Notes* 5, no. 3 (Jan. 15, 1981): 2.
92. "Tribes Given Opportunity to Revise Program Priorities for 1983 Budget," *Indian News Notes* 5, no. 43 (Nov. 20, 1981): 1.
93. "Smith Appointed Chairman of White House Indian Policy Working Group," *Indian News Notes* 5, no. 30 (Aug. 6, 1981): 1.
94. Department of Interior, "Interior Announces Changes in BIA Organization," News Release, Feb. 19, 1982.
95. Department of Interior, "Interior Announces BIA Reorganization," News Release, May 28, 1982.
96. "Watt to Deliver Indian Policy Statement," *Arizona Daily Star*, Sept. 27, 1982.
97. The White House, "Statement of the President: Indian Policy," Office of the Press Secretary, News Release, Jan. 24, 1983.
98. *B.I.A. Tribal Newsletter* 7, no. 1, Phoenix Area ed., Jan. 27, 1983.
99. "Indian Tribes Skeptical on Policy Shift," *New York Times*, Jan. 30, 1983.
100. *Ibid.*
101. "McCain Heads Task Force for GOP on Indian Affairs," *Arizona Daily Star*, Feb. 25, 1983.

"CONGRESS IN ITS WISDOM": THE COURSE OF INDIAN LEGISLATION

V I N E D E L O R I A, J R.

*I*ndian Affairs is a peculiar province of the legislative branch of our government. Although the Constitution charges the president with the responsibility to deal with Indians through his power to make treaties, and Indians always seem to look to the president for direction, the Constitution allocates power to Congress under the Commerce Clause for all matters relating to Indian tribes.[1] This constitutional power meant little during the formative years of the United States. Indians occupied the vast interior of the continent while non-Indians huddled in settlements on the Atlantic seaboard. Trade with Indians was conducted at important junctions on major rivers, and if Congress occasionally spoke about Indian matters, hardly anyone in direct contact with the Indians was listening.

Although both houses of Congress had formal Indian committees, Congress paid little attention to its role as the architect of Indian fortunes apart from providing legislative confirmation of presidential policies such as forced removal. By about 1850, however, Congress began to assume a more active role; it authorized various commissions to deal with Indians in California, the Great Plains, and the Pacific Northwest.[2] Congressional initiative in these matters was very important because it altered the role of the president from that of a negotiator of treaties to an administrator of domestic statutes. Indians continued to look to the Great Father as intercessor on their behalf, but Congress increasingly determined the nature of Indian policy. The sixty years it had taken Congress to assert its prerogatives was not through oversight. Although the *Cherokee* cases dealing with Indian removal had clearly upheld the primacy of federal law in Indian affairs, it was only after the United States made a determined effort to settle the entire continent, best represented by the California and Oregon migrations, that Congress grasped its role as mediator between whites and Indians.

In 1871, after several years of bickering between the two houses of Congress on aspects of federal Indian policy, the Indian Committee of the House of Representatives attached a far-reaching amendment to an Interior Department appropriations bill.[3] The amendment declared that no tribe would thereafter be recognized as capable of making treaties with the United States, although it also declared that existing treaties would be honored. Between 1871 and 1914, however, the government made over 100 agreements with Indians that resembled treaties. Indeed, at the negotiating table Indians were told they *were* treaties, and federal district courts later acknowledged that these agreements stood on a par with treaties as legal documents. But the congressional attitude was that treaties could be violated at whim because Congress in its wisdom would act in the best interest of the Indians.

Of more significance was the fact that the 1871 amendment represented a new way of handling Indian matters. The federal government no longer went hat in hand to isolated places in the West seeking changes in the status of tribes or the manner in which the federal bureaucracy served them. Instead, a senator or congressman needed only convince his fellow legislators on the Indian committees of the desirability of a revision and it stood an excellent chance of becoming first a federal statute and later an administrative policy. Indians as a subject of congressional debate were moved from the national agenda to an item on a committee agenda, and they were never again seen as having an important claim on the national government.

In the last century a number of statutes were passed in attempts to resolve the Indian problem in one bold stroke. Today these efforts are distinguishable more by their historical context than by their ideology. The goal of almost all this federal legislation was the quick and permanent assimilation of Indians into the American social fabric. Thus the General Allotment Act,[4] the Burke Act,[5] the Snyder Act,[6] the Wheeler-Howard Act,[7] the Johnson-O'Malley Act,[8] House Concurrent Resolution 83-108,[9] the Indian Civil Rights Act,[10] the Indian Education Act,[11] and the Indian Self-Determination and Education Assistance Act [12] were respective legislative milestones in this larger effort to include Indians in the emerging American culture.

A chronological assessment of this legislation tends to hide a persistent congressional belief in the efficacy of statutes to erase Indian cultural traits, so it is best to survey the legislation under topical headings. In this way we can measure the extent to which federal legislation enhanced or eroded the political status of Indians. The legislative pendulum has always swung erratically as the mood of the country shifted between liberal and conservative views. Indeed, no other country has had such a fluctuating relationship with its aboriginal people. Yet there has always been some commitment to remain within the historic guidelines established in early colonial days. Hence no Congress has gone to the limit in either bolstering Indian fortunes or severing the longstanding relationship between tribes and the federal government. We can grant this much: If the United States has rarely fulfilled the spirit of the law, it has nevertheless done better by its native people than other countries that faced this problem.

CORPORATE POLITICAL STATUS AND TRIBAL CLAIMS

Indian tribes were described by Chief Justice John Marshall in 1832 as "domestic dependent nations," and until the 1880s the tribes enjoyed aspects of that status. For the most part, they lived outside the civilized boundaries of the United States and participated in trade relationships with American citizens. They were not domestic in that they seldom integrated with other residents of the several states, but since the United States would have regarded a foreign invasion of tribal lands as an act of aggression against itself, the tribes were an important part of American society. Yet they lacked clear legal relationship to American society, and the cession of treaty-making in 1871 deprived the tribes of their sole means of redress—negotiations and agreements. They were consequently helpless when the federal government began to initiate policies to assimilate tribal members into its citizenry.

In 1883 the Supreme Court reversed the conviction of Crow Dog, a Sioux medicine man who had been convicted in a territorial court of murder of Spotted Tail, a Sioux chief considered friendly to the United States.[13] Citing Revised Statutes section 2146, which granted tribal governments jurisdiction in major criminal offenses, the Supreme Court raised the question of self-government in a wholly unexpected context. Could an Indian tribe, whose mechanisms of self-government varied significantly from the procedures of the white majority, govern itself according to its ancient customs in the midst of a modern nation? The Supreme Court said "yes," but the public outcry following its decision insisted the opposite. In 1885 Congress passed the Seven Major Crimes Act, which effectively precluded any tribes (except the

Five Civilized Tribes) from exercising criminal jurisdiction over crimes of a serious nature.[14] The trying of these offenses was restricted to federal district courts.

The 1885 act virtually eliminated traditional sanctions against tribal culprits. Their knowing that final judgment lay outside the reservation boundaries undercut Indian reliance on their own institutions as a means of resolving disputes. Disturbances thus increased and forced the Bureau of Indian Affairs to seek more power to keep order on the reservations. Indians became more lawless because they were discouraged from using known, traditional codes of conduct, yet did not understand the government's new standards of behavior.

The passage of the Assimilative Crimes Act of 1898 completed the destruction of the native legal system for handling domestic disputes.[15] This law made personal acts, not otherwise regarded as criminal offenses under federal codes, subject to criminal prosecution if they violated state laws. This statute was intended to resolve the conflict of laws which occurred when federal statutes failed to cover minor offenses against the peace. Because Indian reservations were regarded part of the larger federal interest, a measure of state law, that which dealt with minor criminal offenses and misdemeanors, became part of the law that governed Indians.

Prior treaty provisions initially exempted the Five Civilized Tribes from the operation of the Seven Major Crimes Act, but a series of federal acts gradually stripped them of internal political powers. Their losses culminated in the authorization of the Dawes Commission to enroll their members for the purpose of allotting tribal lands. Finally, the Curtis Act of 1898 gave these tribes a choice of securing an allotment agreement with the United States or having the Dawes Commission determine how their lands would be divided.[16] The Curtis Act also abolished their tribal courts and declared tribal laws unenforcable in federal courts. With this pressure, justified by a series of field hearings designed to show that mixed-blood Indians dominated and exploited the full-bloods, the tribes capitulated and accepted allotment. On April 26, 1906, Congress made provision for the final disposition of their affairs. A joint resolution of March 2, 1906, expressed formal recognition of the tribal governments, but their existence was little more than symbolic.[17] The resolution authorized the president to appoint government officers, a practice followed for nearly seven decades. It was not until 1970 that the Five Civilized Tribes regained the right to vote for their own tribal officials.[18]

The dissolution of the governments of the Five Civilized Tribes was an extreme case. Most other tribes in the West managed to retain some aspects of their traditional government. The annual reports of the Commissioner of Indian Affairs are filled with requests by informal tribal councils seeking permission to spend tribal funds on a per capita basis, and for permission to travel to Washington to secure promised annuities or to obtain the right to sue the government for loss of lands or treaty violations. Shadow tribal governments existed on most reservations, and if no longer overt, traditional forms were still active. Some prominent tribal leaders became judges in the Courts of Indian Offenses or Indian policemen. The people recognized their status and often transferred their loyalties to these new institutions because of the presence of traditional leaders.

The Great Depression, ironically, provided the occasion for a revival of tribal fortunes: Franklin D. Roosevelt's landslide election meant a mandate for radical reform. The president chose as his Indian commissioner John Collier, an old adversary of the bureaucratic machinery of Washington. Collier believed deeply in the resiliency of tribal cultures, and in 1932 he had urged Congress to pass legislation authorizing tribal councils on the reservations. Thwarted in this effort, Collier proceeded to draw up a blueprint for political and economic reorganization of the reservations. His plan was introduced in 1934 by Senator Burton K. Wheeler and Representative Edgar S. Howard, and after extensive congresses with Indians to seek their ideas (and substantial, almost crippling amendments by Congress), the Indian Reorganization Act became law.

Both the Indians and Congress believed that Collier had hoodwinked them. Wheeler, quickly disillusioned with his legislative creation, held hearings in an effort to generate support for its repeal. But Collier's energy and efficiency made it difficult if not impossible to reverse the movement toward tribal self-sufficiency. In addition, Collier clearly utilized a series of solicitor's opinions that judged tribal sovereignty to have always existed; it followed that the Indian Reorganization Act merely formalized a traditional relationship between Indians and the United States.

The Indian Reorganization Act (IRA) had major provisions that spelled the end of the allotment policy and vested considerable powers of self-government in the newly organized tribal governments. It made provisions to secure lands for landless Indians, allowed a certain measure of municipal powers with the adoption of a tribal constitution and by-laws, permitted tribes to form business corporations for economic development, established a system of credit for both tribes and individuals, and made Indian preference in employment in the Bureau of Indian Affairs a major goal. Two years later some provisions of the act were made available to Alaska Natives,[19] and to Oklahoma Indians by means of the Oklahoma Indian Welfare Act.[20] Although the Alaskans and Oklahomans did not have the same reservation status as tribes in other states, the provisions for economic development and rehabilitation enabled them to organize as communities in order to provide employment for their members. If we consider the effect of these three acts, it is apparent that Collier was almost wholly responsible for the creation of the modern tribal self-government.

World War II severely disrupted Collier's program for Indian rehabilitation, and he resigned at the end of the war, weary of defending his program against slanderous attacks and severe budget cuts. In 1947 the Hoover Commission was authorized by Congress to discover new ways of reducing the federal government. It suggested a transfer of some Indian programs to state governments and recommended the eventual assimilation of Indians into the American mainstream. In 1954, with Congress controlled by Republicans for the first time in a generation, conservative legislators passed a series of acts designed to rapidly sever the federal relationship and merge the Indians with the rest of society. House Concurrent Resolution 83-108, passed in 1953, declared the sense of Congress in terminating the special relations with Indians as rapidly as possible. The next year Congress passed a series of termination acts which severed the federal ties of a number of tribes. Generally this policy envisioned the congressional task as the transference of federal responsibility to private corporations established to supervise tribal property and assets. In 1958, after a prolonged and profoundly adverse tribal and public reaction, the policy was formally disavowed. Unilateral termination became a discredited congressional option with few advocates.

The status of Indian tribes shifted perceptibly during the sixties, when tribes were made eligible for the multitude of social programs authorized by Congress. Instead of directing their efforts toward Indians specifically, Congress in most instances declared that poverty anywhere in American society was deserving of federal assistance. Indians, who generally fell within any determination of poverty, were cited as examples of groups and geographical regions that required massive aid. Tribal political status thus partially depended upon the economic conditions under which Indians lived, and making tribal sovereignty a partial function and *de facto* part of the federal establishment.

In 1975 Congress finally passed a statute directly addressing Indian needs—the Indian Self-Determination and Education Assistance Act—which basically updated the Indian Reorganization Act. Generally, the 1975 act provided for more extensive subcontracting of certain federal services that Congress believed answered the Indians' basic needs. The act did not formally bolster the political status of tribes, but in expanding the types of functions that tribal governments were allowed to perform, it greatly increased their effectiveness.

The beginnings of the Reagan administration saw massive cuts in federal appropriations. Because Indians derived their operating funds from a variety of federal agencies, they suffered substantially. The political status of the tribes, however, remained basically constant in spite of the ambitious reform program. Their stable political standing, combined with victories in litigation that also expanded tribal political powers, gave Indians considerably more potency as self-governing entities as the 1980s began than they had enjoyed at any previous time in this century.

When treaties were still being forged with Indian tribes, it was possible to include in the negotiations any claims that derived from previous agreements. In 1863, however, the Court of Claims was restricted in its jurisdiction from handling claims based upon treaty articles.[21] This prohibition meant that an Indian tribe seeking justice in a treaty dispute with the government required special legislation giving the Court of Claims jurisdiction over its claim. Tribes were restricted to this cumbersome procedure until the establishment of the Indian Claims Commission in 1946.[22]

Non-Indians were not so restricted, however, and they often became third party complainants under the amity provisions of Indian treaties. At first, settlers with complaints against specific tribes complained to the Secretary of the Interior; the Secretary decided the issue and reimbursed the injured parties from tribal accounts in the federal treasury. As more claims against the Indians were sent to the Interior Department, it became necessary to establish a more sophisticated procedure. Congress passed the Indian Depredations Act on March 3, 1891 to resolve this issue.[23] People with claims against the Indians still filed with the Secretary of the Interior for a decision, but appeals could be taken by the tribe or government to the Court of Claims. As a result, by the first decade of this century most non-Indian claims, valid and fraudulent alike, were settled—leaving only the claims by Indians against the United States unresolved.

The Meriam Report of 1928 emphasized that no solution to Indian problems was possible until the tribal claims were decided in a manner satisfactory to the Indians. During the late 1920s and early 1930s a variety of bills were introduced attempting to resolve the claims issue, but little of significance transpired until the end of the Second World War. Embarrassed that America had not dealt justly with its racial minorities while chastizing other nations for similar behavior, Congress decided to provide a forum for the settlement of Indian claims. Under the provisions of the Indian Claims Commission Act, tribes had five years to file their claims and to cite any cause of action in equity or law that would justify their contentions. The claims subsequently filed were of two kinds: inadequate payment for land cessions a century before, and inadequate administrative supervision of tribal funds, i.e., accounting claims, on Indian monies handled by the United States.

Over 600 claims were filed and nearly half of these resulted in judgments favorable to Indians. But the Claims Commission's work was tedious and prosecution of claims took longer than anyone had anticipated. The commissioners insisted on adopting the outmoded procedures of the Court of Claims instead of acting as a commission with informal rules of evidence and procedure. In this way the ICC became merely another court bogged down with adversary proceedings and courtroom maneuvers. In 1978 the Claims Commission was terminated and the remaining claims were sent to the Court of Claims for final resolution.[24]

In the mid-sixties Indians began to question the refusal of the Indian Claims Commission to consider the restoration of lands to tribes. Some Indian groups insisted that they would prefer the return of their sacred lands to monetary compensation. Most prominent in this movement was the Taos Pueblo of New Mexico, which sought a restoration of its sacred Blue Lake area. The people of Taos mounted a national campaign and convinced the Nixon administration to return this area in 1970 as a partial settlement of their claim.[25] The Yakimas of Washington State and the Warm Springs Indians of Oregon also took this route and received smaller tracts of land. In the East, the Maine tribes and other Indian groups pressed land claims in the late sixties and early seventies, although under different circumstances. Unlike the Claims Commission cases, these later tribes invoked the protection of the 1790 Trade and Intercourse Act, alleging that because their lands had been taken without federal approval, title had never legally passed from the Indians. Litigation by the New England tribes threatened the stability of land titles in the whole region, and finally the various tribes and defendant states, sometimes with the active participation of the Interior Department, agreed to work towards out-of-court settlements. The Indians in Maine and Rhode Island finally effected solutions to their land claims in this manner.[26]

The Alaska Natives had extensive claims against the federal government that had lain unresolved since the purchase of that region from Russia in 1867. Both the acts of May 17, 1884[27] and August 24, 1912[28] outlined procedures for a full civil government, but nimbly sidestepped the subject of native land titles and claims. Even the statehood act in 1959 avoided any definite statement on this subject.[29] The Natives began to litigate their claims in the mid-sixties, and Congress, at the urging of various oil companies and of the state, provided a generous legislative solution to the land claim issue. The legislation, passed in 1971, divided the state into twelve regions and established a corporation to provide an administrative-political entity for the Natives of each region.[30] An additional corporation was formed in Seattle, Washington, to serve Alaska Natives who had relocated to the lower states before the settlement. Both money and lands were given to the corporations who administered this economic bonanza on behalf of their enrolled members.

A subject closely related to land claims was the effort by some Indian communities to obtain formal political acknowledgement of their tribal status. The distinction between federally recognized tribes and the unrecognized communities was in many cases without historical or legal justification, and was primarily a bureaucratic convenience. Approximately 70 groups of Indians had been "recognized" during the twentieth century as tribes for whom the federal government had responsibility.[31] Yet under existing regulations the remaining unrecognized groups could neither become sponsors of poverty and education programs for their people, nor receive any of the other services of the Bureau of Indian Affairs. Recognition, prior to the seventies, was a matter of obtaining the services of a friendly Congressman to sponsor special legislation, or (primarily during the Collier years) required the help of aggressive federal employees to secure a solicitor's opinion recommending the establishment of a federal reservation for a landless Indian group.

In the late 1970s several efforts were launched to define the full legal scope of the term "Indian." The need for the studies arose over intense controversies surrounding programs designed to serve all Indians, such as the large Title IV programs of the Indian Education Act. The Bureau of Indian Affairs was given primary responsibility for establishing eligibility for recognition, and in typical bureaucratic fashion it created a maze of criteria. Most of the requirements imposed were standard profiles and procedures that had little to do with Indian heritage[32] or with federal responsibility for Indians as articulated in numerous statutes and Supreme Court decisions.[33] Nevertheless, when the rules for recognition were published in 1978, nearly a hundred groups filed for federal status.

INDIVIDUAL POLITICAL AND ECONOMIC RIGHTS

The relationship of the federal government to Indians has always had its contradictory aspects. Tribes formally entered into treaty relations with the United States, yet the national government has also assumed responsibility for individual Indians. As a result, there has been frequent confusion as to whether federal proposals are to assist Indians in their individual or in their corporate/political capacities. Individuals had generally been a matter of concern only as a tangible measure of successful assimilation. Early treaties, primarily the Removal treaties of 1808–1835, contained provisions to give individuals a share of tribal assets by requiring them to abandon tribal relations, take allotments within ceded areas, and assume state citizenship. The Constitution, in fact, spoke of Indians being "not taxed" in its provisions for determining representation in Congress—inferring that some individual Indians had indeed been assimilated and were taxed as other Americans.

Individual rights for Indians, therefore, were conceived in a non-Indian egalitarian social context, while internal self-government remained the province of the tribes. The General Allotment Act of 1887 provided the vehicle for "breaking up the tribal mass" by vesting in the individual a tract of land from the larger tribal estate; he and his family were expected to earn their living from it, in a "civilized" manner. Although this act dealt primarily with land, many of its proponents supported it because of the cultural implications. They believed that the division of tribal assets offered a mechanism for freeing the individual Indian from his outmoded past.

Reformers who advocated the allotment of the reservations did not believe, however, that individual Indians could immediately take their place in the American economic system. To eliminate the possibility that Indians might be unlawfully deprived of their property, they insisted upon a twenty-five year period of trust during which the individual was expected to learn to manage his own property. When this trust period expired, it was expected that the Indian allottees would become state (and therefore national) citizens, with attendant responsibilities, in particular that of taxpayer. Although this plan seemed feasible to many people, Congress did not allow its fruition. Only four years after the passage of the General Allotment Act, the statute was amended to provide that the Secretary of the Interior could manage the allotments of Indian minors, or those deemed *non-compos mentis*.[34] Presumably the Secretary would learn the lessons of private property on behalf of the Indians.

In 1906 Congress devised a new way to allot tribal members. The Act of March 2, 1906 had a provision that allowed individuals to withdraw from the tribe and receive a per capita share of tribal assets.[35] Although few Indians took advantage of this provision, it remained a favorite congressional device for vesting rights in the individual, and during the termination period, individual withdrawal became the vehicle for reducing tribal membership of the Klamaths of Oregon and the Utes of Utah. It is worth noting that the early efforts of Congress to provide individual rights centered on the distribution of property rather than on the articulation of traditional personal liberties.

Both the General Allotment Act and the Act of August 15, 1894 established Indian preference in employment in the Bureau of Indian Affairs.[36] As income rather than capital became an issue among Indians, employment on the reservation gained importance. Consequently, preference in federal employment for Indians was emphasized in the Indian Reorganization Act, and Collier elevated the recruitment of Indians for Bureau posts to a high priority. In the seventies this issue emerged once more as both the Nixon and Ford administrations sought to turn Indian administration over to Indians.

A sit-in protest in 1970 at Littleton, Colorado brought back the question of Indian preference in employment, this time revolving around promotion rather than initial hiring. In *Morton v. Mancari* the Supreme Court decided that Congress had intended Indian preference in every level of government and as a political right of the individual Indian rather than as a special privilege of a racial group.[37]

Citizenship as an individual right for Indians has been intimately linked to ownership of private property and preference in employment. Early treaties, however, linked allotment and citizenship, but even the General Allotment Act provided for the assumption of citizenship only after the expiration of the trust period. The Bureau of Indian Affairs, unfortunately, insisted that citizenship came automatically with the issuance of a fee patent, regardless of the period of trust. The Burke Act of 1906 affirmed this administrative practice. Congress rather tamely followed the lead of the executive branch on the issue of citizenship by formalizing practices that had begun as simple administrative expediencies.

Congress also viewed citizenship in a traditional context apart from the connection with trust property relations. In 1919, a grateful Congress made citizens of those Indians who had served in the Armed Forces during World War I, and this sentiment to include Indians as citizens continued to grow.[38] In 1924, another statute made citizens of all Indians born in the United states without infringing on their rights to tribal or other properties.[39] Many traditional Indians then argued that they had dual citizenship, both tribal and American, but the Iroquois, believing that the imposition of American citizenship would injure their tribal affiliation, promptly sent the President notice of their rejection of American citizenship.

Although some states, particularly Utah and Arizona, insisted that persons under legal disabilities could not vote as citizens, the issue of Indian citizenship virtually disappeared until the 1950s when reactionary Republican congressmen insisted that the preservation of the federal property trust made Indians second-class citizens. Much energy on behalf of termination was generated by well-meaning people who did not understand the difference between the intangible privileges of citizenship and the tangible trust protections for Indian property guaranteed by treaties and agreements. With the collapse of the termination policy, however, the co-existence of Indian citizenship with the federal trust relationship became politically acceptable to all but the most extreme right-wing. That Congress could become so confused on such a simple matter illustrated the fact that Indian legislation seldom received the careful consideration of other legislation.

As part of the New Deal efforts to modernize Indian administration, Congress passed a statute on May 21, 1934 repealing twelve sections of the U.S. Code of Federal Regulations that severely restricted individual rights.[40] Some of these measures originated in the early days of the republic, and included a prohibition against sending seditious messages to Indians, the authorization of the military to compel obedience to an agent's order, and the empowering of the Commissioner to expel "detrimental" persons from Indian reservations. Although the remedial legislation addressed civil rights, the two Indian committees responsible seemed unaware they were making great strides in human rights. They perceived the repeal of these provisions rather as mere housekeeping.

The Indian Reorganization Act also provided several measures for the enhancement of individual rights. Individuals (as well as tribes) became eligible for rehabilitation loans and grants, could receive professional training from an educational fund, and most important from a conceptual viewpoint, became eligible to participate in the benefits of the IRA. This provision was carried to somewhat ludicrous lengths during the 1930s when anthropologists working for the Bureau of Indian Affairs in North Carolina measured the heads of several hundred Lumbee Indians and declared twenty-two of them Indians (tentatively Tuscaroras) because their cranial measurements corresponded to the average measurements of the Blackfeet tribe of Montana, for whom the Bureau had statistics. In the 1970s these individuals were still waiting to enjoy the benefits of the IRA, and toward this end had accepted the Bureau's identification of them as Tuscaroras. The Lumbees themselves were later declared American Indians in a statute passed in 1956, although they were denied eligibility for Bureau services.[41]

Congress did not deal with individual Indian rights again until the mid-sixties, when pressure for civil rights encouraged legislation. Extensive hearings were held in various parts of Indian country, and finally Senator Sam Ervin of North Carolina proposed a multipurpose act which introduced concepts of American constitutional law into the tribal judicial system. Title I of the Indian Civil Rights Act prohibited tribal governments from abridging the basic freedoms of speech, religion, press, assembly, and petition for redress. The title also incorporated such protections as the right against unreasonable search and seizure, double jeopardy, self-incrimination, a delayed trial, excessive bail prohibitions, unequal protection of the laws, and prohibitions against bills of attainder and ex-post facto laws. Title I thus summarized the state of American constitutional law at the time of passage and applied it to the relations between tribal governments and their members.

Subsequent litigation concerning procedure and representation in tribal governments greatly expanded the original congressional purpose in passing the Indian Civil Rights Act, and forced tribal courts to introduce many of the procedural protections enjoyed by non-Indians in state and federal courts. In one significant area, however, the ICRA did not intrude. In deference to the Pueblos, some of whom had theocratic governments, an establishment of religion clause was not forced upon tribal governments, allowing religious exclusion where traditions warranted it.

The trend during the past century is clear. Congress has moved from the disbursement of tribal properties to the articulation of personal individual liberties. Even if tribal cultures remain constant in the practice of traditions, the federal government rarely allows tribes' internal cultural functions to supercede the personal legal privileges enjoyed by non-Indians.

CORPORATE ECONOMIC STATUS

Land, its ownership and use, has been a major theme in the federal-Indian relationship. By 1882 most western lands had been taken away from the tribes, although the Indians of the northern plains and Indian Territory still possessed large tracts. The goal of land policy in the 1880s was to provide each Indian with a farm-sized tract of land, thereby ensuring his assimilation into the rural economy.

The decades following the passage of the General Allotment Act saw a bewildering succession of statutes that revealed the contradictory purposes of the assimilation policy. The tendency of Congress was to vest increasing power in the Interior Department to manage and dispose of Indian allotments. Management of Indian resources was gauged according to the cash income derived from it. Indians received less from their property than other citizens, however, because Indian lands were isolated from markets and generally non-productive. Congress tended to blame Indians for this failure, and gradually increased government control over their resources. Yet justification for the allotment policy continued the same—that Indians would become successful only if allowed to own and manage their own property.

The Act of February 16, 1889, which authorized the sale of dead timber on reservations, initiated a domino-like succession of statutes dealing with Indian resources.[42] Later statutes enabled large lumbering corporations to exploit heavily-forested Indian lands in Minnesota, Wisconsin, Washington, and Oregon. Thereafter, Indians waged a continuing struggle to make the Bureau of Indian Affairs give them an accurate appraisal of their timber assets; even so, they were hard put to prevent fraud by corporations that secured government contracts to cut their timber.

Indian irrigation projects began in the 1850s when Congress appropriated funds to construct an irrigation canal on the Colorado River Indian reservation in Arizona.[43] Appropriations thereafter were sporadic until the federal government entered the field of irrigation and reclamation with the Newlands Act of 1902.[44] Because Indian lands constituted a significant portion of federal land-holdings in the West, the passage of this act made Indian irrigation a high priority in the Interior Department. In the Act of May 18, 1916, Congress authorized the leasing of allotted lands susceptible to irrigation if the Indian owner was disabled, aged, or could not personally occupy them.[45] This provision allowed non-Indians to secure a foothold on reservation lands considered potentially fertile; it also increased government control over the property of individual Indians. Many of the irrigation projects developed by the Interior actually served to transfer Indian water to non-Indian irrigators who lived on or adjacent to the reservations.

The problems of Indian allotments were addressed in the Omnibus Act of June 25, 1910.[46] The act provided for the administration of the estates of allottees, made unlawful any attempt to transfer an Indian allotment to a non-Indian, provided protection against timber trespass and fire damage on allotted lands, and allowed an exchange of allotments if they were needed for power or reservoir sites. Coupled with the Burke Act, which dealt with the removal of trust provisions on allotments, the Omnibus Act also served to enhance the power of the Secretary of the Interior to deal arbitrarily with Indian lands.

The Secretary was generally authorized to sell timber on allotted lands and had significantly expanded his already considerable power to lease lands for the benefit of the allottees. The resulting income was deposited in Individual Indian Monies (IIM) accounts and then parceled out to allottees believed by the Bureau to be "worthy" recipients. This practice led to scandal a decade later when fullbloods of the Five Civilized Tribes with IIM accounts totalling in the hundreds of thousands of dollars were found dead of malnutrition or living in abject poverty while the Bureau diverted their income to schools and churches.

The mobilization of natural resources for the war effort during World War I made exploitation of Indian lands inevitable. With its usual tardiness Congress did not face the problem until June of 1919, well after the hostilities had ended. It then passed a general statute authorizing the Secretary of the Interior to grant leases and prospecting permits on Indian lands in nine western states—Arizona, California, Oregon, Washington, Idaho, Montana, Wyoming, and New Mexico.[47] This statute proved much too broad, however, and was superseded by the Act of May 29, 1924, which required public auction of mineral leases by the Secretary and the approval of the tribal council before the successful bidders could begin their activities.[48]

The unilateral use of Indian lands by the Interior Department, or by persons it designated, gradually ceased after the 1924 statute, which required some form of tribal consent for almost everything done with Indian lands. The Act of March 3, 1927, for example, while expanding the Secretary's authority for oil and gas leasing on unallotted land, also provided for the deposit of rentals, royalties, and production bonuses in the Treasury of the United States to the credit of the tribe involved.[49] Tribal councils were free to spend these funds, although they could not issue per capita payments without the permission of Congress. The admission that tribes owned the income derived from their lands proved a profound turning point in the congressional view of Indian property. Having admitted that Indians possessed subsurface and other land rights as did any other owner, Congress began to accept the idea that Indians, both individually and as tribes, might someday achieve economic independence from federal largess and still enjoy the protection of the federal government. This idea fit exactly the beliefs of John Collier, who incorporated it into his reform of Indian affairs in the IRA.

An important step in this process was the passage of the Leavitt Act of July 1, 1932.[50] Indian irrigation projects had been burdened from their inception by the practice of charging construction and maintenance costs against the allotments irrigated. Neither the Indians nor the white farmers who shared these projects could afford to pay the sometimes exorbitant costs, and many irrigation projects failed because of it. Indian lands were initially exempt from the charges as long as they remained in trust status, but it became apparent as the Great Depression deepened that it would never be possible to repay the full cost of the projects. The Bureau of Indian Affairs had the power to waive the charges in some instances, but the Leavitt Act empowered the Secretary of the Interior to adjust or eliminate debts standing against the lands, a corrective measure that enabled some of the projects to regain financial health.

The major statute dealing with Indian natural resources in this century was the Indian Reorganization Act of 1934. Although many commentators emphasize the self-government measures of this act, Collier and the Bureau saw it equally as a measure for achieving Indian economic independence. Most important in their thinking was the fact that further allotment was forbidden on those reservations which accepted the act. Collier was optimistic if naive about the revitalization of Indian culture that would follow. He envisioned individual allottees eagerly ceding back their lands to tribal ownership and living once again in communal harmony. But Indians who owned oil wells in Oklahoma quickly disabused him of this notion, and only one tribe actually consolidated their lands using Collier's formula.

A revolving loan fund was established for the repurchase of tribal lands, so that land consolidation became an acceptable measure of economic progress of the reservations. A variety of business enterprises began that involved the use of tribal lands, and while many of these activities were simply upgraded cattle and farming cooperatives, the IRA programs significantly increased the ability of Indians to develop their own resources. Irrigation ditches were cleaned and repaired, timber resources were developed, some tourism was initiated, and reservations were encouraged to look beyond simple agricultural activities to bolster tribal and individual income. Most loans taken out by Indians were promptly repaid when their enterprises became successful. In fact, the revolving loan funds enjoyed one of the best records in this regard of any federal activity in the Depression years.

At the height of the termination era, on August 9, 1955, Congress enacted a measure which proved important in the development of

Indian natural resources.[51] This act allowed long-term leasing of Indian lands, primarily by tribal councils, to attract industries and agricultural activities to the reservations. Over the next two decades many tribes sought additional waivers of the trust responsibility, and received permission to issue leases on some tracts for ninety-nine years.

The following year (1956) Congress passed an act that let Indian allottees mortgage their allotments but prohibited foreclosure of these lands in state courts.[52] With these two statutes, the attention of Congress seemed diverted from exploitation and sale of Indian assets. This trend has continued in recent years; in fact, the discovery of energy resources has accelerated the rate at which tribes develop their own land. Congressional concerns now involve establishing ground rules for the exploitation of resources, and the old questions regarding ownership of minerals and other natural resources have faded into obscurity.

If one had to choose the dominant feature of Indian legislation of the past century that dealt with natural resources, it would be the continuing failure of Congress to understand the economics of the times. The reservations were allotted when the family farm was becoming an anachronism and when agriculture required a substantial investment in machinery. Tribes were finally given the right to veto Interior leases of their lands in the 1920s, during the final years of the first great industrial surge before the Great Depression. The termination period also saw the squandering of tribal riches on useless experiments in private capitalism. Today's emphasis on mineral extraction (to the exclusion of other forms of community economic development and of alternative energy resource use) again makes Indian development of natural resources outmoded and suspect.

No legislative proposal considered by Congress dealt with the Indians' potential choices for the development of their lands. The urgency of Congress to be rid of the "Indian Problem" allowed for only short-term and seemingly simple solutions. Rarely did anyone in either house of Congress compare the actual economic realities of the nation with the solutions imposed on the tribes. Impatience at Indian reluctance to participate in the expanding American economy, which was bolstered by the attitude that large non-Indian interests should have priority in using Indian resources, prevented the formulation of any fair plan for Indians' use of their own lands.

INDIVIDUAL AND CORPORATE
SOCIAL RIGHTS

Early treaties authorized some social services, but generally these benefits were authorized for a limited time, during which Congress assumed that Indians would learn to provide for themselves. No one ever bothered to see if the tribes were learning how to live in an increasingly complex world. Consequently, no matter how hard Indians tried to provide for themselves, the pace of settlement and technological development made their efforts all but futile. As it became clear that the government would have to engage in extensive social programs to prepare Indians to live in American society, treaty provisions began to contain more specific descriptions of the services the national government was willing to provide. The 1867–1868 Peace Commission treaties, for example, promised a schoolhouse and a teacher for every group of thirty children who could be induced to attend school. Since neither the federal government nor the Indians were eager to see this provision implemented, it remained an unfulfilled promise until the 1960s when large-scale social service programs became popular.

The 1880s saw the emergence of an extensive network of off-reservation boarding schools that symbolized the first national commitment to educate Indians. The Act of July 31, 1882, for example, authorized the use of abandoned military posts for Indian schools.[53] Although these facilities were welcomed, the act really indicated that Indians could expect to receive the discards of the larger society. Thus, surplus lands and properties, obsolete machinery, and finally, food commodities came to represent the most tangible form of federal aid to Indians.

Missionary schools provided the backbone of Indian educational programs until the turn of the century. Despite the development of federal boarding schools, the Bureau of Indian Affairs was unable to meet the needs of so many tribes. As the churches were still politically influential on many reservations, the government came to rely on them for education. But as might be expected, conflict broke out between Catholic and Protestant missionaries, resulting in the Appropriation Act of June 7, 1897, which prohibited the use of federal funds for sectarian education.[54] The Protestants supported this policy in order to deprive Catholics of federal funds in their mission schools. The Catholics devised a means whereby the government allowed them to use tribal funds for parochial school financial support, and in spite of objections by other tribal members and Protestant missionaries, the Supreme Court upheld this kind of expenditure in *Quick Bear v. Leupp*.[55]

Debates over Indian appropriations marred the early twentieth-century sessions of Congress. Tribal annuities were expiring, yet reservations badly needed a continuing source of income. Congressmen with destitute tribal constituents often sought to include them as beneficiaries of federal largess, using the argument that services should be uniformly administered. Finally, a compromise was reached in the Snyder Act of November 2, 1921, which authorized the Secretary of the Interior to expend funds for certain social services without regard to previous treaty commitments. Continuing treaty obligations were henceforth regarded as a part of the general Indian appropriations, and no further effort was made to record expenditures by tribe or to link such costs to specific treaty items. From this more convenient allocation of Indian monies came the general belief that the federal government had promised a large variety of social services to Indians simply because they were Indians.

The Act of February 15, 1929 foreshadowed programs of the New Deal.[56] It permitted agents and employees of any state to enter Indian lands for health inspections and for the enforcement of both sanitation regulations and compulsory school attendance. The act represented a growing belief that states had a major responsibility for Indians because of their recently acquired status as citizens. The major statute encouraging states to extend their social services to Indians was the Johnson-O'Malley Act (JOM) of 1934, which authorized the Secretary of the Interior to sign contracts with states, their agencies, and private institutions to provide a variety of welfare services using federal funds. JOM became the major vehicle for supporting educational programs for Indians in public schools. It has lately become a controversial program because of the requirement, added in the last decade, that Indian parent committees be consulted in the expenditure of federal monies. A careful reading of the statute suggests that it was never intended to assimilate reservation children into public schools but rather to assist those who had already left the reservations in their adjustment to the larger society.

During World War II, Congress embarked on an ambitious program to compensate all local school districts for sudden massive shifts of population that occurred when war industries and military installations sprang up in sparsely populated areas. When the Korean War made it clear that the United States would need a continuing defense system, Congress formalized federal educational aid by passing two statutes, popularly known as public law (P.L.) 874 [57] and P.L. 815.[58] P.L. 874 gave financial assistance to school districts faced with meeting extraordinary demands on the annual operating budget, while P.L. 815 provided construction funds for expansion of school facilities. It was not long before Congress had expanded the concept of education subsidies beyond defense-related activities to include national parks and forests and, eventually, Indian reservations.

During the rush of social legislation in the late sixties and early seventies, Congress substantially amended P.L. 874 and 815. The Indian Education Act of 1972, an amendment to P.L. 874, established a National Advisory Council on Indian Education and formalized many of the programs for research and development available previously to Indian communities as part of the general national social legislation. Out of a national purpose, then, Indians were eventually linked to the domestic programs available to all other Americans and were understood by Congress as simply another, albeit needy, American ethnic group.

This transition—from special client with specific treaty claims against the United States to one of a number of equally deserving groups eligible for national social welfare legislation—completed the assimilation of Indians into the general society, at least in the eyes of the federal government. Congress had finally abandoned its belief that cultural change could be commanded by legislative fiat. Ironically, making federal social programs available to Indians achieved social integration more quickly than assimilation policy ever had. Indians were henceforth concerned with formal institutions that could bring them federal largess, and tended to adopt a view of the world compatible with their new status as a client group.

CONCLUSION

A century ago, Indians constituted one of the most important groups in the domestic affairs of the nation, but they have lost status during the intervening decades. The Senate and House of Representatives both had full committees dealing with Indian Affairs at the beginning of this century. By 1976, Indian matters were handled by minor subcommittee assignments in the House and by a "Select" committee of the Senate that had to be renewed periodically by Senate resolution. Part of this decline in importance can be traced to the Congressional Reorganization Act of 1946, which eliminated the old Indian committees and placed Indians under Public Lands (and later under Interior) in subcommittee status.[59] But the frustration of dealing with Indians on minor issues and the tedious nature of Indian legislative work also contributed to the decline in importance of Indians. No western senator or congressman wished to spend time on Indian matters when he could sit on a prestigious committee such as Space, Armed Forces, or Judiciary, where issues of national scope and importance were being debated.

One can easily trace the erosion of congressional concern with Indian legislation by examining efforts to bring order to the field of Indian affairs. In 1928, in conjunction with the spirit of reform exemplified in the Meriam Report of that year, the Senate Indian Committee under Senate Resolution 79 authorized a continuing investigation of the conditions of Indians in the United States.[60] Members of that committee took their work seriously and spent the next eight years holding field hearings in various parts of the West. Their work documented the existence of certain Indian needs that were met later both by the New Deal legislation sponsored by John Collier and by the establishment of the Indian Claims Commission. Most important, however, was the willingness of the senators to visit Indian reservations and spend countless hours examining how the Bureau of Indian Affairs programs actually worked.

In the Indian Delegation Act of August 8, 1946, Congress gave the Department and Secretary of the Interior authority to delegate administrative responsibility to lower-ranking federal employees; this move substantially diluted the trust responsibility of the Department.[61] In effect, Congress washed its hands of Indians and assumed that Indian matters could be handled administratively. Thereafter, the information that Congress received regarding Indians was carefully screened by the Interior Department, and of course represented the bureaucratic view of things. An indication of congressional unconcern was the Act of July 14, 1956, which directed the Secretary of the

Interior to make a study of Indian education.[62] In former years a congressional committee or its staff would have undertaken this kind of study.

In 1976, following the occupation of Wounded Knee and the subsequent demands by a large segment of the Indian community and liberal press for fundamental reforms in Indian affairs, Congress authorized the American Indian Policy Review Commission.[63] Nicknamed the Abourezk Commission after the senator who proposed it, the commission was divided into eleven "task forces" composed of Indian members. The Task Forces quickly politicized both selections to their membership and topics to be covered, and little significance was accomplished in the two years the commission existed. The Abourezk Commission adequately reflected the contemporary status of Indians: they had become a small (if vocal) ethnic pressure group which had to be placated by Congress, but they were no longer a matter of grave national concern.

Congress still retains all powers allocated by the Constitution with respect to Indians. Yet there is no reason to suppose that we will see a new direction in policy for the remainder of the century. Indian affairs have become burdensome for everyone, Indians and congressmen alike, chiefly because of complex organizational structures that have arisen since the Indian Reorganization Act.

Consequently, there is little incentive for anyone in Congress to adjust the federal laws and bureaucracy that govern Indians, no matter how necessary the adjustments. The political relationship between Indians and the national government may finally have lapsed into terminal inertia. If so, we might as well accept the present configuration of Indian affairs as a permanent fixture in our lives.

N   O   T   E   S

1. U.S. Constitution, Article 1, section 8, clause 3, 1 Stat. 10, at 13, Sept. 17, 1787. All statute citations are from the *United States Statutes at Large*.
2. See Act of June 5, 1850, 9 Stat 437; Act of March 25, 1864, 13 Stat. 37; Act of June 30, 1864, 13 Stat. 324; Act of June 15, 1866, 14 Stat. 358; Act of March 14, 1867, 15 Stat. 1; Act of July 20, 1867, 15 Stat. 17.
3. Act of March 3, 1871, 16 Stat. 544, 566.
4. Act of Feb. 8, 1887, 24 Stat. 388.

5. Act of May 8, 1906, 34 Stat. 182, P.L. 59-149.
6. Act of Nov. 2, 1921, 42 Stat. 208, P.L. 67-85.
7. Act of June 18, 1934, 48 Stat. 984, P.L. 73-383.
8. Act of April 16, 1934, 48 Stat. 596, P.L. 73-167.
9. Act of Aug. 1, 1953, 67 Stat. B132, H.Con.Res. 108.
10. Title II, §201, Apr. 11, 1968, 82 Stat. 77, P.L. 90-284.
11. 86 Stat. 334, P.L. 92-318, Title IV, "Indian Education Act" (1972).
12. "Indian Self-Determination and Education Assistance Act," Jan. 4, 1975, 88 Stat. 2203, P.L. 93-638.
13. *Ex Parte Crow Dog*, 109 U.S. 556 (1883).
14. Act of March 3, 1885, 23 Stat. 362.
15. Act of July 7, 1898, Sec. 2, 30 Stat. 717.
16. Act of June 28, 1898, 30 Stat. 495.
17. Act of March 2, 1906, 34 Stat. 822.
18. Act of Oct. 22, 1970, 84 Stat. 1091, P.L. 91-495.
19. Act of May 1, 1936, 49 Stat. 1250, P.L. 74-538.
20. Act of June 26, 1936, 49 Stat. 1967, P.L. 74-816.
21. Act of March 3, 1863, 12 Stat. 765.
22. Act of Aug. 13, 1946, 60 Stat. 1049, P.L. 79-726.
23. Act of March 3, 1891, 26 Stat. 851.
24. Act of Oct. 8, 1976, 90 Stat. 1990, P.L. 94-465.
25. Act of Dec. 15, 1970, 84 Stat. 1437, P.L. 91-550.
26. Maine Indian Claims Settlement Act, 94 Stat. 1785, Oct. 10, 1980, P.L. 96-420, and Rhode Island Indian Claims Settlement Act, 92 Stat. 813, Sept. 30, 1978, P.L. 95-395.
27. Act of May 17, 1884, 23 Stat. 24.
28. Act of Aug. 24, 1912, 37 Stat. 512, P.L. 62-334.
29. Act of July 7, 1958, 72 Stat. 339, P.L. 85-508.
30. "Alaska Native Claims Settlement Act," Dec. 18, 1971, 85 Stat. 688, P.L. 92-203.
31. See House Report no. 2503, 82nd Cong., 2d sess., Dec. 15, 1952, pp. 687–716.
32. See "Federal Acknowledgment Process," Hearings before Sen. Select Committee on Indian Affairs, 96th Cong., 2d sess., June 2, 1980.
33. See *United States v. Sandoval*, 231 U.S. 28 (1913) and *United States v. Candalaria*, 271 U.S. 432 (1926).
34. Act of Feb. 28, 1891, 26 Stat. 794.
35. Act of March 2, 1907, 34 Stat. 1221, P.L. 59-182.
36. Act of Aug. 15, 1894, 28 Stat. 286.
37. Morton v. Mancari, 417 U.S. 535 (1974).
38 . Act of Nov. 6, 1919, 41 Stat. 350, P.L. 66-75.
39. Act of June 2, 1924, 43 Stat. 253, P.L. 68-175.
40. Act of May 21, 1934, 48 Stat. 787, P.L. 73-242.

41. Act of June 7, 1956, 70 Stat. 254, P.L. 84-570.
42. Act of Feb. 16, 1889, 25 Stat. 673.
43. Act of March 2, 1867, 14 Stat. 492.
44. Act of June 17, 1902, 32 Stat. 388, P.L. 57-161.
45. Act of May 18, 1916, 39 Stat. 123, P.L. 64-80.
46. Act of June 25, 1910, 36 Stat. 855, P.L. 61-313.
47. Act of June 30, 1919, 41 Stat. 3, P.L. 66-3.
48. Act of May 29, 1924, 43 Stat. 244, P.L. 68-158.
49. Act of March 3, 1927, 44 Stat. 1347, P.L. 69-702.
50. Act of July 1, 1932, 47 Stat. 564, P.L. 72-240.
51. Act of Aug. 9, 1955, 69 Stat. 539, P.L. 84-255.
52. Act of March 29, 1956, 70 Stat. 62, P.L. 84-450.
53. Act of July 31, 1882, 22 Stat. 181.
54. Act of June 7, 1847, 30 Stat. 62.
55. *Quick Bear v. Leupp*, 210 U.S. 50 (1908).
56. Act of Feb. 15, 1929, 45 Stat. 1185, P.L. 70-760.
57. Act of Sept. 30, 1950, 64 Stat. 1100, P.L. 81-874.
58. Act of Sept. 23, 1950, 64 Stat. 967, P.L. 81-815.
59. "Legislative Reorganization Act of 1946," Aug. 2, 1946, 60 Stat. 812, P.L. 79-601.
60. Senate Res. 79, 70th Cong., 1st sess., Feb. 1, 1928.
61. Act of Aug. 8, 1946, 60 Stat. 939, P.L. 79-687.
62. Act of July 14, 1956, 70 Stat. 531, P.L. 84-702.
63. Act of Jan. 2, 1975, 88 Stat. 1910, P.L. 93-580.

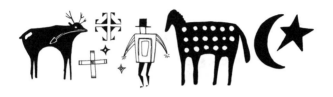

THE INDIAN
REORGANIZATION ACT

L A U R E N C E   M.   H A U P T M A N

*I*n a recent interview for *Indian Truth*, Suzan Shown Harjo stressed the importance of reevaluating the Indian Reorganization Act: "It's an issue that's worth taking a serious look at, especially since we're approaching the fiftieth anniversary in 1984. It shouldn't be looked at stereotypically, but as any law is looked at: in the context of its passage, and what it hoped to accomplish, what it did or did not accomplish, and what might be a future direction."[1] Harjo's sentiments represent a widely held attitude among Indians about the legislation that undergirds presently-existing tribal governments. The fiftieth anniversary will no doubt produce a torrent of articles and conferences dealing with the effects of this legislation.

The Indian Reorganization Act, the most important legislation affecting Native Americans in this century, has been the subject of heated debate in Indian communities since its passage in 1934.[2] To some Native Americans—such as the Oneidas of Wisconsin, who had lost a 65,000-acre reservation because of allotment provisions under the Dawes Act,[3] and had less than 90 acres of land in tribal ownership at the beginning of the New Deal—the IRA provided the mechanism for beginning tribal economic restoration, political reform, and meaningful self-government. Most of all, the IRA provided the Oneidas with hope for the future. As one tribal elder observed, the act was "the best thing that ever happened" to them because "no tribal governing mechanism to stop fraudulent land sales existed before the IRA."[4] Not all Indians felt the same. The New Deal years marked an era of increased discord and factionalism between traditional tribal leadership and leaders under the new systems of tribal government created under the IRA. Whether traditional or newly elected, Indian leadership often felt subjected to undue non-Indian tampering with the existing tribal political systems.[5] To one prominent Rosebud Sioux, the IRA represented "a blueprint for elected tyranny."[6]

Recent assessments condemn more than they praise the IRA and the Indian New Deal. The report of the American Indian Policy

Review Commission (the Abourezk Commission), for instance, faulted all government policymakers since 1934 both for neglecting to promote aggressive land acquisition for tribes and for failing to protect the existing Indian land base. From 1934 to 1974, the report pointed out, only 595,157 acres were purchased for tribal use, while government agencies condemned 1,811,010 acres of Indian land for other purposes.[7] The blame, of course, rests with subsequent Congresses and administrations who failed to provide funds for land purchase, not with the originators of the land purchase program. Yet it is noteworthy that both Indians and policymakers alike look back to the Indian Reorganization Act of 1934 as the foundation upon which to make these judgments— as if the mere passage of the act guaranteed the actions and attitudes of subsequent generations of Indians and Congressmen.

In recent years, historians have also tended to qualify their praise of New Deal Indian policy. They emphasize that the good intentions of Commissioner John Collier, architect of the policy of self-government for Indians, were undermined by his paternalistic attitude toward Indians, by his naive and often romantic perceptions of modern Indian life, by his abrasive and authoritarian personality, and even by his general lack of understanding of Native American cultures and diversity. There is no question that Collier possessed all these human failings, that he based his conception of modern Indian life primarily on his experiences of the Navajos and Pueblos, and that his single-minded devotion to his goal often alienated potentially valuable Indian allies. Nevertheless, he provided a steady hand upon the bureaucratic wheel that made permanent change possible.

Consequently, historians now view the New Deal as a golden opportunity to build a reservoir of trust between Indian and non-Indian—which the national government missed. This failure at least partially explains the enduring economic hardships that Indian communities have experienced in the half-century since IRA.[8]

Much of the commentary on the IRA has ignored a central fact: that it was largely an administrative reorganization following a century of mismanagement and mistaken policies that had seriously depleted Indian resources and reduced the Indian population to subsistence. Much of the reorganization was an in-house effort that involved changes in attitudes and perceptions, reallocations of administrative powers and responsibilities, and revision of ad-hoc rules and regulations that had accumulated over the preceding century. It was clearly time to clean house, but it is ironic that the governmental bureau responsible for the situation both sponsored the remedial legislation and was charged with carrying out the reforms. This dual role of the Bureau of Indian Affairs is a major reason why many Indians look at the IRA with both admiration and suspicion.

Indians had come to view the Interior Department with suspicion by the turn of the century. The lavish promises they had been given during negotiations for allotment had proven ephemeral. Instead of material prosperity and wealth they had been reduced to paupers and seen most of their land stolen. The 1891 amendment to the Dawes General Allotment Act of 1887 had given the Secretary of the Interior authority to lease allotments on a discretionary basis, and the 1906 Burke Act had accelerated the rate at which Indians, once given their patent-in-fee, saw their lands removed from trust.[9] Between the passage of the Dawes General Allotment Act of 1887 and the Indian Reorganization Act in 1934, the Indian land base had shrunk by over 90 million acres.[10] Even worse, some reservations were still being allotted, although almost every policy-maker knew that allotment was a discredited policy.[11] In 1933 Indians retained approximately 48 million acres of land, much of it arid, unusable, and non-productive. The Great Dust Bowl conditions made substantially more land unliveable.

Moreover, 49 percent of the Indians on allotted reservations were landless. Even before the onset of the Great Depression, 96 percent of all Indians earned less than $200 per year.[12] Much of this income was derived from leasing their allotments to whites who could afford to invest in the necessary equipment to farm. When these farmers went broke, the leases were cancelled and the Indians were returned their badly eroded lands without any income or the possibility of making the land productive.

The federal government was not unaware of these conditions. In 1922, Secretary of the Interior Hubert Work asked a blue ribbon commission composed of prominent citizens, the Committee of One Hundred, to investigate Indian affairs and make recommendations, but their recommendations were forgotten in the general prosperity of the 1920s.[13] Several years later, another investigation was authorized. This time, in order to get maximum political impact, Work asked the prestigious Brookings Institute to do a complete survey, including significant field work and on-site visitations of the Bureau of Indian Affairs and its programs. Beginning work in 1926 under Lewis Meriam, the staff of this study included Henry Roe Cloud, a nationally respected Indian leader, W. Carson Ryan, Jr., a prominent educator and head of the Bureau's educational programs, and Edward Everett Dale, a well-known historian.

The study was released in 1928 as *The Problem of Indian Administration*, but it is popularly known as the Meriam Report. The report severely criticized Bureau health care delivery to Indians, who suffered from much higher rates of infant mortality, trachoma, and tuberculosis than other Americans. It was especially critical of Bureau efforts to educate Indian children at boarding schools, pointing out overcrowded conditions, lack of qualified school personnel and uniformity of curriculum, improper diet, poor medical care, and harsh discipline. It added that the overall quality of Indian Service employees was lower than that found in other government agencies and remarked that they showed little empathy for the people they were serving.[14] The Meriam Report stirred up considerable controversy. Its description of problems and its careful identification of areas for reform made it impossible to ignore, as had happened with previous reports. But with the country soon gripped by the Great Depression, the Meriam recommendations—most of which required a substantial federal investment in programs—did not fare well in the federal budget.

Indian Commissioner Charles Rhoads and Assistant Commissioner J. Henry Scattergood, reformers formerly associated with the Indian Rights Association, were given control of the Indian Bureau during the remaining years of the Hoover administration, but their efforts were regarded as too little too late. By the early 1930s the Bureau of Indian Affairs faced an uncertain future. It was continually at war with private reform groups interested in the conditions of Indians; these included the Indian Rights Association and more especially the American Indian Defense Association led by the fiery John Collier. Always alert to bureaucratic abuses, Collier clashed with Albert Fall on the Pueblo Lands Bill, defeating the Secretary of the Interior before he was driven from office in disgrace over the Teapot Dome scandal. He also helped organize the All Pueblo Council, which represented the first continuing aggressive effort by a large group of Indians to achieve self-government.

In 1932 Collier and Nathan Margold asked Senator Lynn Frazier of Montana to introduce legislation so that the tribes could organize councils that the federal government would recognize. Their proposed legislation provided for a committee to draft a constitution and by-laws for any reservation on which one-quarter of the adult tribal members wished to organize. Once the constitution was adopted, the tribal councils would be empowered to represent their tribes before Congress, the executive branch, and the courts. The legislation proposed to vest all existing powers of Indian tribes or councils in the new councils approved by the reservation people, including the power to approve the sale or lease of lands and to employ an attorney to represent the tribe. One important provision, Section 9, authorized the Secretary of the Interior to dismiss any employee or officer under his jurisdiction who interfered with the tribe or its members in the free exercise of the powers which tribal councils gained under this act.[15]

The Collier proposal was revolutionary in its scope. By shifting power to the newly approved tribal councils and away from the office of the Secretary of the Interior, it sought to reverse a century of federal encroachment on the right of local self-government. Collier's belief in the inherent right of self-government, derived primarily from his experiences with the Pueblos and Navajos, was the keystone of his vision of Indian reform. It became the rallying point for his attack on the Bureau's inefficiencies.

With the election of Franklin Delano Roosevelt and his appointment of Secretary of the Interior Harold Ickes, the New Deal became a reality for Indians. Ickes recommended John Collier as Commissioner of Indian Affairs, no doubt believing it better to bring the zealot inside the government than have him outside setting brushfires of protest, as he had during the previous administration. Along with Collier came two attorneys who made significant contributions to reform: Felix S. Cohen and Nathan Margold. Together they provided the legal talent needed to orient the massive bureaucracy toward reform. When the second year of the New-Deal Congress began in 1934, the Interior team submitted the Indian Reorganization Act to Congress with full presidential support.

It was apparent, however, that Collier had little support outside the administration. The Indian Reorganization Act proposed to stop allotments, form tribal governments, create a Court of Indian Affairs, and establish radical changes in land tenure. As reactions to the proposal mounted, Collier requested a short period in which to gather Indian support for his bill. The Bureau quickly convened a series of Indian "congresses" in various parts of the country designed to explain the proposal and obtain enthusiastic Indian endorsements. When the various tribes learned that Collier expected them to cede their allotments back to the tribe, they rejected his four-title bill. It was all Bureau employees could do to prevent a complete rout of the new policy. The Oklahoma tribes in particular rejected the Indian Reorganization Act; they believed they would have to return their oil wells to tribal governments that existed only as paper organizations.

Congress radically altered Collier's proposal, eliminating the four-title bill and substituting a new bill which contained several provisions not germane to self-government, but vital for congressional passage. The final version provided for the establishment of tribal elections to accept or reject the provisions of the legislation and of tribal constitutions and corporations. It established a revolving loan fund to assist organized tribes in community development, and by waiving civil service requirements, it offered preference to Indians who sought employment in the Bureau of Indian Affairs. The act also created an educational loan program for Indian students seeking a vocational, high school, or college education. Perhaps most important, the act ended the land allotment policies of the Dawes Act for those tribes accepting the new provisions, and provided for the purchase of new lands for Indians. Unallotted surplus lands were authorized to be returned to tribal governments. Conservation efforts were encouraged by the establishment of Indian forestry units and by herd reduction on arid land to protect range deterioration. This later program cost Collier the support of the Navajos because it meant a radical reduction of their sheep herds.

Sections 16 and 17, the tribal and business organization provisions, were the heart of the IRA. According to Section 16:

> Any Indian tribe, or tribes, residing on the same reservation, shall have the right to organize for its common welfare, and may adopt an appropriate constitution and by-laws . . . at a special election authorized by the *Secretary of the Interior*. . . . Amendments to the constitution and by-laws may be ratified and approved by the *Secretary* in the same manner as the original constitution and by-laws [emphasis added]. . . . In addition to all powers vested in any Indian tribe or tribal council by existing law, the constitution adopted by said tribe shall also vest in such tribe or its tribal council, the following rights and powers: To employ legal counsel, the choice of counsel and fixing of fees to be subject to the approval of the *Secretary of the Interior*; to prevent the sale, disposition, lease, or encumbrance of tribal lands, interests in lands, or other tribal assets without the consent of the tribe; and to negotiate with the Federal, State, and local Governments. The

Secretary of the Interior shall advise such tribe or its tribal council of all appropriation estimates or Federal projects for the benefit of the tribe prior to the submission of such estimates to the Bureau of the Budget and the Congress [emphasis added].

Section 17, which was concerned more with business organization, allowed the Secretary of the Interior to issue a charter of incorporation upon request and to establish the electoral machinery to vote on it. If approved, the incorporated tribe could "purchase, take by gift, or bequest, or otherwise, own, hold, manage, operate, and dispose of property of every description, real and personal, including the power to purchase restricted Indian lands and to issue in exchange therefor (sic) interests in corporate property, and such further powers as may be incidental to the conduct of corporate business" as long as it was not inconsistent with the law. It added that "no authority shall be granted to sell, mortgage, or lease for a period exceeding ten years any of the land included within the limits of the reservation," with a caveat that this provision could be revoked only by Congressional legislation.[16]

The IRA achieved some noteworthy initial successes. It helped some tribes increase their tribal landbase, and (especially when contrasted with the allotment period) helped some gain better control of tribal property. Yet according to Commissioner Collier, the act was designed to overcome a situation where "the Department has absolute discretionary powers over all organized expressions of the Indians. . . . Tribal councils existed by the Department's sufferance and had no authority except as . . . granted by the Department."[17] Sections 16 and 17 indicate that the attempt to provide the tribes with self-rule served mainly to increase the personnel and supervisory responsibilities of the Interior Department and its agency, the BIA. In effect, the IRA "added a new layer of permanent administration to the agency [BIA], while all the staff and activities established by the General Allotment Act were continued for the benefit of the remaining allottees."[18]

Collier had claimed that the bureaucratic nature of Indian affairs and the lack of home-rule was the real issue in designing the Indian Reorganization Act. During congressional hearings on the bill, the commissioner maintained its aim was to "extend to all Indians that minimum of home-rule in domestic and cultural matters which is basic to American life."[19] On a separate occasion, he added: "Any American community that was at the mercy of such a bureaucracy would move out or rise in rebellion."[20] Yet ironically, Collier gave the BIA, an agency already viewed by many Native Americans as the germ responsible for the sickly state of Indian affairs, increased authority in their supervision. Thus, even when the majority of a tribe valued the opportunity to rebuild a landbase or participate in the revolving loan program, many viewed the increased federal supervision as a necessary but unpleasant trade-off.

Having been betrayed by allotment, Indians could be excused for their suspicion. One Seneca Indian said: "You can't make me believe that the [U.S.] Government offers loans to us without asking security. Suppose we don't make money without plows. Suppose our horses die before we can pay back. What then?"[21] He added that the government, upon default, would undoubtedly appropriate Indian homes. Another Seneca, despite his faltering English, put it most accurately: "We have been fooled time after time that most of the Indians have lost faith in the Saxon race we certainly have had some raw deal in back history we have never had a square deal."[22] Many agreed with Ray Jimerson, a Seneca leader, that the act was "too long and complicated, is full of new rules and regulations, and is subject to Bureau interpretation."[23] Especially among the Iroquois, although perhaps less among the western tribes, most people expected that government intervention would only be bad news for them.

The administration attempted to develop a pro-IRA spirit within the bureaucracy, but there were problems. On April 30, 1934, Secretary Ickes warned all Bureau employees: "If any employee wishes to oppose the new policy he should do so honestly and openly from outside of the Service."[24] But this effort to change traditional Bureau thinking was severely criticized by Roger Baldwin, the founder of the American Civil Liberties Union. Baldwin was a strong supporter of the new policy who nevertheless felt that mandatory IRA support denied free speech to civil service workers.[25] The administration was damned if it did and damned if it didn't. In addition, many Bureau employees turned their energies to the promulgation of the act among the tribes with a frantic zeal. Eager superintendents in California and on the Northern Plains made extravagant promises to the tribes in an effort to persuade them to adopt the act. Extra food rations and Emergency Conservation Work jobs were used as enticements. In some cases elections were hurried and unpublicized.[26] Opponents of the legislation sometimes found themselves without the means of publicizing their views.

The Bureau attempted indirectly to manipulate the congressional hearings; they looked more favorably on requests for travel funds from supporters than from opponents of the measure. Some Indian informants identified the sources of opposition, and as early as 1938 the FBI was directed to trail dissidents.[27] In addition, despite the major structural changes that the Indian reorganization achieved, it failed to correct a sore point in Indian-federal relations: the everyday abuses of authority and the corruption of BIA reservation superintendents. Thomas Sloan, the prominent Omaha attorney and former president of the Society of American Indians, castigated Collier's "new day for Indians" before a congressional committee in 1935; he claimed it represented a "business as usual" approach to Indian problems. Describing the alleged criminal actions of a superintendent on the Klamath Reservation in Oregon in 1935, Sloan insisted that the local operations of the Indian Service had changed only in form since Collier's appointment. He added that "in spirit and execution it is the same system, and in substance it is the old arbitrary power of superintendents that control."[28]

Nor did the Indian Service appear to change very much in the 1930s. Some of the most glaring abuses described in congressional hearings were committed by superintendents of the Cherokee Reservation in North Carolina. Although some of their actions were criticized by Washington officials, the men were not removed from their positions and continued to exercise rigidly authoritarian policies. The superintendents faced open rebellion by a sizable body of Cherokees partly because of an Interior Department plan to build the Blue Ridge Parkway directly through the heart of the reservation. The intent was to stimulate tourism in the newly opened Great Smoky National Park. The superintendents tried to silence their critics by suspending government contracts for apples and farm products granted to the opponents of the IRA and the parkway plan; they also fired teachers who disagreed with the new government program (including the teaching of a new curriculum prepared by progressive educational specialists); and they denied mailing privileges to the duly elected vice chief of the tribe. Furthermore they suspended Cherokee students from school on the grounds that their parents were protesting the school system, the curriculum, the IRA, the parkway project, and the superintendents themselves.[29]

By 1940 critics of the IRA sought a nationwide repeal of the act. In a congressional hearing, Alice Lee Jemison, a Seneca and the Indian New Deal's major critic among the Iroquois, maintained that there "is no self-government in the act; all final power and authority remains in the Secretary of the Interior, which is exactly where it always has rested heretofore."[30] She added that in certain areas, including grazing and timber operations, the Secretary of the Interior had in fact expanded his power.

In sum, the IRA was destined by its design to limited success. Historians should focus not on why the IRA achieved less than its sponsors envisioned, but why the agency with the most to lose by Indian self-government was allowed to administer the reform legislation without supervision from any other federal agency. Indeed, one can trace the manner in which career bureaucrats systematically subverted the provisions of the IRA. Scudder Mekeel, the former head of Collier's applied anthropology unit within the Department of the Interior, described the treatment of the referendum provisions:

> The election provision in the Indian Reorganization Act immediately put the Indian Service in the position of a campaigner— at least to the extent of informing and educating the Indians as to what acceptance or rejection of the Act entailed, what benefits would be had from acceptance, and what the Indians would be giving up by rejecting it. This, of course, put the burden of proof on the Indian Office—an administrative organization already felt by many Indians to be hostile and inimical to their interests. Therefore many Indians felt that the Indian Reorganization Act was some grand scheme to get more land away from them, or at least a scheme by which the white man would profit in some way but not the Indian.[31]

Under the best of conditions it would have been impossible for the agency to escape the burden of its history. And because many Bureau employees did not wish Indians to develop self-government, it was a foregone conclusion that things would not progress smoothly.

One of the most important aftershocks of the IRA was its impact on Indians associated with its administration; the effects still shape Indian politics today. Collier, in formulating the IRA, based his overall plan on the British colonial policy of "indirect rule."[32] This modified colonial structure—rule through the use of native peoples in local institutions—was resented by many Indians and did irreparable damage to distinguished Indians connected with the Collier administration. Indians such as Henry Roe Cloud, Ben Dwight, D'Arcy McNickle and others, who were brought into the Bureau by Collier to help their people, were faced with a thankless and impossible task because "Bureau Indians" had been viewed as traitors by many Indians since the days of Carlos Montezuma.[33]

Carlos Montezuma was one of the most well-respected national Indian leaders in the first two decades of this century. An orphan educated by a kindly white army officer, Montezuma became a physician and devoted the last years of his life to one fundamental reform: the abolition of the BIA. Giving up a career in the Indian Health Service because of what he considered its colonial nature, Montezuma worked from his Chicago-based home to create a national network devoted to exposing the conditions of the reservations and destroying the bureaucracy that he believed shackled his people.[34] He represented a minority of Indian people at the time, but his disciples carried forward his beliefs with zeal.

An irony of the IRA period is that John Collier had come close to the position of Montezuma in his days as leader of the American Indian Defense Association. But Collier's fiery attacks on the bureaucracy dwindled when he became the Indian commissioner. D'Arcy McNickle, commenting on this change, said that Collier had to "turn around and win the confidence of the Indian people as chief of the bureau he had vilified. It was an awkward situation to be in and he never entirely succeeded in extricating himself."[35] Montezuma, however, had never recommended reform. Reform to him meant only strengthening, not diminishing, bureaucratic control over the lives of Indians, as he explained: "Reorganization means to strengthen and improve. No amount of reorganization of the Indian Bureau will abolish the Indian Bureau. Without much thought one can see that this reorganization business of the Indian Bureau will strengthen and enlarge the Indian Bureau."[36] These were prophetic words for a man who died a decade before Collier began his social engineering; they should have been heeded.

Tribal business committees and councils fared little better than individual Indian leaders under the IRA. Despite a sincere commitment by some of these new organizations for economic, educational, and political development, many Indians labelled these committees tools of the BIA from the very beginning.[37] As early as October 1946, the secretary of the Sioux Indian Rights Association wrote to Ben Dwight, then acting secretary of the National Congress of American Indians, that 30 percent of the Oglala Sioux, who had opposed the IRA, were boycotting all tribal elections conducted under the provisions of the act.[38] It is little wonder that by the 1970s these "IRA councils" became the focus of "Red Power" militancy that sought to restore traditional government to some reservations.

The road to Wounded Knee in 1973 was blazed by the paradoxes and inconsistencies of the Indian Reorganization Act. Although today's critics of the act should remember that self-government was a radical policy for the 1930s, there is no question that the IRA was and is a seriously flawed piece of legislation. The IRA was not designed to recognize tribal sovereignty, nor did its operations encourage it. The Secretary of the Interior, after all, had the final voice in every major policy decision made by Indians. It is no wonder that many Indians believed that the Bureau, under the IRA, "set up puppet governments on the reservations and somehow mysteriously governs all aspects of tribal life by remote control."[39]

Collier's paternalistic viewpoint, although progressive and even radical for his time, should not be taken as a model for future Indian policy. Ultimately, neither Collier nor Ickes trusted Indians to regenerate themselves. Perhaps they saw in the drastic cultural erosion of the previous decades the Indian's final separation from their ancient way of life. Perhaps they only wished to provide a modern vehicle with elements of traditional ways—although Collier's later writings and reflections indicate that his belief in the permanency of Indian culture was sincere and deeply felt.

Policies put into effect since the IRA, with the exception of the brief termination period of the 1950s, have generally followed Collier's lead in paying lip service to Indian culture while linking Indians ever closer to federal bureaucracy. The Indian Self-Determination and Education Assistance Act of 1975, for example, although heralded by its congressional sponsors as a major development in Indian policy, was actually only a footnote to the original ideas of self-government promulgated by John Collier four decades before.[40] The 1975 act merely sought to formalize the tenuous relationships which had grown up in the 1960s when Indian tribes became sponsoring agencies of federal poverty programs.

Creating tribal business committees, as did the IRA, or contracting federal programs from the Bureau and other federal agencies, as we have seen in the more recent past, can never produce true self-determination. The nature of the present federal-Indian relationship must be altered from one of paternalism, no matter how well disguised, to true self-rule. This change will require Congressional awareness of problems and the courage to provide Indians with a vested legal status immune from its intrusions and manipulations. Considering the increase in educated and professional Indians with management and administrative skills, it is time for a *real* "Indian New Deal."

N   O   T   E   S

1. *Indian Truth* 260 (July–Aug. 1981): 9. Harjo is presently executive director of the National Congress of American Indians.
2. Act of June 18, 1934, P.L. 73-383, 48 Stat. 984.
3. Act of Feb. 8, 1887, 24 Stat. 388.
4. Interview with Anderson Cornelius, conducted by Laurence M. Hauptman, Oct. 20, 1978, Oneida, Wisconsin. Mr. Cornelius is the last surviving member of the original Oneida Tribal Council organized under the Indian Reorganization Act. For the Oneidas in the period, see Laurence M. Hauptman, *The Iroquois and the New Deal* (Syracuse: Syracuse University Press, 1981), ch. 5.
5. Interview with Rupert Costo (Cahuilla), April 20–21, 1979, Geneva, New York; Joseph DeLaCruz (Quinault), "On Knowing What is Good for the American Indian," Letter to the Editor, *New York Times*, Aug. 2, 1978, p. 20; *Voices From Wounded Knee, 1973* (Rooseveltown, N.Y.: Akwesasne Notes, 1974), pp. 4, 10–11, 55.
6. Robert Burnette (Rosebud Sioux) and John Koster, *The Road to Wounded Knee* (New York: Bantam Books, 1974), pp. 115, 117, 132, 168–169, 182–187.
7. American Indian Policy Review Commission, *Final Report*, vol. 1 (Washington, D.C.: U.S. Gov't. Printing Office, 1977), pp. 309–310.
8. The four major monographic treatments of this period are: Donald L. Parman, *The Navajos and the New Deal* (New Haven: Yale University Press, 1976); Kenneth R. Philp, *John Collier's Crusade for Indian Reform, 1920–1954* (Tucson: University of Arizona Press, 1977); Graham D. Taylor, *The New Deal and American Indian Tribalism: The Administration of the Indian Reorganization Act* (Lincoln: University of Nebraska Press, 1980); and Hauptman, *The*

Iroquois and the New Deal. For a review of the literature, see Laurence M. Hauptman, "Big Deal?," *Journal of Ethnic Studies* 9, (Summer 1981): 119–124.

9. Act of Feb. 28, 1891, 26 Stat. 794. Act of May 8, 1906, 34 Stat. 182.

10. D. S. Otis, *The Dawes Act and the Allotment of Indian Lands*, ed. Francis Paul Prucha, S.J. (Norman: University of Oklahoma Press, 1973), pp. 92–93.

11. See, for example, the Act of Feb. 14, 1931, 46 Stat. 1006, which extended the time allowed for homesteaders to pay for allotments taken on the Cheyenne River Sioux and Standing Rock Sioux Indian Reservations in North and South Dakota.

12. National Resources Board, Land Planning Committee, *Indian Land Tenure, Economic Status, and Population Trends* (Washington, D.C.: U.S. Gov't. Printing Office, 1935), pp. 56–57.

13. *The Indian Problem: Resolution of the Committee of One Hundred Appointed by the Secretary of the Interior and a Review of the Indian Problem*, Jan. 7, 1924 (Washington, D.C.: U.S. Gov't. Printing Office, 1924).

14. Lewis Meriam and Associates, *The Problem of Indian Administration* (Baltimore: Johns Hopkins University Press, 1928), pp. 3–51, 447–448.

15. See S. 3668, 72d Cong., 1st sess., 1932, introduced by Senator Lynn Frazier of Montana.

16. By 1940, 252 Indian tribes had voted in the referendum as required by the act: 174, including 99 separate California Indian bands totaling less than 25,000 people, voted in favor of the act, while 78 tribes rejected the act. Nationwide, 38,000 Indians voted for the IRA, 24,000 against, and 35,000 eligible voters did not participate, perhaps as a sign of silent protest against the legislation. Moreover, 150 Indian groups failed to adopt constitutions as required under the IRA, allegedly to provide them an element of self-rule. As a result, fewer Indians adopted constitutions under the IRA than those who did not. Lawrence C. Kelly, "The Indian Reorganization Act: The Dream and the Reality," *Pacific Historical Review* 64 (Aug. 1975): 291–312.

17. "Tribal Self-Government and the Indian Reorganization Act of 1934," *Michigan Law Review* 70 (April 1972): 966.

18. Russel L. Barsh, "The BIA Reorganization Follies of 1978: A Lesson in Bureaucratic Self-Defense," *American Indian Law Review* 7 (1979): 12.

19. Quoted in Russel L. Barsh and James Y. Henderson, *The Road: Indian Tribes and Political Liberty* (Berkeley: University of California Press, 1980), pp. 105–106.

20. Barsh and Henderson, *The Road*, p. 106.

21. Quoted in Carl Cramer, *Listen for a Lonesome Drum* (New York: Farrar and Rinehart, 1936), pp. 110–111.

22. George F. Newton to John Collier, Oct. 28, 1934, no. 4894-1934-066, pt. 12-A, Records Concerning the Wheeler-Howard Act, Box 9, RG 75, National Archives.

23. *Hearings on H.R. 7902*, U.S. House of Representatives, Committee on Indian Affairs (Washington, D.C.: U.S. Gov't. Printing Office, 1934) IX, p. 389.

24. U.S. Senate Subcommittee on Indian Affairs, *Hearings on S. Res. 79: Survey of Conditions of the Indians of the U.S.* (Washington, D.C.: U.S. Gov't. Printing Office, 1928–43), pt. 37, p. 20645.

25. Roger Baldwin to John Collier, May 29, 1934, John Collier MSS, Correspondence, 1933–1945, vol. 1, pt. 2, Series 1, Box 2, "Roger Baldwin," Yale University.

26. On the extravagant promises of agents and their misuse of ECW work relief, see *Hearings on S.R. 79*, pt. 37, pp. 21502, 20630–20631, 21438, 21466; on the use of bribery in the form of food rations, see *Hearings on S.R. 79*, Pt. 37, pp. 21489–21490; on the scheduling of referenda at inopportune times of year, see *Hearings on S.R. 79*, pt. 37, p. 21502. According to Rupert Costo, Indians who opposed the IRA were denied the use of public meeting facilities. Interview conducted by Laurence M. Hauptman of Rupert Costo, April 20–21, 1979, Geneva, N.Y.

27. FBI Main File on Alice Lee Jemison, FOIPA no. 60,431, released to Jeanne Marie Jemison (copy in author's possession) Aug. 17, 1978; John L. Freeman, "The New Deal for Indians: A Study in Bureau-Committee Relations in American Government" (Ph.D. diss., Princeton University, 1952), pp. 199–201; Alice Lee Jemison's speech to the Black Hills Treaty Council on July 27, 1938 (verbatim, notarized by Sioux informants), in Office File of Commissioner John Collier, "Alice Lee Jemison," RG 75, NA; John Snyder (Seneca) to Alice Lee Jemison and Jemison's reply, June 12, 1935, Office File of Commissioner John Collier, "Alice Lee Jemison," RG 75, NA; Frank D. Williams (Tuscarora) to John Collier, Sept. 27, 1934, no. 48622-1934-066, Records Concerning the Wheeler-Howard Act, RG 75, NA; Ben Dwight, organization field agent of the BIA, Memorandum on American Indian Federation meeting in Tulsa to Mr. Monahan, Aug. 22, 1938, Office File of Commissioner John Collier, "American Indian Federation," RG 75, NA.

28. *Hearings on H.R. 7781: Indian Conditions and Affairs*, U.S. House of Representatives, Subcommittee of the Committee on Indian Affairs, 74th Cong., 1st sess. (Washington, D.C.: U.S. Gov't. Printing Office, 1935), pp. 599–601.

29. *Hearings on S. R. 79*, pt. 37, pp. 20596, 20630–20631, 20645–20854. Alice Lee Jemison to President Franklin D. Roosevelt, Aug. 11, 1937, BIA Central Files, 1907–1939, no. 747-1935-155, General Service, RG 75, NA; *Hearings on S. R. 79*, pt. 37, pp. 20586–20670; Fred B. Bauer, *Land of the North Carolina Cherokees* (Brevard, North Carolina: George Buchanan, 1971), pp. 34–53; "Those on Qualla Reservation Refuse to Grant Federal Government Right-of-Way for Blue Ridge Parkway; Legend Cited," *New York Times*, Aug. 27, 1939, p. 23. Interview of Catherine Bauer, April 6, 1978, Cherokee, North Carolina. Interview by Laurence M. Hauptman of Rupert Costo, April 20–21, 1979. Collier wrote Superintendent Foght on May 7, 1935 that "such shortsighted action of removing dissident Indian children from school is harmful rather than helpful to your cause and is a direct injury to children withdrawn" (pp. 20645–20646 in the *Hearings on S.R. 79*, pt. 37). Charles J. Weeks interprets these events as merely a conflict between assimilationist "White Cherokees" and more traditional tribal members, with the Indian Service siding with the traditionalists, but admits that "Foght had little previous experience in dealing with Indians." Weeks ignored Ickes' letter of May 20, 1935, which is reprinted in the hearings report and reveals that the Secretary of the Interior was concerned merely with white tourist development, not with the Indians. See *Hearings on S. R. 79*, pt. 37, pp. 20615–20616. Moreover, the hearings report gives the exact details of where the parkway was originally to be built, not where it was finally built years later. The initial plan would have condemned some of the best Cherokee land to make way for a thoroughfare. Weeks adds that neither an IRA constitution nor charter of incorporation was accepted by the Cherokees during the Collier years, indicating that Weeks misread the size of the opposition to Collier, the internal tribal political divisions deeper than the White Cherokee-traditionalist schism, and the importance of the Blue Ridge Parkway controversy to the Cherokee New Deal. Weeks, "The Eastern Cherokee and the New Deal," *North Carolina Historical Review* 53 (July 1976): 303–319.

30. U.S. House of Representatives, *Hearings on S. 2103: Wheeler-Howard Act—Exempt Certain Indians*, 76th Cong., 3d sess. (Washington, D.C.: U.S. Gov't. Printing Office, 1940), p. 20596.

31. Scudder Mekeel, "An Appraisal of the Indian Reorganization Act," *American Anthropologist* 46 (April–June 1948): 213.

32. Mekeel, "An Appraisal," p. 209; see also Philp, *John Collier's Crusade*, pp. 140–141.

33. Interview with Louis R. Bruce, Jr., Dec. 11, 1980, conducted by Laurence M. Hauptman, Washington, D.C.

34. For the extraordinary career of Montezuma, see Peter Iverson, *Carlos*

Montezuma (Albuquerque, N.M.: University of New Mexico Press, 1982). For Montezuma's ideas, see "The Bureau Indians," *Wassaja* 3 (March 1919): 1; "Aim, Fire, Shoot Straight!" *Wassaja* 7 (Oct. 21, 1921): 1–2; *Let My People Go*, pamphlet of Speech Before Society of American Indians, Sept. 30, 1915 (n.p., n.d.): *Abolish the Indian Bureau* (n.p., n.d.).

35.   D'Arcy McNickle, *They Came Here First: The Epic of the American Indian*, rev. ed. (New York: Harper & Row, 1975), p. 242.

36.   "The Difference Between the Indian Bureau and Other Bureaus of the Government," *Wassaja* 8 (Oct. 1922): 3.

37.   See notes 4 and 5. Moreover, the vitriolic debate over the merits of the IRA has spilled into academic journals, receiving much attention by non-Indian scholars. In 1978 and 1979, the *Journal of Ethnic Studies* published a series of responses and replies by Wilcomb Washburn, Joseph G. Jorgensen, and Richard O. Clemmer that in part dealt with the IRA among the Hopi and its aftermath.

38.   Harry Conroy to Ben Dwight, Oct. 16, 1946, National Congress of American Indians MSS., *National Anthropological Archives*, Smithsonian Institution.

39.   Vine Deloria, Jr., *Custer Died for Your Sins* (New York: Macmillan Company, 1969), p. 147.

40.   Indian Self-Determination and Education Assistance Act, 88 Stat. 2203, Jan. 4, 1975, P.L. 93-638.

INDIAN LITIGATION

A L V I N J. Z I O N T Z

INTRODUCTION

*I*ndian tribes have challenged American notions of justice since the founding of the Republic. Many of the issues arising from their survival have been decided by the courts, for as De Tocqueville shrewdly observed, "Scarcely any political question arises in the United States that is not resolved, sooner or later, into a judicial question." Indeed, no other nation has evolved a more extensive body of jurisprudence devoted to its indigenous people.

Most of what is called Indian law developed within the past hundred years. By the latter part of the nineteenth century, the reservation system was firmly established and the policy of detribalizing or Americanizing the Indian was in full swing. At the same time, white population in the West was growing swiftly, and with it came conflicts over lands, water, fish, and game. As the western territories became states, the problems were cast in the form of governmental conflicts among federal, state, and tribal authorities. State governments were to become the Indians' relentless adversaries. States asserted political authority over all lands and persons within their borders, and repeatedly challenged the federal government's supremacy in Indian affairs. Many of these challenges found their way to the Supreme Court. Because the Supreme Court has carved out a dominant role in the American polity, its decisions have established the contours of Indian tribal sovereignty in the United States.

The early seminal decisions of the Court in Indian affairs are well known: *Johnson v. McIntosh*,[1] *Cherokee Nation v. Georgia*,[2] and *Worcester v. Georgia*.[3] These three cases, decided between 1823 and 1832, set forth the fundamental principle of tribal sovereignty. The opinion in each case was authored by John Marshall, the greatest Chief Justice in the Court's history. Unfortunately, many later decisions have lacked the breadth of vision displayed in these early cases. Yet a survey of the past hundred years reveals an effort by the Court to balance the primordial sovereignty of the tribes with the *realpolitik* of national ambitions and values.

This article reviews some of the decisions of the past century in order to outline the evolution of American law respecting Indian tribes. The choice of cases is selective, with an emphasis on the principle of tribal sovereignty, and for this reason the article omits many important cases that do not bear directly on that principle.

THE EROSION OF THE TERRITORIAL SOVEREIGNTY OF TRIBES

After *Worcester v. Georgia* was decided in 1832, the law was clear that political authority within Indian country reposed in the tribe, limited only by federal external supremacy. The erosion of this principle by the intrusion of state authority began in 1881 with the case of *United States v. McBratney.*[4]

McBratney was charged with the murder of one Thomas Casey. Neither McBratney nor Casey were Indians, but the murder had occurred on the Ute Indian Reservation. Since it was assumed that federal criminal law applied in Indian country, McBratney was tried in federal court, where he was convicted. McBratney's attorney challenged the conviction, claiming that the federal court did not have jurisdiction over the crime. A crime did not become a federal offense, he argued, merely because it occurred on an Indian reservation. Because no Indians were involved, he claimed that the case should be governed by the law of the state in which the Ute reservation was located—Colorado—and he took an appeal to the Supreme Court.

At first blush, the case seemed to present only a technical jurisdiction issue. But at stake was nothing less than state penetration of the bulwark around Indian country which had been established fifty years earlier in *Worcester v. Georgia*. In that case, the Court had ruled that state laws were inoperative in Indian country. All matters occurring within Indian country were solely within the authority of the tribe or the federal government. As in *McBratney*, the affected tribe did not participate in the case. Yet tribal interests were implicated in *Worcester* because it was clear that any decision opening the way to Georgia's exercise of power in Cherokee country would be fatal to the political life of the tribe. Marshall's opinion was an unqualified rejection of the claim of state authority.

In 1881, the Supreme Court chose to ignore *Worcester* and decided in McBratney's favor. He was subject, said the Court, only to the laws of Colorado, which had acquired the power to punish crimes in Ute territory through the law which admitted the state into the Union. That law, enacted by Congress in 1875, gave the citizens of the territory the power to create a state which could enter the Union "upon an equal footing with the original States in all respects whatever." The Court said Colorado would not be on equal footing with the original states if its powers did not extend over whites everywhere within its borders. Since the statute contained no exception for Indian lands, the Court interpreted it as demonstrating a congressional intention to override all prior legislation, including the provisions of the Ute treaty which set apart a territory to be the home of the Ute people.

This reasoning was totally inconsistent with the holding of *Worcester*, in which the Court had held that the laws of Georgia, one of the original thirteen states, did not extend to a white man in Cherokee country. If the equal footing clause were to be given effect, Colorado should have no greater powers than Georgia. Instead, the Court turned *Worcester* on its head with no explanation or even mention of this reversal.

The *McBratney* ruling might have been limited to states that were admitted to the Union without restrictions on their jurisdiction, but fifteen years later, in *Draper v. United States*[5] the Supreme Court applied the *McBratney* rule to a case in Montana—a state which had been admitted to the Union on condition that Indian lands there "remain under the absolute jurisdiction and control of the Congress of the United States." The Court rejected the argument that Congress intended to restrict Montana from enforcing its laws against non-Indians on reservations. The Court's thinking may have been affected by the General Allotment Act of 1887, which looked towards the ultimate dissolution of Indian country and the melding of Indian and white populations.

Draper legitimized the exercise of State power over crimes in Indian country everywhere. No longer was the government of Indian territory limited to the tribes and the United States; state authority there was now firmly established as well. But state authority proved to be almost totally incompatible with tribal sovereignty. Jealous of their authority and intolerant of Indian enclaves within their borders, the states fought to extend their power over Indians and their lands. *McBratney* and *Draper* became significant beyond the narrow issue of jurisdiction over crimes on Indian reservations; as William Canby points out, *McBratney* and *Draper* opened the door to judicial balancing of state and tribal interests.[6]

CROW DOG: A PYRRHIC VICTORY FOR TRIBAL AUTONOMY

In the year following *McBratney*, the Court decided *Ex Parte Crow Dog*,[7] a case involving a Sioux Indian sentenced to hang for the murder of another Sioux. The defendant, Crow Dog, had allegedly taken revenge for the victim's improper behavior with Crow Dog's wife. The question was whether he could be prosecuted under the laws of the United States.

The federal criminal laws excluded crimes committed by one Indian against another. However, the treaty with the Sioux provided that Indian wrongdoers were to be turned over to the United States for trial and punishment under federal law. The treaty also provided that the Sioux would be subject to the laws of the United States, and that each Indian individual would be protected in his rights of property, person, and life.

The Supreme Court was not persuaded that this language gave the federal government the power to execute an Indian for the murder of another Indian. The Court's reasoning was rather strained. The treaty clause requiring the Sioux to "deliver up" to the United States "bad men among them" was construed to mean Indians of other tribes. The provision subjecting the Sioux to the laws of the United States was read to mean laws to be enacted in the future.

The scheme envisaged by the treaty, said the Court, was federal tutelage to achieve self-government and economic independence. Self-government meant maintenance of internal law and order by administration of tribal laws and customs. The Court saw the treaty as a charter for a continuing tribal society, and held that individual Indians were not subject to the laws of the United States in their personal and domestic relations.

To subject the Indians to an alien legal system whose rules, procedures, and penalties were unknown to the Sioux was fundamentally unfair, said the Court. To be sure, underlying the Court's concern for fairness was the prevailing view in white society that the Sioux were ignorant savages. Nevertheless, the Court showed sensitivity to the separateness of the Sioux culture and the enormity of allowing white government to intrude into Sioux personal relations.

The Court's sensitivity was not shared by the agents of the Indian Service, who saw the decision as a serious obstacle to their mission of acculturation and detribalization. How could they be expected to Americanize the Indian if misconduct were dealt with by the Indians in their own way? The taking of life must be stopped; the white man's code must be imposed; and murderers, after all, should hang. Congress was easily persuaded, and two years after the *Crow Dog* decision, Congress made major crimes involving Indians punishable by federal law.

The *Crow Dog* episode contains an important lesson: litigation may produce only short-term results. If a court decision stirs strong feelings among influential groups or sufficiently offends the values of the dominant society, Congress may act to reverse the decision.

KAGAMA: THE UNEASY CASE FOR PLENARY CONGRESSIONAL POWER OVER INDIANS

The power of Congress over Indians was brought to the high court in *United States v. Kagama*.[8] Two Hoopa Valley Indians were charged with murder of another Indian on the reservation under the new federal Major Crimes Act. Their attorney challenged the legality of the indictment and argued that the Major Crimes Act was unconstitutional.

The argument went to the very heart of federal authority over tribes and presented the Supreme Court with serious difficulties. What was the source of Congress's power to govern the internal relationships of Indians within their own reservations? After all, under American constitutional doctrine, the federal government was a government of limited powers. The source of federal power must be found somewhere in the Constitution. The only clause that could remotely lend support to such a claim of power was Article I, Section 8, the

Commerce Clause: "The Congress shall have power . . . to regulate Commerce with foreign Nations, and among the several States, and with the Indian Tribes."

The Supreme Court conceded that this clause did not provide authority over the internal affairs of tribes and their members. The Court could have concluded that the power to govern the internal affairs of Indian communities was simply not to be found among the enumerated powers in the United States Constitution. Indeed, one could hardly look to the United States Constitution to find such a power since the tribes had taken no part in the forming of the political compact. Unlike the colonists, the Indians had not delegated any power to the national government over them. They were aliens to the United States, and the Commerce Clause implicitly recognized that fact. The enumeration of any power over Indian tribes in the Constitution could operate only as an agreement concerning the division of political authority between the national government and the states.

However, the Commerce Clause suggested to the *Kagama* Court a theory of political sovereignty that would place the Indian nation firmly under the authority of the federal government. The Commerce Clause treated the Indian nations as a category separate from foreign nations, the Court pointed out. The Court had decided in *Cherokee Nation v. Georgia* that the tribes were neither foreign nations nor states. From here the Court took a giant leap: sovereignty within the geographical limits of the United States must repose *in either* the government of the United States or the states of the Union. Since the state governments had no law-giving authority over Indians within the reservation, sovereignty must reside in the United States. This might be called the two-sovereign theory.

This is hardly a constitutional argument, however, but rather an exercise in political abstraction, and one that begs the question. The *Kagama* Court simply *assumed* that sovereignty must inhere in the federal government or the states rather than the tribes themselves. But this was inconsistent with the principle expounded in *Worcester*, that the tribes, by placing themselves under the protection of the United States, did not lose their internal sovereignty. The two-sovereign theory, nevertheless, furnished one leg for the *Kagama* construct of federal power over Indians.

A second leg was based on the analogy of Indian country to United States territories. The federal government, explained the Court, asserted the power to govern territories of the United States until they had attained statehood. This power did not derive from the Constitution, but rather from the "ownership of the country in which the territories are."

The Court was apparently aware that this reasoning fell short of supplying a persuasive and principled argument. While *Worcester* had held that the external relations of tribes were impaired by the sovereign authority of the United States, no case had suggested that the United States had acquired authority to govern the internal relations of the tribes. Nevertheless, the territorial analogy supplied the second leg of a theory: ownership of the land.

But a landlord does not, at least under common-law principles, enjoy any authority over the private lives of his tenants. The Court found a rationale for such extraordinary authority in the dependent status of the Indians. They were described as weak, helpless, and subject to danger from the people of the states who were often, said the Court, "their deadliest enemies." The federal government had assumed responsibility amounting to guardianship through its dealings with the Indians, and from that duty there arose a power to protect them. In one final rhetorical flourish the Court declared that power over the Indians must exist in the federal government "because it never has existed anywhere else, because the theater of its exercise is within the geographical limits of the United States, because it has never been denied, and because it alone can enforce its laws on all the tribes."

The *Kagama* decision is interesting not as constitutional analysis, but as an exercise in the dialectic of power politics. Perhaps it was realistic for the *Kagama* Court to speak of only two sovereigns in 1886. The detribalization policy had been in effect for ten to fifteen years; traditional tribal government had become severely crippled or had disappeared altogether. The tribes were "programmed" for extinction as social units. In these circumstances there may indeed have been a vacuum of political power that state governments would have filled had not the federal government insisted on its sovereignty.

Kagama is one of the principal sources of what has come to be known as the "plenary power" doctrine, which in practice means that Congress has the power to do virtually as it pleases with the Indian tribes. It is an extraordinary doctrine for a democracy to espouse. It would justify abolishing the political existence of the tribes. Short of that, it justifies the imposition of controls over the lives and property of the tribes and their members. Plenary power thus subjects Indians to national powers outside ordinary constitutional limits.

The justification for the plenary power doctrine rests in part on the assumption that there exist only two sovereign authorities—the federal and state governments. What happens, however, when the tribes reconstruct themselves as functioning governments and it becomes necessary to admit that there are three sovereignties? Can plenary power be justified by federal "ownership" of the continental United States? In 1828, the Supreme Court had found that this was an adequate basis for federal political control of territories.[9] But as Chief Justice Marshall pointed out at that time, federal power to govern a territory *which has not acquired the means of self-government* results from the fact that it is not within the jurisiction of a particular state. The right to govern, said Marshall, may be the inevitable consequence of the right to acquire territory. But that analogy does not comfortably fit self-governing Indian tribes.

Nor does national "ownership" of territory support the right of a government based on the consent of the governed to impose its political authority on the inhabitants. For the *Kagama* court, an additional element was necessary: the analogy to guardianship—the power arising from the weak and dependent state of the Indians. But as the Indians achieve political cohesion, establish functioning governments, and become less dependent, the *Kagama* rationale is fundamentally challenged. Applying *Kagama* to modern circumstances must lead to the conclusion that federal power can no longer be plenary without doing violence to the fundamental principles of a democratic state.

LONE WOLF: DUE PROCESS DENIED

Kagama became the foundation for a series of decisions of the Supreme Court regarding the doctrine of plenary power.[10] The principle reached its apotheosis in *Lone Wolf v. Hitchcock*;[11] in which the Supreme Court upheld the constitutionality of an act of Congress that breached the treaty made between the United States and the Kiowas and Comanches.

Lone Wolf, decided in 1903, shocks the conscience of many, because it is thought to be the source of the doctrine that the United

States Congress may abrogate an Indian treaty. Actually, the Supreme Court had decided that in 1871 in *The Cherokee Tobacco*.[12] Indeed, the principle that Congress has the constitutional authority to abrogate treaties, whether with Indian tribes or foreign nations, is of long standing.

What is important about *Lone Wolf* is its evasion of the constitutional issue raised by the plaintiff. Lone Wolf did not rest his claim on lack of power in Congress to repeal or abrogate a treaty. Rather, he argued that the treaty with the Kiowa and Comanche created property rights secured by the Fifth Amendment which could not be abridged by the United States without due process of law. The Supreme Court held that the plenary power of Congress over Indians could not be limited even by the Fifth Amendment. The Court offered this justification: to admit the constitutional claim would be to admit that the authority of Congress could be limited "in respect to the care and protection of the Indians [and would] deprive Congress, in a possible emergency, when the necessity might be urgent for a partition and disposal of the tribal lands, of all power to act, if the assent of the Indians could not be obtained."

Lone Wolf, like *Kagama*, was an act of judicial *realpolitik*. Indians could expect little constitutional protection from Congress. The doctrine of plenary power meant a judicial "hands-off" attitude in cases involving Congress' relationships with the Indians.

THE IMPORTANCE OF THE GOVERNMENT SIDING WITH THE INDIANS: *WINTERS* AND *WINANS*

Lone Wolf illustrates another important point. In Indian litigation, tribal challenges to federal power, particularly to congressional action, face almost insurmountable barriers. The Supreme Court has always been reluctant to expend its limited credit in opposing Congress. It has been particularly deferential in Indian affairs, considering the area, like foreign relations, to involve peculiarly sensitive questions of national policy that are not well-suited for judicial management.

The Supreme Court has, however, exhibited quite a different attitude where the United States has associated itself with tribal interests. Two remarkable cases arising during the early twentieth century are illustrative.

Two years after *Lone Wolf*, the Supreme Court decided *United States v. Winans*.[13] The case involved the claims of the Yakimas to cross private lands to conduct their traditional salmon fishery from riverbank lands. The non-Indian landowners operated their own fishery, employing a fish wheel. They claimed rights arising from their ownership of the land and under their license from the State of Washington, which, they argued, gave them monopoly rights along the stretch of river adjoining their property. The Yakimas, on the other hand, claimed rights under their treaty with the United States, and the federal government sued the property owners to enforce the treaty. The decision was a sweeping affirmation of the superiority of Indian fishing rights under federal treaties. It also established an important concept—the doctrine of reserved rights. These words of the Supreme Court in *Winans* have been quoted in many later cases: "[t]he treaty was not a grant of rights to the Indians,—but a grant of rights from them, a reservation of those not granted."[14]

Three years later, in 1908, the Court ruled in *Winters v. United States* that the establishment of a reservation impliedly reserved water for the use of the Indians.[15] This reserved water right was superior to the right of any non-Indian off the reservation to use water flowing through the reservation, if the non-Indian's claim arose after the reservation was established. The reserved right was based, not on words found in any treaty or federal act, but rather upon circumstances. The Court said it did not believe the United States would expect the Indians to settle on an aride wasteland. Therefore, it must be implied that the United States intended to reserve sufficient water for both the present and future needs of the reservation. The implications of this ruling were far-reaching. Indeed, the Indian rights created by the decision are still commonly known throughout the West as "Winters rights."

The two decisions were extraordinary. Both upheld claims that the Indians had broad rights to natural resources—in *Winans*, fish, in *Winters*, water. In *Winans*, the Court went so far as to hold that a treaty guarantee of a right to fish at "usual and accustomed grounds and stations" imposed burdens of passage and temporary occupancy upon lands far from any Indian reservation. In *Winters*, the Court created a new species of water rights that would have major effects on farmers and ranchers throughout the arid West. It is highly doubtful that the

Court would have reached these conclusions had the United States not been the Indians' advocate for these claims.

THE MODERN ERA BEGINS: *WILLIAMS V. LEE,* 1959

The Supreme Court has generally been influenced by the government's prevailing Indian policy. When that policy shifts, it does not take long before the Court's decisions reflect it. The Indian Reorganization Act of 1934 signalled a shift from detribalization to its opposite—promotion of tribal self-government.[16] The Supreme Court's first real opportunity to protect tribal self-government came in a case which symbolizes the beginning of the modern era in Indian law: *Williams v. Lee.*[17]

Williams v. Lee arose out of a suit brought by a merchant against a Navajo and his wife to collect for goods sold to them on credit. The merchant, who operated under an Indian trader's license on the reservation, had sued in Arizona state court, no doubt a common practice. But in this case the Navajo tribe went to the aid of its member. The tribe had followed its attorney's advice to strengthen its tribal court system in order to provide a forum on the reservation for this type of dispute.[18] *Williams v. Lee* would decide whether the Navajo courts would be ignored in favor of the Arizona courts.

The case presented the same question that had faced the Supreme Court 127 years earlier in *Worcester v. Georgia:* to what extent could state law reach onto Indian reservations? Two substantial Indian interests were involved. There was first the interest of individual Indians. Subjecting them to collection suits in off-reservation state courts put them at a serious disadvantage. Not only were they required to travel to distant courts, but once there, they were subjected to proceedings under laws with which they were largely unfamiliar. They were often not represented by counsel and in many cases were not fluent in English. No doubt the Indians also felt they suffered from racial prejudice.

There was a second and equally important interest at stake: that of the tribe in preserving its sovereignty and the integrity of its tribal court system. If white merchants doing business on the reservation could ignore that court system and take their disputes to state courts, the sovereignty of the tribe would be seriously impugned.

The Supreme Court of Arizona held that the courts of Arizona had jurisdiction over the suit, but the tribe appealed and the United States Supreme Court reversed. The latter Court said that the treaty with the Navajos impliedly reserved the Indians' right of self-government, which would be undermined if state courts could exercise jurisdiction over Indians concerning on-reservation transactions.

Whether a state could assert authority over the reservation, said the *Williams* Court, depended on whether its action infringed on the right of reservation Indians to make their own laws and be ruled by them. Unfortunately, this "test" was somewhat ambiguous. The tribes understood the case to stand for the principle that reservations were under tribal jurisdiction, and that unless there was an express congressional delegation of power to the states, they could not invade the sphere of tribal authority. The states interpreted the case to mean that state power over the reservation and its inhabitants was unfettered except where the tribes could demonstrate that the exercise of state power constituted an infringement upon tribal self-government. This created enormous uncertainty. What was included under the rubric of "self-government" and what constituted "infringement?"

Some of this ambiguity was resolved by the Court in 1973, in *McClanahan v. Arizona State Tax Commission*.[19] The Supreme Court made it clear that the infringement test of *Williams v. Lee* was intended to describe the reach of state power within Indian reservations only *where non-Indians are involved*. Where only Indians are involved and the transaction or activity occurs wholly within the reservation, the *Williams* test has no application and tribal laws prevails. Where non-Indians are involved, the Court will look to expressions of Congress and the relevant treaty, against the backdrop of the tribe's inherent sovereignty, to determine whether there is any scope for state authority over the transaction. The legal analysis is made in terms of federal preemption. This is the constitutional doctrine that states may not act in a sphere of authority reserved by the Constitution for the national government unless Congress expressly delegates such authority.

With the decision in *McClanahan*, the doctrine of infringement was overshadowed by the Court's emphasis on federal preemption. But *Williams v. Lee* remained a landmark decision and sent a message to the tribes: if they would exercise their governmental power and begin to fill the vacuum created by its long suppression, the federal courts might support them. The tribes might then expand their powers over their lives and their lands. The tribes were on notice that if they remained passive, others would take the initiative.

THE RECONSTRUCTION OF TRIBAL GOVERNMENT AND THE BEGINNING OF LEGAL ACTIVISM

The contemporary movement to reconstruct tribal government began with the Indian Reorganization Act of 1934. It suffered a severe setback during the termination era, which falls roughly between 1947 and 1963. In the mid-1960s, however, tribal self-government received substantial momentum from the Great Society program of President Lyndon Johnson. The program provided funds for new community projects aimed at the problem of poverty. Many of these programs were promptly adopted by tribes. Federal monies provided a means to hire Indians and put them to work serving their own communities within the framework of tribal government. Although this may have been the intent of the program, the administrative infrastructure of tribal government was being set in place.

At the same time, tribes were beginning to appreciate that the courts could provide them with a means to reclaim their sovereign powers. In the past, few tribes were able to secure the services of private attorneys. Indian litigation had been largely under the control of the federal government, whose attorneys were often hampered by the government's complex and conflicting interests. Tribes were frequently advised to go slowly and to refrain from asserting new authority. When the government was willing to take a tribal case to court, the legal claims asserted were often timid and tentative. After all, the federal government had discouraged the tribes from asserting their authority for a hundred years and had no desire to lead the way in a fight for expansion of tribal sovereignty.

By the mid-1960s, a new spirit of militancy had begun to permeate the thinking of tribal councils. At the same time, a new breed of lawyers was beginning to enter the field of Indian law. Some of these were private law firms and some were publicly funded. The Legal Services Corporation and non-profit legal foundations like the Native

American Rights Fund began to provide legal support to the tribes. The older organizatons like the Indian Rights Association and the Association on American Indian Affairs now had valuable new allies in their struggle to preserve and reconstruct tribal sovereignty. This effort vastly increased the ability of tribes to wage campaigns in the courts.

Tribal attorneys began to advise tribal governments to expand their governmental activities: to adopt codes, to strengthen the tribal court system, to actively govern the entire reservation and all those on it. The legal boundaries of tribal authority were uncertain, but the tribes and their attorneys were ready to embark on a course of aggressive litigation. They would seek to establish new legal boundaries—to engage in a pioneering effort to employ litigation as a tool for reconstructing tribal sovereign power.

The new spirit of legal activism is perhaps best typified by the fishing rights litigation brought by the salmon-fishing tribes of the Pacific Northwest. Beginning first with Indian willingness to fish at treaty-guaranteed places in defiance of state law and to risk jail, the Indian movement rapidly accelerated into a full-scale battle in the courts. Commencing with a Washington State decision in 1954 overturning the conviction of an Indian violating state fishing laws, the cases multiplied as the Indians and the States of Washington and Oregon became locked in battle. Three times the issue came before the United States Supreme Court in what has come to be known as the *Puyallup* series.

The efforts by the Indians to vindicate their treaty rights aroused the hostility of non-Indian sports and commercial fishing organizations. Interracial tensions rose. The federal government was forced to enter the dispute, and finally in 1973 the United States felt compelled to bring suit against the State of Washington. The attack was joined by all the Northwest tribes. *United States v. Washington* went to trial before a federal district judge, George Boldt. Its sweeping affirmation of the Indians' right to share equally in the salmon harvest created a shock wave of anger among non-Indian fishermen. They vilified the judge so persistently that the decision came to be known in the Pacific Northwest as the "Boldt Decision."[20] The case was affirmed by the Ninth Circuit the following year,[21] and when the Supreme Court denied review, the Indians and their supporters thought that they had finally secured the rights which had been denied by Washington for 100 years. But the struggle was not over.

Commercial and sports interest groups combined with state fish and game agencies in efforts to relitigate the case in state courts. They challenged the authority of state officials to carry out the orders of the federal court. The Washington Supreme Court ruled in favor of the non-Indian fishermen on this point. The situation on the waters of Puget Sound grew ugly as law enforcement was virtually abandoned by state officers. Washington's fishermen also launched an unsuccessful campaign to persuade Congress to abrogate treaty fishing rights. Finally, the State of Washington and its fishermen's association persuaded the United States Supreme Court to hear their appeals.

The Supreme Court's 1979 decision in *Washington v. Fishing Vessel Association*[22] affirmed the Indians' treaty fishing rights and was in most respects a sweeping victory for tribal interests. But the Court introduced a disturbing modification. The Indians' right to an equal share of the resource was qualified: They were entitled to a "moderate livelihood." There was no such restraint on non-Indian fishermen and the Court did not trouble to explain the basis for the rule, or set forth any standards to interpret it. This language portends more litigation to constrict the scope of the Indians' rights.

Meanwhile, apart from the fishing rights litigation, the tribes were heartened by decisions in both state and federal courts recognizing tribal governmental powers in such areas as child custody,[23] divorce,[24] extradition,[25] hunting,[26] and automobile licensing.[27] The growing judicial support for the authority of tribal governments received impetus from two Supreme Court cases. A 1975 decision, *United States v. Mazurie*,[28] seemed particularly significant because it involved the delicate question of tribal authority over non-Indians. The Mazuries were non-Indians who were convicted for operating a tavern on the Wind River Reservation in defiance of tribal licensing regulations—a federal offense. The Mazuries contended that the tribe could exercise no governmental authority over non-Indians, but the Supreme Court held that Indian tribes were governments which could exercise federally-delegated powers.

The following year, in *Fisher v. District Court*,[29] the Supreme Court preemptorily reversed a Montana state court decision and held that a state court had no jurisdiction over an adoption where all parties were members of the Northern Cheyenne Tribe residing on the reservation. The Court invoked the *Williams v. Lee* doctrine and held that any attempt by the state to exercise jurisdiction would infringe upon tribal self-government. Barring Indian access to state courts in this kind of question was not racial discrimination, said the Court, because the jurisdiction of the tribal court does not derive from race but rather from the political status of the tribes.

THE SUPREME COURT BEGINS TO APPLY CONSTITUTIONAL SCRUTINY TO INDIAN LEGISLATION

By the 1970s, tribes could begin to feel that their place in the American federal system was becoming secure. They had survived the allotment policy of the late nineteenth century and the termination of the mid-twentieth. The government seemed to be committed to a policy of self-determination and gave repeated assurances that the commitment was permanent. But the tribes and their supporters became alarmed by the anti-tribal movement which surfaced in the mid-1970s. It had arisen out of the hunting and fishing disputes in the West and was spurred by the land claims of the eastern tribes. The anti-tribal movement attained sufficient political force to significantly inhibit Congress in its legislative treatment of Indians. While tribes had their supporters, they would be badly outnumbered in any national political fight. The spectre of tribal termination could not be eradicated. Even if the prospect of full-scale termination was remote, less extreme measures, such as treaty abrogation and diminishment or disestablishment of reservations, were not beyond possibility. So long as the courts denied protection to tribal political rights from congressional excesses, the tribes were ultimately defenseless.

Since *Kagama*, the Supreme Court had treated federal Indian legislation affecting tribal rights as non-justifiable political questions, citing the plenary power doctrine. When a case was deemed to involve such questions, the aggrieved parties were told that in effect their remedies lay in the political process. The result was to leave the tribes to the mercy of Congress— their very existence arguably a matter of congressional license.

Perhaps it was inevitable that the Supreme Court would ultimately come to view the plenary power doctrine as unsound. The beginning of that process can be traced to the 1962 decision in *Baker v. Carr*.[30] This is the best known as the "one man, one vote" case, but for legal scholars it is equally famous for its treatment of the political question doctrine. That doctrine had led the Court to refuse to hear constitutional challenges to electoral districting in 1946. By 1962, however, the Court was ready to apply equal protection standards because they were "well-developed and familiar." After *Baker v. Carr*, the political question doctrine was a much less substantial barrier to constitutional inquiry by the Supreme Court.

Before the Court would exercise judicial review of Indian legislation, it first had to develop constitutional principles which related to the uniqueness of the Indians' status. That process may be said to have begun with *Morton v. Mancari* in 1974.[31] A group of non-Indian employees of the Bureau of Indian Affairs had sued the Bureau, charging that the Indian preference clause of the 1934 Indian Reorganization Act was unconstitutional. That clause required the Bureau to give preference in hiring and promotion to tribally-affiliated Indians. The plaintiffs claimed this was a racial preference which denied them due process and equal protection of the laws.

The Supreme Court disagreed. The separate treatment accorded Indians was not based on their race, the Court said, but rather on their membership in quasi-sovereign tribal entities. The relationship between the tribe and the federal government was a political one and employment in the Bureau of Indian Affairs was tantamount to political representation. The position of Indians was legally unique and justified their special treatment:

> As long as the special treatment can be tied rationally to the fulfillment of Congress' unique obligation toward the Indians, such legislative judgments will not be disturbed. Here, where the preference is reasonable and rationally designed to further Indian self-government, we cannot say that Congress' classification violates due process.[32]

At last, a constitutional yardstick had been fashioned which might be used to preserve tribal rights. *Morton v. Mancari* is a landmark decision in Indian law. Not only did it apply a constitutional test to Indian legislation, it also defined the relationship between the tribes and the federal government in a new way. It is no accident that following *Mancari* the Interior Department began describing the relationship between the tribes and the United States government as one of "government to government."

Three years after its *Mancari* decision, the Court was faced with an Indian challenge to the constitutionality of an act of Congress. The case was *Delaware v. Weeks*.[33] It involved distribution of money to the Delawares as a result of a claim against the United states. A group known as the Kansas Delawares maintained they were entitled to share in the award. Congress thought otherwise and excluded them. The disappointed claimants sued, arguing that their exclusion amounted to a congressional denial of due process of law. Though the Supreme Court upheld the constitutionality of the act, it declined to rely on the doctrine of plenary power. Instead, it applied the *Mancari* due process test: Was the legislation rationally tied to the fulfillment of Congress' unique obligation toward Indians? The Court then scrutinized the legislation and satisfied itself that the test had been met. There was even a dissenting Justice who thought the law was unconstitutional. For the first time, the Supreme Court had applied a due process standard to Indian legislation.

Delaware suggests that the Supreme Court may no longer follow *Lone Wolf* in denying constitutional review to Indians challenging an act of congress. This idea was furthered by the views expressed in the Court's recent decisions in *United States v. Sioux Nation of Indians*.[34] Here the Court rejected the government's assertion that the Sioux were subject to the plenary power of the United States Congress, declaring that this view had been expressly laid to rest in *Delaware*. While the Court was careful to distinguish the *Lone Wolf* decision, saying there was some showing there of a good-faith congressional effort to compensate the tribe, *Sioux* strengthens the *Delaware* principle that plenary power will no longer be regarded by the Court as a doctrine which bars judicial review of congressional Indian legislation.

While it is premature to say that the plenary power doctrine is dead, it is surely correct to say that it no longer provides Indian legislation with a near-impenetrable shield against judicial review. The Supreme Court is likely to be ever more willing to regard Indian constitutional challenges as justiciable. It may be a very long time before the Court strikes down congressional lawmaking on Indian affairs, but the court has given its warning in terms of a rule of constitutional law specifically applicable to Indian tribes. That is a far doctrinal journey away from *Kagama* and *Lone Wolf*.

THE SUPREME COURT IMPOSES
LIMITS ON JUDICIAL INTRUSION
INTO TRIBAL AFFAIRS

The 1968 Indian Civil Rights Act was a major congressional intrusion into the internal affairs of tribal governments. Its main purpose was to subject tribal governments to the restraints of the Bill of Rights. The Bill of Rights, however, derives from an individual-centered political philosophy. Tribal societies had no such concept historically and still operate largely on the principle of the primacy of the tribe.

The Indian Civil Rights Act seemed to impose on the Indian world a large and expanding body of constitutional law resting on hundreds of court opinions. Could Congress have intended that tribal action should be measured by the sophisticated and complex doctrines of American constitutional law? More importantly, did it intend that tribal actions should be subject to scrutiny in federal courts by non-Indian judges? It seemed not, for the act provided only one legal remedy—habeas corpus. Habeas corpus challenges the legality of restraint of physical liberty, and applies only in limited circumstances. However, almost as soon as the act went into effect, a suit was brought against the Navajo tribe challenging its expulsion of a non-member from the reservation. The trial judge ruled that the case was subject to adjudication by the federal courts even though the plaintiff had not asked for a writ of habeas corpus, but for an injunction against the tribe. As for the argument that the act gave the federal courts no such wide-ranging jurisdiction, the judge ruled that such remedies must be implied, or else the purposes of the act could not be achieved. Other federal courts followed the same reasoning and reached the same result.

Tribes were thus subjected to suits under the Indian Civil Rights Act challenging a wide variety of tribal actions on grounds that they violated the act. This seemed to violate the well-established principle that tribes could not be sued unless Congress and the tribe consented. But for ten years following 1968, the federal courts ignored the principle of sovereign immunity and allowed such suits to proceed. Finally, in 1978, the issue reached the United States Supreme Court.

The case of *Santa Clara Pueblo v. Martinez*, presented the question of whether a tribe could defend discrimination against its female members on cultural grounds.[35] The tribe had denied membership to offspring of women, but not men, who married outside the tribe. Before reaching that issue, the Supreme Court had to decide whether the lower courts had been correct in their assumption that they could override tribal immunity from suit and exercise their jurisdiction to grant every kind of remedy, even money damages.

The decision of the Supreme Court came as a surprise to many observers. It held that the federal courts had been wrong in assuming they had jurisdiction over tribes under the act. The Court said that the act provided only the remedy of habeas corpus, and that Congress had not intended to create any other remedy. The courts could not expand the act by implication.

The *Martinez* decision virtually closed the doors of the federal courthouse to suits against tribal governments regarding claims that they had denied individual liberties. Individual rights, except for habeas corpus, would have to be vindicated in tribal forums.

In the wake of the *Martinez* decision, there were some who urged the Department of the Interior to devise a method of administrative enforcement of the Indian Civil Rights Act. Some tentative steps in this direction were taken by the Bureau of Indian Affairs, but were abandoned after protests by tribes. Others urged that the Indian Civil Rights Act be amended to provide a limited waiver of sovereign immunity. In the years which have passed since *Martinez*, the agitation for remedial action seems to have died away.

The effect of *Martinez* was to preserve, at least temporarily, a wall of separation between the American courts and Indian tribal governments. The effect of this separation, it is generally agreed, has been to strengthen the powers of tribal governments, albeit at the expense of their accountability.

TRIBAL CRIMINAL AUTHORITY OVER NON-INDIANS

The question of the extent to which Indian tribes may exercise authority over non-Indians has long been a thorny one for the American judicial system. It is one thing to acknowledge the power of tribes over their own members, but quite another to concede their power over non-Indians.

It was not until 1968 that tribes were required to extend to anyone the protections found in the Bill of Rights of the United States Constitution. With the passage of the Indian Civil Rights Act in that year, tribes became obligated to respect the individual rights enumerated in that act. But the *Martinez* decision in 1978 denied complainants access to the federal courts, except, of course, to challenge physical detention by use of the writ of habeas corpus.

There has always been an emotional undercurrent to arguments by non-Indians against the exercise of tribal authority over them. Some of it is simply racist and chauvinistic. But it is also claimed that it is fundamentally unfair to subject non-Indian residents to a tribal government in which they are not and cannot be represented.

The issue of tribal jurisdiction over non-Indians has historically received little attention in the courts. In 1904, the Supreme Court did rule that Indian tribes may tax non-members on the reservation to raise revenue.[36] That case was followed in subsequent decisions in lower federal courts.[37] But aside from taxation, the scope of tribal authority over non-Indians remained unclear.

Prior to the 1960s, no tribe had dared assert criminal authority over non-Indians because of the federal government's disapproval. Some treaties contained language suggesting that tribes retained such power, but for the most part there was no principle or rule of law recognized by the American courts which would provide support for any such claim. In 1934, the Interior Department had issued a legal opinion concerning the scope of the inherent powers of Indian tribes. The opinion was written by Felix Cohen, later recognized as the foremost legal scholar in the field of Indian law. It said, "Those powers which are lawfully vested in an Indian tribe are not, in general, delegated powers granted by express acts of Congress, but rather inherent powers of a limited sovereignty which has never been extinguished."[38]

Cohen later expanded on the principle, saying that except as limited by treaty or statutes of Congress, tribes retain all the powers of any government. This doctrine came to be called the doctrine of residual sovereignty. It had far-reaching implications, for it meant that anyone challenging the exercise of tribal power must find a statute or treaty which explicitly withdrew that authority. Such limitations were in fact quite few in number. So the doctrine of residual sovereignty seemed to provide a tailor-made vehicle for the reconstruction of tribal government.

With the resurgence of tribal government in the 1960s, tribes began to seek ways of reasserting their authority over their reservations. Lawlessness on the reservation was a particularly critical problem. Although major crimes committed by whites on the reservation were subject to state or federal criminal prosecution, minor crimes were largely ignored. Local non-Indian law enforcement authorities had little incentive to send their personnel onto Indian reservations. The result was that traffic offenses, trespasses, violations of tribal hunting and fishing regulations, disorderly conduct and even petty larceny and simple assaults committed by non-Indians went unpunished. The situation cried out for action. Tribal governments began to adopt law and order codes extending their jurisdiction to crimes by non-Indians. By the 1970s, some thirty-three tribes were enforcing criminal jurisdiction over whites. The Suquamish Indian Tribe on the Port Madison Reservation in the state of Washington was one of these.

The Port Madison Reservation is located directly across Elliott Bay from the city of Seattle. The reservation was established by an 1855 treaty which set aside 7,276 acres for the Suquamish Indians. The tribe was a small one. In 1978 it had approximately 550 members, of whom about 150 lived on the reservation. The reservation, however, was checkerboarded with non-Indian land ownership and had a substantial non-Indian population. The Suquamish seemed an unlikely candidate for a large role in the history of Indian litigation, but they were to become the first tribe to present to the United States Supreme Court the claim that Indian tribes had criminal jurisdiction over whites on the reservation.

Oliphant v. Suquamish Indian Tribe had its origins in an incident which occurred during the tribe's 1973 Chief Seattle Days celebration.[39] The tribe had requested police assistance from the county sheriff's office but were told that only one deputy was available for an eight-hour period during the entire weekend. When the tribe requested law enforcement assistance from the Bureau of Indian Affairs agency, they were told that they would have to provide their own law enforcement. Consequently, the tribal police force was the only effective force available for most of the period of the celebration.

At about 4:30 A.M. on a Sunday morning an altercation occurred between tribal police and a young man named Mark Oliphant. Tribal police claimed that they ordered him to leave the grounds because of disorderly conduct and that in the subsequent dispute he punched one of the tribal officers. He was arrested and confined in the tribal jail. He was subsequently released on his promise to appear. Tribal court proceedings were stayed when the attorney for Oliphant advised that he was filing a habeas corpus proceeding in federal court under the Indian Civil Rights Act challenging the jurisdiction of the Suquamish tribal court. The tribe instructed their attorneys to defend its authority.

The federal district court, applying the rule of residual sovereignty, denied the writ and upheld the tribe's position. Oliphant's attorney appealed the case to the Ninth Circuit Court of appeals. in 1976, the Ninth Circuit affirmed the decision of the district court. The court's analysis relied heavily upon the theory of residual sovereignty. Analyzing the treaty with the Suquamish and subsequent legislation, the court could find nothing to support any suggestion that the tribe's criminal jurisdiction had been extinguished or limited by Congress. Oliphant petitioned the United States Supreme Court for review.

When the Supreme Court agreed to review the case, the attorneys for the Suquamish Tribe were gravely concerned. An adverse decision could affect not only the Suquamish, but every tribe. It might be possible to prevent Supreme Court review by dismissing the charges, thereby rendering the case moot. The Suquamish decided to submit the matter to the National Litigation Committee of the National Congress of American Indians for guidance. The committee's members comprised most of the attorneys representing Indian tribes in the United States, as well as Indian leaders and tribal governmental officers. At their meeting in Dallas in 1977, the issues were analyzed and debated intensively. The case had some weaknesses. Non-Indians outnumbered Indians on the reservations. The reservation was not in a remote rural area but near two large cities. The tribe was small and lacked the stature of the larger tribes, such as the Navajos.

On the other hand, the alleged offense had occurred on tribal land. It involved an assault upon a tribal police officer in the performance of duties clearly intended to protect the general safety of Indians and non-Indians. The tribe's handling of Oliphant, including his prompt arraignment before a tribal court and his release on recognizance, were careful and responsible actions.

While one might conceive a case with better facts, no one could be sure that the next to come before the Supreme Court would be as good. Furthermore, the Suquamish enjoyed the advantage of two lower court decisions in their favor. Finally, it might not be possible to moot the case. It was, after all, not the Suquamish who chose to bring the case to the federal courts or to appeal it, and thus the matter was not completely within their control. The NCAI Litigation Committee decided by an overwhelming majority to recommend that the tribe not moot the appeal.

Oliphant v. Suquamish was a serious defeat for the tribes. In a 7 to 2 decision, the Supreme Court held in 1978 that Indian tribes did not have jurisdiction to punish criminal offenses committed by non-Indians. Both sides had focused their arguments on whether the treaty with the Suquamish or any subsequent legislation indicated a congressional intention to deny Indian tribes criminal jurisdiction over non-Indians. On this issue, the Suquamish seemed clearly to have the better of the argument. But they had a problem: How was it that for over 100 years Congress, the courts and the Department of Interior had assumed that tribes had no such power? There was no good answer.

The Supreme Court refused to follow the residual sovereignty analysis. Instead, it created a new gloss on the doctrine. Indian tribes, said the Court, not only lost powers by express congressional action, but they were also proscribed from exercising powers "inconsistent with their status." The Supreme Court viewed tribal punishment of whites as fundamentally incompatible with federal sovereignty. Therefore, said the Court, the tribes "necessarily [gave] up their power to try non-Indian citizens of the United States except in a manner acceptable to Congress." The Court admitted that the problem of local law enforcement facing the tribes was a serious one, but this, it said, was nonetheless a matter for congressional deliberation.

The decision fell heavily on tribal governments. It seemed a death knell to the recovery of lost power. Without criminal authority over its territory, any government is crippled. Worse, *Oliphant* raised questions regarding tribal civil authority over whites. Without that, tribes would be reduced to nothing more than self-governing membership associations. No one knew how far the Supreme Court might go in that direction.

While tribes and their supporters saw nothing good in the *Oliphant* decision, its political consequences may have been beneficial, because the growing tribal assertions of authority over non-Indians had brought on a white backlash in the western states of serious proportions. Legislation had been introduced in Congress to strip Indian tribes of all governmental powers except those narrowly limited to their own members. The *Oliphant* decision seemed to defuse these anti-tribal movements.

TRIBAL CIVIL AUTHORITY OVER NON-INDIANS

Oliphant was a watershed; the Supreme Court could no longer be relied upon to support the growth of tribal government. The decision cast a shadow over the right of tribes to assert any authority over whites. That right would be further tested in the area of taxation. The tax struggle between the tribes and the states arose from the operation of "smokeshops"—Indian or tribally-owned stores selling cigarettes at discount prices. The operators of these stores, relying on the principle that states had no authority to tax Indians, sold cigarettes free of state tax. Business on reservation smokeshops boomed as whites flocked from nearby communities. White business competitors were angered by the loss of patronage, and state revenue officers were indignant at the loss of millions of tax dollars.

In 1976 the Supreme Court decided in *Confederated Salish and Kootenai Tribes v. Moe* that while states could not tax Indians, they could insist that Indian merchants collect state sales taxes from white customers who purchased cigarettes in their shops.[40] The states felt this would put an end to the smokeshop "nuisance." But several tribes in Washington State imposed their own tax on cigarettes. *Moe* had not involved a tribal tax, so the Washington tribes felt they were not bound by that decision. They felt their tax, which was approved by the federal government, should preempt the field. There obviously wasn't room for both tribal and state taxes since that would bring the retail price of reservation cigarettes above the price elsewhere. Because the tribal tax was significantly lower than the state's, Indian cigarettes could be sold at a competitive advantage. The existence of the tribal tax brought the "infringement" test of *Williams* into play: Did the state tax infringe on tribal government? The tribes maintained it did, for it would preclude the tribes from taxing the sales of cigarettes.

The Supreme Court thought otherwise. In *Colville v. Washington* it held the tribes could not preempt the state's tax.[41] The Court refused to follow the infringement test. Instead, it adopted a "balancing of interests" approach. While the tribes have an important interest in raising revenue, that interest, said the Court, is strongest when the revenues came from "value generated on the reservation by activities involving the tribes and when the taxpayer is the recipient of tribal services." This seems to be another way of saying the court saw nothing commendable in Indians bringing merchandise onto the reservation for sale to whites at discount prices. All the Indians were doing, said the Court, was "marketing a tax immunity to non-members of the tribe." The value of the merchandise was generated off the reservation and the white taxpayers were for the most part nonresidents who received no tribal services. Under the balancing of interests test the state won.

From the tribes point of view, *Colville* was a bitter defeat. It seemed to entrench state tax authority over the reservation and it ended an important source of revenue for Indians and tribes. But the authority of the states to require Indians to collect their tax on cigarettes had, in fact, been approved four years earlier in *Moe*. *Colville* did contain two holdings which promised to be useful to the tribes. The state had urged the Court to extend *Oliphant* and rule that tribes had no civil authority over whites and could not tax them at all. This the Court rejected, saying that tribes have inherent power to tax non-Indians doing business on trust lands where the tribe or its members are significantly involved. Second, the decision left open the possibility that the Court would uphold tribal preemption of state tax authority if the state attempted to tax values generated on the reservation when its interests were insignificant compared to those of the tribe.

Colville, like *Oliphant*, was a watershed. The infringement test of *Williams v. Lee* was in tatters. The tribes could no longer rely on it to protect them from state claims of authority even where they could show significant economic loss to tribal government. The *Colville* court had also put a new gloss on the *Oliphant* holding. *Oliphant* had held tribes could not exercise powers "inconsistent with their status." *Colville* modified the rule: tribes could not exercise powers "inconsistent with the overriding interests of the national government." This raised new questions. Must a direct conflict with national interests exist before tribal authority could be restricted? How were such overriding interests to be determined? No one knew, of course, and the lower courts were left to puzzle over the vague new boundary of tribal authority over non-Indians.

In 1981, a year after the *Colville* decision, the Court had the opportunity to clarify the law in a hunting and fishing case, *Montana v. United States*.[42] Hunting and fishing always arouse deep passions. As we saw in the Pacific Northwest treaty fishing controversy, heightened emotions can lead to serious strife between Indians and whites. It generated a bitter controversy between the Crow Tribe and the state of Montana and finally led the tribe to declare the reservation closed to all non-Indian hunting and fishing. The litigation which followed raised the issue whether an Indian tribe could bar non-Indians from hunting or fishing on reservation lands owned by non-Indians or in rivers running through the reservation.

The Supreme Court ruled that regulation of hunting and fishing by non-members of the tribe on non-Indian lands did not fall within the ambit of tribal authority. "[E]xercise of tribal power beyond that is necessary to protect tribal self-government or to control internal relations is inconsistent with the dependent status of the tribes, and so cannot survive without express Congressional delegation." This language would work a devastating restriction on tribal authority. The Court went further. It ruled that title to the bed of the rivers flowing through the reservation had passed to the states when they entered the Union. The only exception was where there was some clear expression, in a statute or treaty, of congressional intent to reserve these bedlands for the tribe. The Court found no such expression in the Crow treaty. Thus, the Court ruled, the state of Montana, not the tribe, owned the bed of these rivers.

Montana v. United States appeared to be a crushing defeat for tribal interests. Depriving tribes of (long assumed) ownership of the riverbeds on their reservation had far-reaching implications. It appeared to open the way for states to claim jurisdiction over rivers and non-Indians fishing activities the length and breadth of reservations. This not only affected fishing but also river uses for the generation of hydroelectric power and irrigation. The regulatory issue was just as important. Non-Indian lands within the reservation appeared to have been placed beyond the regulatory reach of tribal government. But the Court left open an important exception: The tribes might exercise civil authority over the conduct of non-Indians on such lands if it could show that the conduct "threatens or has some direct effect on the political integrity, the economic security, or the health or welfare of the tribe."

The exception was broad enough to provide hope that tribes could defend regulation of non-Indian land, though they would have to meet a burden of jurisdiction not faced by non-Indian governments.

Montana's holdings made deep inroads into long-held Indian beliefs about tribal ownership and tribal sovereignty. But some basic principles of tribal sovereignty seemed unshakeable. One of these was the power of a tribe to tax non-Indians who did business on the reservation. After *Oliphant*, some thought even this hallowed principle might be overturned by the court. Such thinking must have motivated the companies extracting oil and gas on the Jicarilla Apache reservation.

In 1976 the Jicarillas imposed a severance tax on oil and gas produced on tribal land, and twenty-one companies sued, challenging the power of the tribe to tax them. Their principal argument was that an Indian tribe's power to tax non-Indians derived solely from its power as a landowner to exclude them from its lands. Since these plaintiffs were conducting their operations under leases with the tribe, and the leases said nothing about any tax, the tribe had no power to exclude them and thus no power to tax. The argument was rejected by the Supreme Court in 1982.

Merrion v. Jicarilla Apache Tribe held that tribal power to tax non-Indian business transactions derived not from a mere landowner's power to change a fee for entry onto his lands, but from the general power possessed by all governments to raise revenue by taxation.[43] Even if the power stemmed from the power to exclude, the Court said, the tribe was not divested of the power to impose a tax after leasing its land to a non-Indian.

The *Jicarilla* case might be seen as a rather limited victory for tribal sovereignty. After all, its fundamental holding that tribes could tax non-Indians doing business on the reservation had been affirmed in *Morris v. Hitchcock* in 1904. Furthermore, the tribal tax was imposed on activities conducted on tribal lands in a consensual or voluntary transaction. The Court was also careful to point out that the tribe's ability to tax was conditioned on prior government approval of its ordinance. But *Jicarilla* does contain language and ideas which strengthen tribal sovereignty.

Jicarilla says the power to tax is a necessary instrument of self-government and territorial management, both being essential attributes of Indian sovereignty. The Court goes on to analyze tribal taxation in terms of the same criteria historically employed by the court for state taxation. This may signify a conceptual development of some importance; the judicial expansion of federal system analysis to embrace tribal governments.

While the *Jicarilla* opinion contains important and repeated reaffirmations of tribal sovereignty, it remains to be seen whether the Court will sustain broader exercises of tribal taxing power over non-Indians—on non-Indian lands, for example—or in non-consensual situations such as property or income taxes. *Jicarilla* was a 6-to-3 decision and two members of the majority are likely to leave the court in the next four or five years. *Jicarilla*, of course, does not deal with the more difficult questions of tribal sovereignty, including the scope of tribal authority over non-Indians on non-Indian land, the power of the tribe to preempt state taxes and the limits of federal power over tribes. In these areas, the conservative directions taken by the Court since *Oliphant* presage difficulties for tribal efforts to achieve territorial sovereignty.

INDIAN LITIGATION: DISILLUSION AND A SEARCH FOR ALTERNATIVES

Oliphant, Colville, and *Montana* left many tribal leaders bitter and disillusioned with the American judicial system. It seemed that the Supreme Court had arrogated to itself the policy-making authority which the Constitution delegated to Congress. When a rule of law led to a politically uncomfortable position, the Court seemed to abandon the rule and create a new one.

Disillusionment with the judicial process left tribal governments with few alternatives. They could defer the difficult questions by overlooking challenges to their authority and biding their time until circumstances were more propitious. They could sit down with their adversaries, the state governments, and try to negotiate their differences. They could seek legislative solutions from Congress, although this was becoming increasingly difficult because of the controversial character which now seemed to surround every Indian proposal.

Many Indian leaders argued that the tribes should move outside the domestic arena and strengthen their ties to the international indigenous community. At the same time, they argued, the tribes should seek ways to bring their grievances before world forums, such as the United Nations. While suggestions had met with little interest in the past, Indians were now more receptive. Indeed, the 1980 convention of the National Congress of American Indians devoted a substantial part of its agenda to discussions on establishing an international identity.

This new interest in international forums coincides with the growth of the international law of human rights, a body of law which imposes international norms upon nations concerning the treatment of their own citizens. The Indians would seek to invoke the right of self-discrimination, recognized by many international conventions.

However, the United States has not ratified most of these international conventions, including the International Convention on Genocide, the American Convention on Human Rights, the International Covenant on Civil and Political Rights, and the International Covenant on Economic, Social and Cultural Rights. John Murphy, former State Department legal advisor, has written that "the United States has viewed the ethnic approach to self-determination with a jaundiced eye," in part because of Indian and black separatist demands.[44]

Such conventions, if given effect, would enable Indians to seek international remedies. In 1981, for example, the Human Rights Committee of the United Nations ruled on a complaint brought against the government of Canada by a Maliseet Indian woman, Sandra Lovelace. She charged that the Canadian Indian Act violated the International Covenant on Civil and Political Rights because it detribalized Indian women who married non-Indian men while leaving Indian men who married non-Indians unaffected. The committee ruled in her favor and held that Canada was in violation of its international obligations under the Covenant.[45]

Some American Indian tribes have submitted their complaints to the United Nations Human Rights Commission. Because the United States is not a party to any of the international covenants, however, the only procedure available for these individuals' complaints is the so-called "1503 procedure."[46] This calls for examination of the complaints by a working group and submission of selected complaints to the Subcommittee on the Elimination of Discrimination and ultimately to the Human Rights Commission.

In practice, few complaints result in action by the Human Rights Commission. But the potential for political embarrassment of the

United States is substantial. Indian tribes may seek to exploit United Nations human rights forums rather than continue to litigate in American courts that cannot be expected to shed their national loyalties.

CONCLUSION

The heyday of Indian litigation may well be behind us. The Supreme Court is showing a tendency to retreat from the concept of tribal self-determination. This is likely to exacerbated if conservative members are appointed to replace some of the tribes' present supporters on the Court. The tribes themselves are in a period of retrenchment. They have been severely affected by stringent federal cutbacks and by the decline of the American economy in the 1980s. Most have little money or energy for major litigation. On the other hand, the tribes seem to have secured a firm foothold in the American federal system. The question is whether they will be limited to the role of local governments able to exercise only limited powers of home rule, with little authority over non-Indians, or whether they will emerge as broader territorial governments with significant attributes of sovereignty over all persons and activities within their territory. There is some room for cautious optimism here. A few recent lower federal court decisions have upheld tribal regulatory authority over non-Indians either on the ground that the activity had a significant effect on the economy, health, and welfare of the tribe (applying the *Montana* exception) or on the ground that the tribe's action did not impair any significant federal interest (applying the *Colville* rule).[47]

Perhaps the most serious questions will never be definitively answered by the Court. For instance, will the Court abandon the open-ended notion of the plenary power of Congress in favor of a doctrine of constitutional constraints? Tribal attorneys and legal scholars may help to develop the theoretical bases for such constraints from the implications of the Commerce Clause or from the developing doctrines of substantive due process.

A least the existence of tribal governments as sovereign entities within the American federal system no longer seems to be an issue. Tribal sovereignty is becoming more and more familiar to state officials with each passing year, and Congress now perceives tribal government as part of the structure of American local governments.

The underpinnings of the modern doctrine of tribal sovereignty in federal Indian law can be found in the great court decisions of the past hundred years. In those cases, the Supreme Court has preserved the idea of tribes as sovereignties even while the government seemed bent on their extinction. It remained only for the tribes to exercise their sovereignty. That has now occurred. The tribes will no doubt continue to press against the political restraints that bind them.

It may be that the American judicial system will not be elastic enough to meet Indian ambitions, but the judicial arena is where the conflicts between tribal and non-tribal governments will be decided. Congress, after all, acts infrequently and the executive branch responds to many voices. If the past hundred years is any guide, the Indian cry for justice will be answered by the courts. However, the tribes must act with great care; they must litigate prudently and skilfully. The stakes are very high and there is no turning back.

N O T E S

1. *Johnson v. McIntosh*, 21 U.S. (8 Wheat) 543 (1823).
2. *Cherokee v. Georgia*, 30 U.S. (5 Pet.) 1 (1831).
3. *Worcester v. Georgia*, 31 U.S. (6 Pet.) 515 (1832).
4. *United States v. McBratney*, 104 U.S. 621 (1881).
5. *Draper v. United States*, 164 U.S. 240 (1896).
6. William C. Canby, Jr., *American Indian Law in a Nutshell* (St. Paul: West Publishing Co., 1981), pp. 102–103.
7. *Ex Parte Crow Dog*, 109 U.S. 556 (1883).
8. *Untied States v. Kagama*, 118 U.S. 375 (1886).
9. *American Insurance Company v. Canter*, 26 U.S. (1 Pet.) 511 (1828).
10. *Choctaw Nation v. United States*, 119 U.S. 1 (1886); *Cherokee Nation v. Southern Kansas R.R. Co.*, 135 U.S. 641 (1890); *Stephens v. Cherokee Nation*, 174 U.S. 445 (1899); *Cherokee Nation v. Hitchcock* 187 U.S. 294 (1902).
11. *Lone Wolf v. Hitchcock*, 187 U.S. 553 (1903).
12. *The Cherokee Tobacco*, 78 U.S. (11 Wall) 616 (1871).
13. *United States v. Winans*, 198 U.S. 371 (1905).
14. *Id.*, at 381.
15. *Winters v. United States*, 207 U.S. 564 (1908).
16. *The Indian Reorganization Act*, 48 Stat. 984, 25 U.S.C.A. 55 461-479, (1934).
17. *Williams v. Lee* 358 U.S. 217 (1959).

18. See Stephen Conn, "Mid-passage—The Navaho Tribe and Its First Legal Revolution," *American Indian Law Review*: 329 at 362 (1978).

19. *McClanahan v. Arizona State Tax Commission*, 411 U.S. 164 (1973).

20. *United States v. Washington*, 384 F. Supp. 312 (W.D. Wash. 1974).

21. *United States v. Washngton*, 520 F. 2d. 676 (9th Cir. 1975).

22. *Washington v. Fishing Vessel Association*, 443 U.S. 658 (1979).

23. *Wakefield v. Little Light*, 347 A.2d. 228 (Md. 1975).

24. *Whyte v. District Court*, 346 P.2d 1012 (Colo. 1959); *Red Fox v. Red Fox*, 542 P.2d 918 (Ore. 1975).

25. *Arizona ex. rel. Merrill v. Turtle*, 413 F.2d 683 (9th Cir. 1969).

26. *Confederated Tribes of the Colville Indian Reservation v. Washington*, 412 F. Supp. 651 (E.D. Wash. 1976), modified in *White Mountain Apache Tribe v. Arizona* and *Confederated Tribes of the Colville Indian Reservation v. Washington (consol.)*, 649 F.2d 1274 (9th Cir. 1981).

27. *Red Lake Band of Chippewas v. Minnesota*, 248 N.W. 2d. 722 (Minn. 1976).

28. *United States v. Mazurie*, 419 U.S. 544 (1975).

29. *Fisher v. District Court*, 424 U.S. 382 (1976).

30. *Baker v. Carr*, 369 U.S. 186 (1962).

31. *Morton v. Mancari*, 417 U.S. 535 (1974).

32. *Id.* at 555.

33. *Delaware v. Weeks*, 430 U.S. 73 (1977).

34. *United States v. Sioux Nation of Indians*, 448 U.S. 371 (1980).

35. *Santa Clara Pueblo v. Martinez*, 436 U.S. 49 (1978).

36. *Morris v. Hitchcock*, 194 U.S. 384 (1904).

37. *Buster v. Wright*, 135 F.947 (8th Cir. 1905); *Barta v. Oglala Sioux Tribe of Pine Ridge Reservation*, 259 F.2d 553 (8th Cir. 1958).

38. 55 I.D. 14, Oct. 25, 1934; 1 Op. Sol. 445, 447.

39. *Oliphant v. Suquamish Indian Tribe*, 435 U.S. 191 (1978).

40. *Confederated Salish and Kootenai Tribes v. Moe*, 425 U.S. 463 (1976).

41. *Colville v. Washington*, 447 U.S. 134 (1980).

42. *Montana v. U.S.*, 450 U.S. 544 (1981).

43. *Merrion v. Jicarilla Apache Tribe*, 102 S.Ct. 894 (1982).

44. John F. Murphy, "Self-Determination: United States Perspectives," in Yonah Alexander and Robert A. Friedlander, eds., *Self-Determination: National, Regional, and Global Dimensions*, (Boulder, Colo.: Westview Press, 1980), p. 46.

45. CCPR/C/DR (XIII)/R.6/24, Decision of the Human Rights Committee of the International Covenant on Civil and Political Rights, July 30, 1981.

46. ECOSOC resolution 1503, para. 1, 48 U.N. ESCOR, Supp. (no. 1A) 8, U.N. Doc. E/4832/Add. 1 (1970). See M. E. Tordu, "United Nations

Response to Gross Violations of Human Rights: The 1503 Procedure," 20 *Santa Clara Law Review* 559.
47. *Confederated Salish and Kootenai Tribes v. Namen*, Nos. 80-3189, 80-3190, 80-3196, 80-3216 and 80-3274 (CA 9th, Jan. 1, 1982); *Cardin v. DeLaCruz*, No. 80-3244 (CA 9th, March 15, 1982).

B I B L I O G R A P H Y

1. Barsh, Russell L., and Henderson, James Y. *The Road: Indian Tribes and Political Liberty*. Berkeley: University of California Press, 1980.
2. Canby, Jr., William C. *American Indian Law*. St. Paul, Minn.: West Publishing Co., 1981.
3. Getches, David H., Rosenfelt, Daniel M., and Wilkinson, Charles F. *Federal Indian Law*. St. Paul, Minn.: West Publishing Co., 1979.
4. Gibson, Arrell M. *The American Indian, Pre-History to the Present*. Lexington, Mass.: D.C. Heath & Co., 1980.
5. McCloskey, Robert G. *The American Supreme Court*. Chicago: The University of Chicago Press, 1960.

INDIAN LAND RIGHTS

ROBERT T. COULTER
AND
STEVEN M. TULLBERG

*U*nited States policy toward Indian lands has been directed by conflicting motivations. On the one hand, we find the desire to exploit Indian resources, and on the other a more high-minded desire for justice and the rule of the law. As a practical matter, political forces have prevailed, and the United States legal system has provided precious little protection against direct seizure of Indian land by the federal government or against rigid control of Indian resources by the Interior Department. This vulnerability has meant not only the deprivation of land and resource rights, but the loss or compromise of other essential Indian rights and interests as well. Because of the immense cultural and religious significance of land in Indian life, the power to destroy Indian land rights carries with it power to destroy Indian identity.

Indian legal rights have always been surrounded with the appearance of rigorous legal protection. Initially, the British Crown controlled all dealings with Indian land, and formal treaties were the accepted form of securing and transferring Indian real property. The same practice was immediately adopted by the United States, which also established further legal protections. According to Northwest Ordinance of 1789,

> The utmost good faith shall always be observed towards the Indian; their land property shall never be taken from them without their consent; and in their property, rights, and liberty, they never shall be invaded or disturbed, unless in just and lawful wars authorized by Congress; but laws founded in justice and humanity shall from time to time be made, for preventing wrongs being done to them, and for preserving peace and friendship with them.[1]

The due process clause of the Constitution, on its face, protects all property without limitation from federal seizure unless "due process of law" is observed and the seizure is for a public purpose. The Constitution likewise makes treaties, including Indian treaties, the

"Supreme Law of the Land," along with statutes and the Constitution itself. The Fourteenth Amendment to the Constitution specifically forbids discrimination based on race.

Despite the array of legal principles, United States law and the courts have substantially failed to protect Indian lands from arbitrary confiscations, partitioning, bureaucratic control, and treaty violations. A brief list of some of the federal legal powers which effectively deny Indian land rights today helps to explain Indian people's continuing frustration with federal law (we will examine the legal powers in further detail below). This list also highlights the need for further examination and reform of United States Indian law.

1. Indian land, which lacks constitutional protection from arbitrary seizure by the United States, is the only real property in the United States without that protection. The only constitutional restraint against federal seizure is the requirement that compensation sometimes be paid, but even this requirement applies only to "recognized title" lands, which are lands Congress has expressly approved for *permanent* Indian occupancy.

2. The law provides no protection whatsoever against federal confiscation of "aboriginal title" or "Indian title" lands. Aboriginal title lands are those which have been Indian lands from time immemorial, but which have not been expressly "recognized" by Congress for permanent Indian occupancy. It is not clear what percentage of Indian-held land falls within the "aboriginal title" category today, but some believe it may be more than 50 percent.[2] Indians living on these Indian homelands are treated in federal law as mere tenants at the will of the federal government. Indians asserting legal claims in litigation or negotiations for return of such lands are warned by federal officials and members of Congress that the Indian title to their homelands may be "extinguished" on whatever terms Congress might dictate.

3. It is settled federal law that Congress may unilaterally abrogate Indian treaties, the very foundation of United States legal protection for many Indian territories, and that when it does so, the Supreme Court will consider such acts to be "political questions" beyond the realm of judicial review. It is thus politics alone and not law which determines whether Indian treaties will continue to be part of the supreme law of the land as the Constitution commands.

4. The United States government asserts that it, not the Indians, has the ultimate fee or "trust title" to all Indian lands outside the original thirteen colonies. Indians are said to have only a permissive

right of occupancy. An "Indian trust relationship" is said to give the United States government broad legal powers to control and manage Indian land and resources. Yet the Supreme Court has recently made clear that the federal government, as "trustee," is liable for mismanagement and wrongdoing only if the federal government by legislation expressly imposes such legal liability on itself. Legal accountability for violations of this non-statutory "trust relationship" is practically non-existent.

5. When a group of bills to abrogate a broad range of Indian rights was introduced in Congress in the late 1970s, it became evident that political and moral suasion, not law or the courts, were the only barriers against this effort to terminate Indian governments and tribes. The more recent "Ancient Indian Land Claims Settlement Bill of 1982," which sought to extinguish Indian land claims, is additional evidence that long-sought Indian legal victories risk being "legally" swept away by congressional acts, without any hope of judicial protection.

This astonishing lack of legal restraint is of no small consequence, because the federal government has a strong and pervasive interest in acquiring and controlling land, water, and other resources. The federal government, after all, is the largest proprietor of land and resources in the country, and it clearly has the most extensive adverse interest to most Indian land rights and land claims. As though to excuse or counterbalance the lack of legal protection for Indian property rights, federal officials and many others have urged reliance on the federal-Indian "trust relationship" to protect Indian rights. This trusteeship, supplemented by an enlightened political awareness in Washington, is believed to restrain the federal government from exercising the absolute powers over Indians which it in fact possesses.

Advocates of the trust theory have forgotten or overlooked the fact that the federal government itself initiated the destructive policies of Indian removal, allotment, termination and other wholesale denials of Indian rights. Through these policies and a host of other federal acts, the federal government has confiscated massive areas of Indian lands for its own use and that of its non-Indian citizenry. One looks in vain through the historical record for actions by the Supreme Court to protect Indians from these confiscatory actions. (To be sure, in *Worcester v. Georgia* the Supreme Court declared a *state* statute unconstitutional.[3] In that instance, President Andrew Jackson simply refused to enforce the Court's decision, leaving Indians to their fate at the hands of the state.) As might be expected, all of these disastrous federal policies were said to be in the best interest of the Indian "wards" of the federal government. But the denial of Indian rights is not less damaging because it occurs under the rubric of paternalism rather than greed. The cautionary words of Justice Louis Brandeis seem especially apt:

> Experience should teach us to be most on our guard to protect liberty when the government's purposes are beneficient. . . . The greatest dangers to liberty lurk in insidious encroachments by men of zeal, well-meaning but without understanding.[4]

The continuing threat of unregulated federal power was brought home by the Supreme Court's 1978 reaffirmation of the power to terminate Indian tribes altogether: "Congress has plenary authority to limit, modify, or eliminate the powers of local self-government which the tribes otherwise possess."[5] This power was affirmed once again in *Merrion v. Jicarilla Apache Tribe* (1982), a case in which the Court nonetheless upheld certain taxing powers of the tribe.[6]

THE MARSHALL DECISIONS

All students of United States Indian law agree on at least one point: that to understand the origins and development of federal law pertaining to Indian land, one must turn to five decisions of the John Marshall Supreme Court. These are *Fletcher v. Peck*[7] (hereinafter *Fletcher*); *Johnson v. McIntosh*[8] (hereinafter *McIntosh*); *Cherokee Nation v. Georgia*[9] (hereinafter *Cherokee Nation*); *Worcester v. Georgia*[10] (hereinafter *Worcester*); and *Mitchel v. United States*[11] (hereinafter *Mitchel*). Universally used and abused as precedents, the Marshall Court opinions have been cited in support of doctrines as diametrically opposed as Indian sovereignty and termination. They were quoted with approval by British courts upholding England's dominion over the natives of Africa and India, and yet they have always been the source of ringing pronouncements on the rights of Indian nations under international law.

Although Marshall was a slaveholding Virginia gentleman who consistently ruled that the "property right" in slaves must be upheld in law,[12] he had a more compassionate view of Indians and was reportedly moved to tears by arguments made in the *Cherokee* case. Marshall amassed a fortune in terms of thousands of acres in what was then Virginia, a frontier area which Marshall described as having been "claimed and possessed by Indians, who maintained their title with as much persevering courage as was ever manifested by any people."[13] Rejecting the argument that Indians were simply 'an inferior race of people" without legal rights to their homelands, Marshall drew on the law of the United States and on international law, the "law of nations" as it was known, to set the course of federal Indian law.

The Marshall's Court's analysis of Indian land rights centers on an examination of certain opposing legal theories: on the one hand, the theory that the Indian property right was a right of absolute ownership; on the other, the argument that several legal doctrines operated separately and in concert to deny Indian land rights. The principal doctrines asserted in opposition to Indian land rights were the doctrine of discovery and the law of conquest. Although it is sometimes argued today that the Marshall Court upheld United States title to all Indian lands by virtue of discovery and conquest, a reading of Marshall's opinions supports the opposite conclusion.

The Doctrine of Discovery

The doctrine of discovery came into existence with the rapid expansion of European empires in the fifteenth century. Its basic tenet—that the European nation which first "discovered" and settled lands previously unknown to Europeans thereby gained the exclusive right to acquire those lands from their occupants—became part of the early body of international law dealing with aboriginal peoples.

Property rights of the original inhabitants of "discovered" lands—the rights of the hundreds of millions of "natives" who lived outside Europe—were somewhat uncertain in the early years of this European invasion. They depended on the outcome of legal, theological, and scientific debates as to whether the natives were fully human, whether they were susceptible to Christian conversion, and whether they were capable of "civilized" (i.e. European) culture, government, agriculture, and industry. These debates would continue long into the twentieth century; by the time Europeans settled in North America, however, it was well-established in international law that natives had property rights which could not lawfully be denied by the discovering

European nation. The Indian nations in North America were deemed by law to have the right to own, use, and dispose of their homelands.[14]

In the early period, the military power of England and the rest of Europe was inferior to that of the Indian nations. As a matter of both legal principle and practicality, European nations dealt with the Indian nations as they did with other nations of the world. In general, Indian lands were acquired by agreement, through the use of traditional international diplomacy—specifically, through formal treaties of cession. Indian lands were seldom acquired by military conquest or fiat, and the practices of Spain, France, and the Netherlands did not differ in this regard.

The right of discovery served mainly to regulate the relations among European nations.[15] It did not limit the legal powers or rights of Indian nations in their homelands; its major limitation was to prohibit Indians from diplomatic dealings with all but the "discovering" European nation. In much of North America, for example, England was held to be the only nation lawfully authorized to extinguish Indian title. In other areas, only Spain, France, or the Netherlands possessed such authority. Moreover, the right of discovery gave a European nation the right to extinguish Indian title only when the Indians consented to it by treaty.

John Marshall was intimately familiar with the history of this law, and refused to accept the twisted argument that discovery had extinguished Indian land rights. In his first major opinion on the discovery issue (*Johnson v. McIntosh* [1823]), Marshall stated unequivocally that the law of nations and the doctrine of discovery did not operate to deny Indian land rights:

> On the discovery of this immense continent, the great nations of Europe were eager to appropriate to themselves so much of it as they could respectively acquire. Its vast extent offered an ample field to ambition and enterprise of all; and the character and religion of its inhabitants afforded an apology for considering them as a people over whom the superior genius of Europe might claim an ascendency. The potentates of the world found no difficulty in convincing themselves that they made ample compensation to the inhabitants of the new, by bestowing on them civilization and Christianity, in exchange for unlimited independence. But, as they were all in pursuit of nearly the same object, it was necessary, in order to avoid conflicting settlements, and consequent war with each other, to establish a principle, which all

should acknowledge as the law by which the right of acquisition, which they all asserted, should be regulated as between themselves. This principle was, that discovery gave title to the government by whose subjects, or by whose authority, it was made, against all other European governments, which title might be consummated by possession.

The exclusion of all other Europeans, necessarily gave to the nation making the discovery the sole right of acquiring the soil from the natives, and establishing settlements upon it. It was a right with which no Europeans could interfere. It was a right which all asserted for themselves, and to the assertion of which, by others, all assented.

Those relations which were to exist between the discoverer and the natives, were to be regulated by themselves. The rights thus acquired being exclusive, no other power could interpose between them.[16]

In one of his later Cherokee decisions, *Worcester v. Georgia* (1832), Marshall openly ridiculed the "extravagant and absurd idea" that the right of discovery gave European nations absolute title and dominion over Indian lands:

Soon after Great Britain determined on planting colonies in America, the king granted charters to companies of his subjects who associated for the purpose of carrying the views of the crown into effect, and of enriching themselves. The first of these charters was made before possession was taken of any part of the country. They purport, generally, to convey the soil, from the Atlantic to the South Sea. This soil was occupied by numerous and warlike nations, equally willing and able to defend their possessions. The extravagant and absurd idea, that the feeble settlements made on the sea coast, or the companies under whom they were made, acquired legitimate power by them to govern the people, or occupy the lands from sea to sea, did not enter the mind of any man. They were well understood to convey the title which, according to the common law of European sovereigns respecting America, they might rightfully convey, and no more. This was the exclusive right of purchasing such lands as the natives were willing to sell. The crown could not be understood to grant what the crown did not affect to claim; nor was it so understood.[17]

On occasion, later Supreme Court decisions not only glossed over Marshall's careful articulation of the discovery doctrine, but cited the doctrine as legal authority for United States ownership and extinguishment of Indian land title.[18] But the Marshall Court decisions remain the leading statements on the subject, and they establish that the doctrine of discovery gave no legal authority to control, manage or confiscate Indian lands and resources. Discovery conferred no greater right than "the exclusive right of purchasing such lands as the natives were willing to sell." These words from Marshall's opinion in *McIntosh* were recently reaffirmed and applied by the Second Circuit Court of Appeals in a decision concerning Oneida land claims in New York.[19]

The Law of Conquest

It was also argued in the Marshall Court that the legal power to extinguish title to Indian lands had been acquired by right of conquest. Upon conquest, the victor of a just and lawful war (a war in which the victor was not the aggressor) was permitted by the law of nations to subjugate the defeated enemy by disestablishing its government and formally annexing the conquered territory. This subjugation was deemed to vest the enemy nation's land title in the victorious nation, which thereafter had sovereignty over the conquered territory.[20]

The law of nations provided that the victorious nation became the sovereign of the conquered territory *only* if it subjugated the defeated enemy and formally annexed his lands. If the victor chose instead to make a treat of peace and acquire only some of the defeated nation's lands (by forcing to cede them by treaty), the victor acquired title only to those lands ceded. A treaty, therefore, eliminated the possibility of sovereignty over or of title to the non-ceded territory of a defeated enemy.[21]

Both history and legal analysis show that the law of conquest had no effect whatsoever on Indian property rights. In fact, the United States has *never* (with one minor exception) claimed title to Indian land by right of conquest.[22] The United States chose instead to follow the lead of England, France, Spain, and the Netherlands; it made treaties of cession, even in those cases where Indian nations had been defeated in war. Even if the colonizing nations could have established the questionable proposition that their victories were the product of just wars—a proposition which the Marshall Court found essential to the conquest doctrine[23]—the historical fact remains that the European nations never annexed Indian lands.

The overwhelming majority of Indian treaties of cession were the result of peaceful negotiation and purchase. Many Indian nations and tribes never fought any battles with the United States. Moreover, in a number of cases where Indian treaties of cession followed warfare, the Indian nations had not in fact suffered military defeat, but had either won the war or achieved a stalemate. Such was the case, for example, of the Sioux in the the Treaty of Fort Laramie in 1868.

In *Johnson v. McIntosh* (1823), John Marshall expounded at length on the law of conquest.[24] His discussion has at times been cited as evidence that Indian land rights were indeed lawfully acquired by conquest. Yet Marshall concluded that the law of conquest "was incapable of application" to Indian nations.[25] Subsequent Marshall Court decisions emphasized that purchase, not conquest, was the source of United States title to lands acquired from Indian nations.

These early Supreme Court cases should have ended the legal debate over the law of conquest. But a particularly pernicious Supreme Court decision, *Tee-Hit-Ton Indians v. United States* (1955), rendered over a century after the Cherokee cases, revived the conquest rationale and generated new confusion in legal circles.[26] Indeed, the discussion of the conquest theory in *Tee-Hit-Ton Indians v. United States* ranks among the most uninformed ever made on Indian affairs by the Supreme Court:

> After conquest [Indians] were permitted to occupy portions of territory over which they had previously exercised "sovereignty," as we use the term. This is not a property right but amounts to a right of occupancy which the sovereign grants and protects against intrusion by third parties but which right of occupancy may be terminated and such lands fully disposed of by the sovereign itself without any legally enforceable obligation to compensate the Indians.

> Every American schoolboy knows that the savage tribes of this continent were deprived of their ancestral ranges by force and that, even when the Indians ceded millions of acres by treaty in return for blankets, food and trinkets, it was not a sale but the conquerers' will that deprived them of their land.[27]

The application of the conquest theory to the Tee-Hit-Ton Indians—Alaska natives who never fought a skirmish with either Russia or the United States—is particularly absurd. As one legal scholar noted, "The only sovereign act that can be said to have conquered the Alaska native was the *Tee-Hit-Ton* opinion itself."[28] The Marshall Court decisions are compelling authority that the United States has not acquired power over or title to Indian lands by right of conquest.

The Denigration of Indian Title to a
Mere Right of Occupancy

Marshall and other early Americans of property were most concerned that Indian property rights not detract from the security of white land titles. After all, as Marshall noted, "our whole country" has been "granted by the crown, while in the occupation of Indian."[29] The English Crown's policy of making such grants had been continued by the United States. Land grants were made as payment to Revolutionary War soldiers, and both John Marshall and his father received more than 10,000 acres as a result of their military services.[30] Marshall noted in a legal opinion that if Indian title was permitted to cloud the land titles which whites held under these grants, almost every white land title in New England, New York, New Jersey, Pennsylvania, Maryland and part of Carolina would be adversely affected.[31]

Marshall determined that the property rights of non-Indians must be made secure, even if it meant subverting settled legal doctrine and adopting what he termed an "extravagant pretension." This pretension required converting the right of discovery into actual land title, thereby fabricating a secure title for non-Indians to unceded lands still occupied by the original Indian owners. Marshall used the term "extravagant pretension" because the results he sought were dictated by political expediency, personal interest, and by what he perceived as the national interest. He created a theory to correspond to what had already occurred: the discovering European nation could hold or grant to others "absolute title" to lands still in the possession of the original Indian owners and prior to any conveyance or other acquisition of the Indian rights to the land.

Under this theory, Indians were regarded not as owners, as contemporary international law commanded, but "merely as occupants," although their right of occupancy was to be given full legal protection until ceded to the United States government. In the last of the Marshall Court decisions on Indian title, this Indian right of occupancy was characterized as "sacred as the fee simple" title held by white land owners,[32] although clearly of inferior status in the legal hierarchy of land titles. This new theory permitted the United States to claim, grant, or sell to others the ultimate or "underlying" fee to Indian-occupied lands. This fee was said to be subject to the Indian right of occupancy by which the Indian owners continued to live on the land without the express permission of the white fee holder or the United States. The Indian right of occupancy could be terminated only by the United States, and upon such termination or extinguishment of the Indian right, the white fee title was cleared of the encumbrance of Indian occupancy and was thereby perfected.

Marshall preserved one essential Indian right which was ignored in subsequent Supreme Court decisions. He held that the Indian's right of use and occupancy could be terminated only with the consent of the Indian inhabitants. Later courts soon disregarded this require-ment. In *Johnson v. McIntosh* (1823), Marshall candidly admitted that the new rule was designed outside the settled rules of law:

> If the property of the great mass of the [white] community origi-nates in it, it becomes the law of the land, and cannot be questioned . . . However this restriction [on the Indians] may be opposed to natural right, and to usages of civilized nations, yet, if it be indispensable to that system under which the country has been settled, and be adapted to the actual condition of the two people, it may, perhaps, be supported by reason, and certainly cannot be rejected by courts of justice.[33]

Although he deferred to political reality, Marshall revealed his qualms about elevating the land titles of whites to exclusive, fee simple status, a decision which commensurately denigrated the nature of the Indian title. Although Marshall's decision purported to protect the Indians' right of occupancy, it carried within it the seeds of destruction for Indian land rights, for it denied the cardinal tenet of ownership in law. Indian title was deemed imperfect and imperfectable, and could never acquire the absolute fee status which was and is the epitome of property rights under United States law. His decision served to rein-force the widely held view that Indian property rights were a mere impediment to the progress of a higher, white civilization.

Marshall's decision was political rather than legal, and visible within it was the contemporary imperial cant, racial prejudice, and "scientific" view of inevitable white ascendency over non-white peo-ples. Marshall's opinions are replete with references to "savages" and the non-productive nomadic use of the land—prejudices and historical inaccuracies which have long since been discredited.

In taking a middle road between total disregard and clear respect for Indian land rights, Marshall also signaled that some decisions made by the government concerning Indians could be treated by the Supreme Court as political questions not subject to judicial review. This rationale would be used time and again to deny the federal judiciary the power to check the abuse of Indian rights by Congress and the Executive.[34] While the political question doctrine is properly applied in many areas of government action, such as foreign relations, its application to Indian affairs, while perhaps not improper, has meant a broad denial of judicial protection.

Marshall had opened the way for the wholesale erosion of legal protection for Indian title. Some federal judges emphasized that Indian title was *merely* a right of occupancy. In 1955 the Supreme Court ruled that Indian title could be extinguished at the whim of the United States government, without due process of law and without any compensation.[35] In the 1960s Indian title was compared to a tenancy at will; Indians had rights only as tenants of the United States on Indian homelands occupied from time immemorial by Indians. In 1980, the Supreme Court gratuituously reaffirmed the idea that "the taking of the United States of 'unrecognized' or 'aboriginal' Indian title is not compensable under the Fifth Amendment."[36]

The result of this historical trend was coldly summarized by the Deputy Solicitor General of the United States who has been chiefly responsible for representing the government in Supreme Court cases involving Indian rights:

> According to *McIntosh*, it was always understood that legal title to tribal land belonged to the United States—which placed the tribes in a position of vassalage vis-a-vis the national sovereign.
>
> We may well doubt whether those who wrote the Constitution ever contemplated federal power unilaterally to dismember reservations, to transfer jurisdiction to the States, and to "terminate" tribes altogether. But we must accept that they did.[37]

As long as this view of unchecked federal power over Indian lands prevails, the fundamental rights of Indian nations will remain in jeopardy, and their land rights and land claims are likely to remain unresolved.

THE INDIAN TRUST RELATIONSHIP:
RACIAL DISCRIMINATION AND BOUNDLESS
UNITED STATES POWER
DISGUISED AS MORAL AND LEGAL DUTY

Under one theory of federal law, Indian nations and tribes are the permanent "wards" or "beneficiaries" of a "guardianship" or "trusteeship" administered by the United States government. Today this relationship is commonly referred to as the "Indian trust relationship." The trust theory is built upon the United States government's assertion that it holds "trust title" to virtually all Indian lands. The 1981 handbook of the United States Bureau of Indian Affairs recites the claim of official government trusteeship in characteristically altruistic language:

> By the authority vested in it through numerous treaties, congressional acts, court decisions and executive orders, the U.S. today holds in trust some 53 million acres for the benefit of and use by Indian tribes and individuals.[38]

Based on this assertion of trust title, the Bureau of Indian Affairs administers almost all Indian land and resources.

Treaties, however, have never made the United States a "trustee" of Indian lands. The typical treaty terminology that some argue created the Indian trust relationship provides only that Indians "acknowledge themselves to be under the protection of the United States," and only some of the hundreds of different Indian treaties contain such language.[39] There is virtually nothing in the history of the treaties to suggest that such language was intended to create general trusteeship. The United States is a self-appointed "trustee." Cases such as *Gila River Indian Community v. United States* (1970), in fact, require a specific admission of the trust responsibility by the United States in order for the trust relationship to involve binding federal responsibility.[40]

The Indian trust relationship is said to have first appeared in United States law in the Marshall Court's decisions. Chief Justice Marshall in *Cherokee Nation v. Georgia* (1831) that the relation of Indian nations to the United States "resembles that of a ward to his guardian."[41] In fairness to Marshall, his concept of guardianship had little in common with the Indian trust relationship that developed. The

Marshall Court referred only to a consensual guardianship with powers and duties limited by treaty and international law.

The Marshall Court made clear in *Worcester* that the Indian "guardianship" to which it referred was not like the paternalistic guardianship which applied to infants and mental incompetents but was rather an international compact in the nature of an international protectorate relationship or alliance:

> The Indian nations had always been considered as distinct, independent political communities, retaining their original natural rights, as the undisputed possessors of the soil, from time immemorial, with the single exception of that imposed by irresistible power, which excluded them from intercourse with any other European potentate than the first discoverer of the coast of the particular region claimed: and this was a restriction which those European potentates imposed on themselves, as well as on the Indians. The very term "nation," so generally applied to them, means "a people distinct from others." The constitution, by declaring treaties already made, as well as those to be made, to be the supreme law of the land, has adopted and sanctioned the previous treaties with the Indian nations, and consequently admits their rank among those powers who are capable of making treaties. The words "treaty" and "nation" are words of our own language, selected in our diplomatic and legislative proceedings, by ourselves, having each a definite and well-understood meaning. We have applied them to Indians, as we have applied them to the other nations of the earth. They are applied to all in the same sense.[42]

Although the Marshall Court characterized Indians as "domestic dependent nations" in a "state of pupilage,"[43] it explained that this characterization did nothing to deny Indian nations the sovereign rights to their Indian lands. Any legal dependency was held to arise solely out of the operation of specific treaties and international law. Nothing in the rulings of the Marshall Court even remotely suggested that the United States could unilaterally impose a guardian-ward relationship on Indians, that it held trust title to Indian lands, or that, as trustee, it could dispose of lands without Indian consent.

Unfortunately, the emphasis Marshall placed on "dependency," combined with his other disparaging comments about Indians (who, he believed, needed instruction in the ways of civilization), paved the way for the paternalistic trusteeship that soon gained prominence in

United States law. Marshall had not, in fact, accepted the argument made in *Johnson v. McIntosh* (1823) that Indians were "an inferior race of people under the perpetual protection and pupilage of the government."[44] But during the mid-nineteenth century the Supreme Court adopted the notion of a permanent trusteeship. This shift reveals an expectation that the "semi-barbarous" Indians would simply give way to a "higher civilization." The Supreme Court would write in 1877:

> The right which the Indians held was only that of occupancy. The fee was in the United States, subject to that right, and could be transferred by them whenever they chose . . . It is to be presumed that in this matter the United States would be governed by such considerations of justice as would control a Christian people in their treatment of an ignorant and dependent race. . . . The power of the United States to make such transfer has in no instance been denied. . . . Congress undoubtedly expected that at no distant day the State would be settled by white people, and the semi-barbarous condition of the Indian tribes would give place to the higher civilization of our race.[45]

As the military and economic power of the United States rapidly expanded during the middle decades of the nineteenth century, the U.S. courts began to treat Indians as infants and incompetents. Power to take unilateral action replaced the limited legal authority based on treaty agreements and international law. This revised view of the Indian guardianship reflected the racial prejudice and ethnocentric assumptions of that era: that white, European peoples constituted a superior race whose "civilized" religion and way of life must be emulated, and if possible, assimilated by the "lower races" of the world. During this period, the colonizing nations of Europe were also justifying their practices in Africa, Asia and elsewhere by claiming to be trustees. European imperial theorists had begun to view the non-white "natives" of the European empires as beneficiaries of a "trusteeship for civilization" whose lands, resources, and governmental affairs would be managed under "imperial tutelage."[46]

The United States increasingly relied on the role of trustee to justify the seizure of Indian lands. The General Allotment Act of 1887, for example, was designed by Congress to divest Indian nations of their land titles and to divide up all Indian lands into individually owned homesteads. The United States decided that "breaking up the tribal mass" would free Indians from the debilitating restraints of

Indian tribal society. Heads of Indian families would receive private title to allotments of 160 acres each. For a short period, these allotments would be free from taxation. Thereafter the property was taxable and subject to seizure for non-payment. All unallotted "surplus" Indian land would be sold by the United States to whites. This disposition was said to be "in the best interest of the Indians." Congress, as "trustee," intended to end communal ownership of Indian lands and to instruct Indians in the "competitive selfishness" they needed to thrive in white America.

As a result of the allotment policy, Indian nations and tribes lost two-thirds of their lands to whites. The language of trusteeship was used to justify this massive confiscation, which the law of the United States officially described as "cessions in trust." Fortunately, many Indians successfully resisted the various allotment efforts, retaining control over at least part of their lands until the allotment policy was formally repudiated by the Indian Reorganization Act of 1934.

The Indian trust relationship itself, however, has not been repudiated, and it has been used before and since to deny Indian rights. The power that this trusteeship gives to federal administrators was well described in a 1953 article by Felix Cohen, the most eminent scholar of Indian law:

> [T]he term [wardship] soon became a magic word in the mouths and proclamations of Indian agents and Indian Commissioners. Over the years, any order or command or sale or lease for which no justification could be found in any treaty or act of Congress came to be justified by such officials as an act of "guardianship," and every denial of civil, political, or economic rights to Indians came to be blamed on their alleged "wardship." Under the reign of these magic words nothing Indian was safe. The Indian's hair was cut, his dances forbidden, his oil lands, timber lands, and grazing lands were disposed of, by Indian agents and Indian Commissioners for whom the magic word "wardship" always made up for any lack of statutory authority. . . . The paternalistic attitude of Indian Bureau administrators during recent years has unfortunately served to buttress that illusion. But it remains an illusion, unsupported by legal authority.[47]

In his classic treatise on United States Indian law, Cohen concluded that Congress used its "wardship powers" as a "justification for federal legislation which would be considered 'confiscatory' if applied to non-Indians."[48] That is, it was a justification for theft.

The Indian trust concept was used in an especially perverted manner to justify the Indian termination policy of the 1950s. This policy forced the dissolution of a number of Indian nations and tribes, caused much hardship in the terminated Indian communities, and led to further loss of lands. The United States asserted that it had the legal power unilaterally to terminate its trust relationship, and by so doing to subject Indian lands and communities to both state taxation and state law. By the 1950s the United States had come to view the Indian trust relationship as a gift to Indians that served as the sole foundation of all Indian rights to self-determination and property. That gift, under the contemporary thinking, could be retracted at whim.

The trust doctrine still permeates federal Indian law today, and the United States continues to rely on the "Indian trust relationship" for broad, unfettered powers over Indian property and affairs. It is said to include the power to seize or sell land without Indian consent as well as the power to extinguish Indian land claims without compensation. "Trusteeship" has been used by the Bureau to justify intervening in internal tribal government and even to justify suspending tribal governments altogether. The authority of the trustee's chief agent, the Bureau of Indian Affairs, cannot be ignored, even in matters not directly related to the land. The Bureau of Indian Affairs and other federal agencies, in fact, have enormous power to control or influence Indian governments in regard to questions of jurisdiction, domestic relations, relations with state and local governments, commercial activity of all kinds, education of Indian children, religious ceremonies and practices, and practically every other aspect of reservation life.

In a few specific cases, Indian governments have expressly consented to placing land in trust with the United States, and in those instances trusteeship can hardly be doubted. But apart from these exceptions, the asserted trusteeship is without support in treaties, general international law, or domestic law.

Some have seen the Indian trust relationship as a source of legal responsibilities toward Indians. Beginning in the early 1970s, an intensive effort was made to urge the United States to declare the Indian trust relationship a legal basis from which Indians could challenge the United States' management of Indian resources, advance Indian land claims, secure federal funding for Indians, and protect the existence and jurisdiction of Indian governments.[49]

These efforts have not proven very successful. Indian rights advocates have been unable to secure the principle that the United States should be fully accountable as a fiduciary under the same strict standards which apply to all fiduciaries who manage the property of others. In 1980, the Supreme Court ruled that the only legally enforceable federal duties towards Indians are those expressly set forth in specific laws enacted by Congress.[50] In 1983, the Supreme Court expressly declared that when the United States as trustee represents Indians in a water rights case, and *also* represents conflicting interests in that same case, it is not bound by the traditional law of trusteeship requiring faithfulness to the interests of the "beneficiary." The Court left unclear just what obligation the "trustee" does owe to Indian "beneficiaries."[51]

These decisions echoed the position of the Attorney General of the United States (1979) that the United States has no fiduciary obligations to pursue Indian claims on behalf of Indian tribes unless those obligations are found "in specific statutes, treaties, and Executive Orders."[52] In sum, under United States law, the government has no legal trusteeship duties toward Indians except those it specifically imposes on itself. Stripped of its legal trappings, the Indian trust relationship becomes simply an assertion of unrestrained political power over Indians, power that may be exercised without Indian consent and without substantial legal restraint. An early twentieth century critic of the European colonial "trusteeship for civilization," which is closely related to the American model, summed it up as "an impudent act of self-assertion."[53]

CONTEMPORARY LAND ISSUES

Perhaps American settlers of every age have felt it their particular misfortune to be troubled by the problems of Indian land rights. Most if not all of the earliest colonial settlements were soon involved in violent conflicts with Indians over land. George Washington and his administration devoted a major part of their energy to negotiations, treaties, and military actions revolving around this issue, for land was the principal means by which the new nation hoped to pay for the costly revolution. As a source of potential conflict, it also presented the single greatest threat to national security.

The last century has been not unlike the one that preceded it. Although the growing military superiority of the United States has brought a virtual end to pitched battles over land, there has been no lessening of conflict. Increasingly, conflicts have been fought politically in Congress and elsewhere and legally in the courts. Physical conflict, however, still occurs, particularly in recent instances when Indians took occupation of claimed lands. The Mohawk occupation in the Mohawk Valley of New York in 1957, the occupation by Pitt River Indian peoples in California in the 1970s, the Mohawk repossession of Ganienkeh in the Adirondacks in 1974, and the encampment of Sioux people in the Black Hills in 1981, are but a few of the recent examples. Nor is this a phenomenon only of recent years; for well over 100 years the Seminoles in Florida have "squatted" on land which they claim and which they successfully fought to keep, but which non-Indians now claim to own.

In 1946 Congress established the Indian Claims Commission to settle all Indian land claims.[54] But the Commission, which went out of existence in 1978, failed to conclude many of its cases, all of which were filed by 1951. In fact, it generated a new round of claims and controversy, partly because the Commission interpreted its mandate to permit money awards only; no other relief could be given. The lawyers for the Indians never questioned that decision. After all, the act establishing the Commission provided that the lawyers receive as much as ten percent of any awards, which frequently ran into the millions of dollars. So powerful was this incentive that lawyers filed claims to recover money damages for land their clients still owned and occupied, as in the claim filed for the Florida Seminoles.[55]

Often the Indian clients did not know that their attorneys were making such claims.[56] In some cases the Indians sought to stop claims because the payment of an award would extinguish their right to the land.[57] Yet the Commission and the Court of Claims, which heard appeals from the Commission, steadfastly refused to permit claims to be amended or withdrawn to avoid this extinguishment. (The one notable exception was the case of the Blue Lake of the Taos Pueblo.)[58] The attorneys for the Western Shoshones in Nevada and California, for example, constantly encouraged their clients to believe that a claim would have no effect on their land rights. Yet some of the Shoshones were still living on the land in question, and all authorities agreed that no treaty with the federal government had ever transferred or extinguished the Indian right to the land. A federal court later held that the Western Shoshones indeed still possessed aboriginal title to the land in question, at least until payment of the award.[59] The federal Court of

Appeals for the Ninth Circuit agreed with this decision.[60] Efforts are still underway to gain recognition of the Western Shoshones' rights to their original lands in Nevada. The Bureau of Indian Affairs has not yet paid the money award, and the controversy continues.

The Western Shoshone case is by no means unique. Claims for land such as the Black Hills in South Dakota have continued unabated for over one hundred years. That claim commenced almost as soon as the United States had confiscated the 7.3 million-acre area from the Sioux Indians in 1877. For years the several Sioux bands met in councils to make plans for recovering the hills, but were hampered by extreme poverty, great distances, and a limited understanding of the English language and the processes of United States law. At last they retained an attorney who in 1923 filed the first formal claim. But at that time the Indians could sue the United States only for monetary damages, not for the restoration of land as most of the Sioux had wanted and expected. The case made its way slowly through the United States Court of Claims, where it was dismissed through procedural technicalities in 1942, and the decision was affirmed by the Supreme Court.[61]

Eventually the Black Hills case was filed before the Indian Claims Commission. The case continued until 1980, when the Supreme Court upheld the decision of the Commission (as modified by legislation to include payment of interest), and the Sioux Indians were awarded in excess of $117 million for their lands.[62] Yet because the claim was for money only, and because the Oglala Sioux (the largest of the Sioux bands) as well as most other Sioux bands have refused to accept money in place of their right to the land, the case has remained alive. New suits have been filed and more are planned, amid lobbying efforts to persuade Congress to return a portion of the hills. The treatment of Sioux rights to the Black Hills has been repeatedly brought to the attention of the United Nations Commission on Human Rights.

Indian land claims have hardly been limited to those by western tribes. In 1909, a parcel of land which belonged to the Oneida Nation, a part of the Six Nations Iroquois Confederacy in upstate New York, was lost through foreclosure on a mortgage illegally entered into by an Oneida individual. But the treaties made by the United States with the Six Nations[63] as well as the Federal Trade and Intercourse Act of 1790[64] made any conveyance of Indian land, including a foreclosure, illegal and void unless done by treaty and with the approval of the United States. The United States brought suit and recovered the land for the Oneidas, which sent a wave of concern through land owners and politicians throughout the state in 1919.[65] The case established the precedent that Indian land lost in violation of the Trade and Intercourse Act could be recovered by a lawsuit in the federal courts. A special commission was established by the New York legislature to study the problem, but its report was suppressed because its results supported Indian rights to recover lands.[66] Other Indians attempted to recover lands by bringing lawsuits, but it was not until 1974 that the Supreme Court decided that such claims could be brought by the Indians themselves in federal courts.[67]

Some Indian tribes were never informed of the establishment of the Indian Claims Commission, or refused to file their claims there. However, when they discovered that they could pursue legal actions to confirm their land titles, a considerable number of cases were filed in federal courts, particularly by Indians of the eastern United States. The governing councils of the Passamaquoddies and Penobscots of Maine were successful in resolving their land claims with the federal and state governments. A suit was filed in 1972 to seek a declaratory judgment concerning the applicability of the Federal Trade and Intercourse Act of 1790 to the Indians in Maine.[68] If the tribes came under the provisions of that statute, the subsequent loss of land would be illegal because no Indian land could be legally transferred to a third party without the presence and approval of an official representing the United States, and without a treaty ratified by the Senate or an act of Congress approving the transfer.

In 1975 the First Circuit Court of Appeals held in favor of the Maine tribes and set the stage for a negotiated settlement of their claim. Eventually, in 1980, Congress approved an agreement which provided for federal services to the tribes, a trust fund of $27 million, and a sum of $54,500,000 to purchase approximately 300,000 acres designated for tribal use under certain restrictions.[69]

In 1978 Congress enacted the Rhode Island Indian Claims Settlement Act, which confirmed an agreement reached among the federal government, the Narrangansetts, and the state of Rhode Island, which provided the tribe with an additional 900 acres.[70] Other tribes pursuing their claims have not been so fortunate, however, partly because Eastern courts tend to be unfamiliar with Indian law. The Mashpees of Cape Cod, for example, lost a jury decision involving the question of whether they were a political entity throughout their history—which effectively precluded them from proceeding with their land claim.[71]

The Alaskan Natives completely avoided the Indian Claims Commission. When the United States purchased Alaska from Russia in 1867, it promised to recognize the existing claims of the Natives. Over the years white settlement proceeded apace, but Native title was a subject studiously avoided by both Congress and the territorial governors. With the coming of statehood in 1958, the question of Native claims became unavoidable; the clash between the interests of the federal government and the new state grew pronounced. In 1968, as he was leaving office, Secretary of the Interior Stewart Udall placed a freeze on all land selections that could be made by the new state under its enabling act until the question was resolved.

Incoming Secretary of the Interior Walter Hickel, former governor of Alaska, was expected to remove the freeze and allow the state to claim its land prior to any resolution of the Native claims. But Hickel continued the freeze, and his refusal to show preference motivated both the Natives and the state officials to seek an agreement. Legislation was introduced in several Congresses, but the first offers made by the federal government were extremely restrictive, offering little of advantage for the Natives. The discovery of oil at Prudhoe Bay in the late 1960s spurred Congress to action. The proposed pipeline to southern Alaskan ports could not be started until the oil companies were certain they would not be blocked by Native land claims. In 1971 Congress passed the Alaska Native Claims Settlement Act which provided the Natives with the right to select 40 million acres of land.[72] The act provided for the establishment of 13 Native corporations with smaller village corporations representing the various Native settlements. These corporations, regional and local, were to share $462,500,000 over an eleven-year period (paid by the federal government), and an additional $500 million which would accrue to the Natives from mineral royalties. Because of the complexities of the Alaska situation, the legislation necessarily led to the reorganization of Native social and cultural patterns; it also provided for modern business organizations and devices to ensure that the money would go to its intended recipients. Today, a decade later, there are many complaints about the use of the corporate form to distribute claims moneys, and considerable rethinking by the Natives of their role in Alaska's future. The massive amount of land involved, however—a total of 365 million acres—was a major reason for the unwillingness of Congress to frame a more suitable solution.

The religious character of the land and the fundamentally different concept of land tenure of many Indian people has played a determining part in many of the unresolved conflicts. It partly explains the phenomenal tenacity of Indian peoples in their land claims, and it certainly lies at the root of the conflicts between the Indian and non-Indian worlds. Western civilization has tended to regard land as an important economic resource which may be bought and sold, whereas Indians commonly regard land as a sacred gift of the Creator to be held in common for both present and future generations. The concept of exclusive individual ownership is sometimes entirely absent among Indians, and even today some Indian peoples regard it as fundamentally wrong to "own" land—much as every civilization now regards it wrong to own another human being.

Traditional Hopi leaders expressed this sentiment in an eloquent 1971 statement issued to protest the "sale" of their land through Indian Claims Commission proceedings and the strip-mining of their land:

> This land was granted to the Hopi by a power greater than man can explain. Title is invested in the whole makeup of Hopi life. Everything is dependent on it. The land is sacred and if the land is abused, the sacredness of Hopi life will disappear and all other life as well.
>
> To us, it is unthinkable to give up control over our sacred lands to non-Hopis. We have no way to express exchange of sacred lands for money. It is alien to our ways. The Hopis never gave authority and never will give authority to anyone to dispose of our lands and heritage and religion for any price. We received these lands from the Great Spirit and we must hold them for him, as a steward, a caretaker, until he returns.[73]

This spiritual attachment to the land is apparent in most if not all contemporary claims, and helps to explain their extraordinary longevity in the face of legal theories and technicalities that barred tribes from recourse in the courts for generations.

CONCLUSION

Conflicts over Indian land rights have been part of United States history from its beginning. They have not changed significantly in that time, largely because this nation has neither dealt with them justly nor established an equitable process for their resolution. And so the conflicts continue.

It is frequently said today that the United States government has "plenary power" over Indian lands and affairs, a term which has come to mean virtually absolute, legally unfettered power. In fact, there has been little advance in federal Indian law since 1903, the heyday of Teddy Roosevelt's jingoism, when the Supreme Court ruled in *Lone Wolf v. Hitchcock* that Congress had the unrestrained power to abrogate Indian treaties, "paramount power over the property of the Indians by reason of its exercise of guardianship over their interests, and that such authority might be implied, even though opposed to the strict letter of a treaty with the Indians."[74]

The failure to resolve Indian land conflicts has its origin in the courts. The Marshall Court was particularly responsible for bypassing the settled rules of law in order to fabricate a new "rule," under which Indian land rights dwindled into mere rights of occupancy, subject to extinguishment by the federal government. This capitulation of the federal courts to political expediency became the usual judicial response to violations of Indian land rights by the United States. The political question doctrine has been the mechanism most frequently employed to deny legal protection to Indian land rights. Likewise, the federal trust relationship, with its claim to judicially unrestricted federal political powers over Indian lands and resources, has denied Indians legal resources while shielding the federal government from legal accountability.

Each of these disabling legal doctrines stems from the colonialist theory and racial discrimination of the nineteenth century. At root is the belief that Indian peoples, their property and affairs, are properly subject to the control of a superior white civilization. Marshall unabashedly cited the colonial law and practices of Spain, Portugal, France, Holland, and England as legal precedents.[75] The premise of Indian racial inferiority is sometimes only implicit, but it is always the underlying justification for involuntarily subjecting a dependent people to the tutelage or trusteeship of another race.

Reforming this body of law is essential if we are ever to resolve Indian land issues. There is reason for hope. The vast body of constitutional law, particularly in the fields of civil rights and due process, provides ample authority for the needed change. Universally recognized principles of human rights suggest that Indian peoples must attain a level of legal protection equal to that of other races. Establishing this basic proposition in United States law will be no easy task, but recent far-reaching reforms, in a broad range of basic human rights offer us grounds for optimism.

N O T E S

1. Art. 3, Act of Aug. 7, 1789, 1 Stat. 50.
2. See, for example, C. Wilkinson and J. Volkman, "Judicial Review of Indian Treaty Abrogation: 'As Long As Water Flows, or Grass Grows Upon the Earth'—How Long a Time is That?" *California Law Review* 63, no. 70 (1975): 601, 616.
3. *Worcester v. Georgia*, 31 U.S. 515 (1832).
4. *Olmstead v. United States*, 277 U.S. 438 (1928), p. 479.
5. *Santa Clara Pueblo v. Martinez*, 436 U.S. 49 (1978).
6. *Merrion v. Jicarilla Apache Tribe*, 455 U.S. 130 (1982).
7. *Fletcher v. Peck*, 10 U.S. 87 (1810).
8. *Johnson v. McIntosh*, 21 U.S. 543 (1822).
9. *Cherokee Nation v. Georgia*, 30 U.S. 1 (1831).
10. *Worcester*.
11. *Mitchel v. United States*, 34 U.S. 711 (1835).
12. D. M. Roper, "In Quest of Judicial Objectivity: The Marshall Court and the Legitimization of Slavery," *Stanford Law Review* 21 (1969): 532.
13. L. Baker, *John Marshall: A Life in Law* (New York: MacMillan Pub. Co., 1974), pp. 79–80; McIntosh, p. 583.
14. F. Victoria, *De Indis et De Jure Belli Relectiones*, J. Bate, trans. (Washington, D.C.: Carnegie Institution, 1917; original ed. 1557), Sec. 1, title 24; M.D. Vattel, *The Law of Nations* (Philadelphia: T. & J. W. Johnson Pub., 1855), American ed., pp. 160–161; F. Cohen, *Handbook of Federal Indian Law* (Washington, D.C.: U.S. Gov't. Printing Office, 1942), pp. 46–47.
15. L. Oppenheim, "Peace," *International Law*, vol. 1 (London: Longmans, Green & Co., 1955), pp. 558–9.
16. *McIntosh*, p. 572.
17. *Worcester*, pp. 544–545.
18. See, for example, *Martin v. Waddell*, 41 U.S. 367 (1842).
19. *Oneida Nation of Wisconsin et al. v. New York State et al.*, 691 F.2d. 1070 (2nd Cir. 1982).
20. Oppenheim, "Peace," pp. 566–567.
21. Oppenheim, "Peace," pp. 566–567.

22. C. Thomas, "Introduction," *Indian Land Cessions in the United States*, 18th Annual report of the Bureau of American Ethnology, pt. 2 (1897), p. 640.

23. *Worcester*, p. 546.

24. *McIntosh*, pp. 590–591.

25. *McIntosh*, p. 591.

26. *Tee-Hit-Ton Indians v. United States*, 348 U.S. 272 (1955).

27. *Id*. at 289–290.

28. N. Newton, "At the Whim of the Sovereign: Aboriginal Title Reconsidered" *Hastings Law Journal* 13 (1980), p. 1244.

29. *McIntosh*, p. 579.

30. Baker, *John Marshall*, p. 80.

31. *McIntosh*, p. 579.

32. *Mitchel v. United States*; see also *Cherokee Nation v. Georgia* (J. Baldwin concurring).

33. *McIntosh*, p. 590.

34. R. Coulter, "The Denial of Legal Remedies to Indian Nations under U.S. Law," *American Indian Journal* 3, no. 9 (Sept. 1977): 5.

35. *Tee-Hit-Ton Indians v. United States*, 348 U.S. 272 (1955).

36. *Sioux Nation of Indians v. United States*, 448 U.S. 371 (1980).

37. Louis R. Claiborn, "The Trend of Supreme Court Decisions in Indian Cases," unpublished, National Indian Law Library, Boulder, Col. (n.d., circa 1980).

38. Department of the Interior, *BIA Profile: The Bureau of Indian Affairs and American Indians* (Washington, D.C.: U.S. Gov't. Printing Office, 1981), p. 7.

39. See, for example, Wilkinson and Volkman, " 'As Long As Water Flows.' "

40. *Gila River Indian Community v. United States*, 427 F.2nd 1194, *cert. denied*, 400 U.S. 819 (1970).

41. *Cherokee Nation*, pp. 17–18.

42. *Worcester*, p. 559.

43. *Cherokee Nation*, p. 17.

44. *McIntosh*, p. 567.

45. *Beecher v. Weatherby*, 95 U.S. 517 (1877), pp. 525–526.

46. P. Curtin, *Imperialism* (New York: Walker, 1972), p. xxiii.

47. F. Cohen, "Indian Wardship: Twilight of a Myth," *The American Indian* 4 (1953), p. 331.

48. Cohen, *Handbook of Federal Indian Law*, p. 170.

49. See, for example, R. Chambers, "Judicial Enforcement of the Federal Trust Responsibility to Indians," *Stanford Law Review* 27 (1975), p. 1213.

50. *United States v. Mitchell*, 445 U.S. 535 (1980).

51. *Nevada v. United States*, 103 S.Ct. 2906 (1983).

52. "Statement of Attorney General Griffin B. Bell to Secretary of the Interior Cecil B. Andrus, May 31, 1979," *Indian Law Reporter 6,* p. M–19.

53. J. A. Hobson, *Imperialism, A Study* (Ann Arbor: University of Michigan Press, 1965), p. 240.

54. Act of Aug. 13, 1946, 60 Stat. 1049.

55. "Report to Congress: Seminole Land Rights in Florida and the Award of the Indian Claims Commission" in *Distribution of Seminole Judgement Funds,* Indian Law Resource Center; Hearings before the U.S. Senate Select Committee on Indian Affairs, 95th Cong. 2d sess. (March 2, 1978).

56. See, for example, *Pueblo of Santo Domingo v. United States,* 647 F.2d. 1087 (Ct. Cls. 1981).

57. 25 U.S.C. 70u.

58. *Western Shoshone Identifiable Group, Represented by the Temoak Bands of Western Shoshone Indians, Nevada v. United States,* Docket 326-K in the U.S. Court of Claims; "Memorandum of the Duckwater Shoshone Tribe, the Battle Mountain Indian Community and the Western Shoshone Sacred Lands Association in Opposition to the Motion and Petition for Attorney's Fees and Expenses" (July 15, 1980).

59. *United States v. Dann,* U.S. District Court for the District of Nevada, Civ. no. R-74-BRT.

60. *United States v. Dann,* 706 F.2d 919 (9th Cir. 1983).

61. *Sioux Tribe v. United States,* 316 U.S. 317 (1942).

62. *United States v. Sioux Nation,* 448 U.S. 371 (1980).

63. Treaty of Fort Stanwix, 7 Stat. 15 (1784); Treaty of Canandaigua, 7 Stat. 44 (1794).

64. See 25 U.S.C. 177.

65. *United States v. Boylan,* 265 F. 165 (2nd Cir. 1920) affirming, 256 F. 468 (N.D., N.Y. 1919).

66. Laws of New York, Ch. 590 (May 12, 1919); H. Upton, *The Everett Commission in Historical Perspectives: The Indians of New York* (Albany, N.Y.: New York State American Revolution Bicentennial Commission, 1980), p. 102ff.

67. *Oneida Indian Nation v. County of Oneida,* 414 U.S. 661 (1974).

68. *The Joint Tribal Council of the Passamaquoddy Tribe v. Rogers C. B. Morton et al.,* 528 F. 2nd 370 (1975).

69. Maine Indian Land Claims Settlement Act of 1980, 94 Stat. 1785.

70. Rhode Island Indian Claims Settlement Act of 1978, 92 Stat. 813.

71. *Mashpee Tribe v. New Seabury Corp.,* 427 F. Supp. 899 (D. Mass., 1977), aff'd. 592 F. 2nd 575, *cert. denied,* 444 U.S. 866 (1979).

72. Alaska Native Claims Settlement Act, 85 Stat. 688 (1971).

73. Quoted in *Report to the Hopi Kikmongwis and Other Traditional Hopi Leaders*, Indian Law Resource Center (Washington, D.C.: 1979), pp. 162–163.
74. *Lone Wolf v. Hitchcock*, 187 U.S. 553 (1903).
75. *McIntosh*, p. 574.

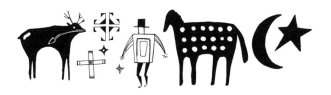

LONE WOLF
V. HITCHCOCK:
THE LONG SHADOW

A NN L A Q U E R E S T I N

*W*hen Commissioner of Indian Affairs J. D. C. Atkins arrived at the Kiowa, Comanche, and Kiowa-Apache reservation during the winter of 1886–1887, his purpose was to enlist Indian support for the allotment acts pending in Congress. Sponsored by Senator Henry L. Dawes and other reform-minded congressmen and organizations, the acts were intended to divide tribal lands into small homestead-sized farming tracts and distribute them to the Indians. The reformers believed that the ownership of their own lands would transform the Indians into a modern agricultural people, separate from their tribal past.

Instead of gaining enthusiastic Indian support, Commissioner Atkins encountered the "determined opposition" of the southern plains tribes; his visit in fact spurred the Indian leaders into action. Defying efforts by the local agent to keep them on their reservation, Lone Wolf of the Kiowas and Chief Jake of the Caddos traveled by train to Washington to fight the proposed legislation.[1] Lone Wolf and Chief Jake arrived too late; the General Allotment Act had been passed on February 8, 1887.[2] The two Indians demanded to see Commissioner Atkins, and then returned home to Indian territory to rally the tribes against the policy.

For Lone Wolf, called Guipagho by the Kiowa, the fruitless trip to Washington marked the start of a long fight to protect his tribe's land and community. His unrelenting efforts won him the enmity of a succession of Indian agents and commissioners, but he persisted for more than fifteen years against increasingly impossible odds. Lone Wolf's final defeat came at the hands of the Supreme Court in *Lone Wolf v. Hitchcock* (1903), his suit to enjoin the allotment of the tribe's reservation.

The Kiowa, Comanche, and Apache reservation has long since disappeared into Oklahoma history, but the Court's decision in *Lone Wolf v. Hitchcock* has remained a cornerstone of federal Indian law. The case is still cited frequently for its principal holding: that Congress has plenary power to abrogate the terms of Indian treaties. As a legal doctrine, the plenary power rule has prevented the courts from reviewing federal Indian legislation, effectively leaving the tribes at the mercy of shifting congressional moods and majorities. Although based on the idea that Congress acts as a guardian for the nation's dependent Indian wards, the rule's function is to facilitate continued congressional appropriation of tribal lands and resources.

Both in Congress and before the Supreme Court, the Kiowas were assisted in their efforts by the Indian Rights Association. Despite its firm support for the goals of allotment policy, the Association insisted that tribal consent was essential whenever Congress tried to modify the terms of Indian treaties; it believed that a great injustice had been done the Kiowas. It was also clear to the Association (after several decades of involvement in Indian policy) that Congress could not be trusted to consider fairly the interest of Indian communities. After the Court's ruling, the Association editorialized:

> It is now distinctly understood that Congress has a right to do as it pleases; that it is under no obligation to respect any treaty, for Indians have no rights which command respect. What is to be hoped for by an appeal to Congress can readily be anticipated by the history of the legislation by which Lone Wolf and his tribe have been deprived of that which had by express treaty stipulation apparently been secured to them.[3]

NEGOTIATING ALLOTMENT: THE JEROME AGREEMENT

On the arrival of the Cherokee Commission at Fort Sill in 1892, allotment became an unavoidable issue with the Kiowa, Comanche, and Apache reservation. Led by David H. Jerome, the three-man panel was established by Congress in 1889 to travel through Indian Territory and convince the tribes to agree to terms for allotment of their lands and sale of the "surplus" remaining after allotment.

Conditions for these Indian people had changed dramatically since the previous round of federal treaty-making a generation earlier. For the Kiowas and Comanches, the 1867 treaty of Medicine Lodge Creek was still in effect, with annuity payments due until 1898. Article XII of the treaty provided that any further cessions of tribal land required the signatures of "at least three-fourths of all the adult male Indians occupying the same."[4] Collecting these signatures on the proposed allotment agreements was the primary task of the commission.

Commissioner David H. Jerome addressed the Kiowa, Comanche, and Apache in council at Fort Sill. He began with a description of the changes in Indian Territory during the twenty-four years since the Medicine Lodge Treaty: the disappearance of the buffalo and other game from the southern plains, growing dependence on government rations, and significantly, a doubling in the region's white population while the three tribes had not increased in number. Jerome then presented allotment as the means of alleviating the hardships of the past decades.

> If the Indians will do what the Great Father wants them to do, and do their part well, it will result in your having plenty of food and clothing; and instead of having, as you sometimes do, only one meal a day, you will have three meals a day and have plenty of clothing and things that will make you comfortable through the winter. Instead of having to wait for an issue of beef every two weeks, you can go out and kill a beef of your own and have a feast every day if you please. I told you a little while ago that for twenty-four years the Indians had increased very little if any in numbers. Now, if you follow the plan that we have told you about you will not have your babies die from the cold, but you will have them grow up good, strong, healthy men and women, instead of putting them in the ground.[5]

Jerome's cynical reliance on this sort of appeal reflected the increasingly desperate situation of the Plains tribes. During the early reservation years, the Indians had been able to supplement their treaty annuity income and the unreliable government rations with hunting (and periodic raids on Texas ranches). Within a decade of the Medicine Lodge Treaty, however, their subsistence economy had been destroyed, and the tribes were kept under tight control by the Indian agents and military at Fort Sill.[6] For Lone Wolf, who had only recently come to leadership, the contrast with the Kiowas' former life was particularly sharp. His foster father, also called Lone Wolf, had been a renowned fighter and raider and the principal chief of the Kiowas during their last years of relative freedom.[7] Originally called Mamayday-te, the younger Lone Wolf was himself an experienced fighter, and had been a childhood friend of Lone Wolf's son. At the time of the

Kiowas' last military resistance, Mamay-day-te was given the name of Guipagho, or "Lone Wolf."[8] By 1892, the new Lone Wolf was well established as principal chief of the Kiowas, representing the people of the reservation with Quanah Parker, a savvy Comanche half-blood, and White Man, a Kiowa Apache.

Disarmed and dismounted, the three tribes faced this fresh assault from the United States government with a new sort of courage. With their tribal autonomy and independence at a nadir, the tribes turned to their treaty, negotiated at Medicine Lodge Creek in 1867, to define their relationship with the federal government. An old Comanche named Howear, who had been present at the treaty council, presented a copy of the document to the commissioners before the negotiations began.

When the Indians were given an opportunity to speak during the second day of the council, the chiefs and headmen of the three tribes rose in turn to speak about the Medicine Lodge Treaty. Although the Indians who spoke called the "white man's road" a good one to travel, the almost unanimous view was that the tribes wished to wait another four years, until the annuity provisions of the treaty expired, before considering a new deal.

What terms the commissioners were prepared to offer was not made clear until the middle of the second session. With prodding from Quanah Parker, Commissioner Jerome presented a proposal to give every member of the three tribes a 160-acre allotment and to pay $2 million for the surplus land remaining after allotment. Jerome refused to estimate a cost per acre, but his report to the President later put the reservation land base at 2,968,893 acres, with only an estimated 453,000 required for the Indian allotments. Of the 2.5 million acres remaining, Jerome considered 350,000 barren and worthless, which left 2,150,000 acres of "surplus" for white settlement. The quoted price, however, was all the tribes would be paid for their reservation.[9]

Jerome was glib about how much $2 million would mean per Indian.

> That $665 would buy . . . 25 fat steers . . . 30 good ponies; it would buy enough blankets and ribbons and pretty things to bury all the Indians on the reservation under. That sum of money will build more houses, dig more wells, and plant more orchards, and build more fences than these Indians will use in forty years. This money that we propose to pay you is so much that the Indians would not want it all at one time if they could get it, for they would not know what to do with it.[10]

Because it was so much money, Jerome explained, only a quarter of it would be distributed among the Indians; the rest would be kept in the United States Treasury to generate five percent interest, or an estimated $75,000 per year to pay an estimated $25 per capita.

After Jerome presented the offer, Commissioner Warren Sayre made certain that the Indians assembled in council understood the iron fist in the velvet glove: he claimed that under the Dawes Act the President could order tribes to take allotments whether they wanted to or not. Sayre admitted that the President had not made such an order for the Kiowa, Comanche, and Apache reservation, and might never do so, but he cited the examples of other tribes: "The Shawnees, Pottawatomies, Tonkawas, the Pawnees, the Otoes, the Missourias, and Poncas have been required to take allotments of land whether they desired to or not."[11]

Despite their desperate condition and the strong inducements offered by the commissioners, the three tribes decided in a council held before the third day's session to keep their treaty land. Although willing to move in the direction which Jerome was urging, Lone Wolf and the others foresaw that allotment could not be forced on their people without disastrous results. At the start of the third day of meetings, Lone Wolf addressed the three commissioners and made the tribes' position clear.

> Look on Quanna's people, they are Indians; look on Lone Wolf's people and Whiteman's people, they are Indians; they are not educated, they do not know how to till the ground. They do not know how to work. Should they be forced to take allotments it means sudden downfall for the three tribes. . . . If each of us were given 160 acres we would not be able to work it like white people—a white man is taught from his youth up to work, we are not—and instead of this 160 acres being a blessing it will be disastrous.[12]

Lone Wolf was concerned that his people were not yet farmers, but he also identified a threat from the non-Indians who would come onto the reservation lands after allotment.

> Very few of our young men and women are educated or partially educated. Here is Joshua Givvens, myself, Quanna Parker, and a few others, you can talk to them and they will answer you in English. Look at them; the rest are not dressed as well as they are. When the worst comes, they will be the only ones that will be able to cope with the white man when he comes to this country. The rest will not know what to do.[13]

With the other members of the three tribes, Lone Wolf knew that the ultimate danger was the loss of their last remaining tribal lands and their identity as a people.

Lone Wolf's pleadings were not intended to turn back the clock or attempt to avoid change. The Kiowa chief agreed that the road set out by the Medicine Lodge Treaty "is about the best that we can travel." He described the "good advice" he had received in Washington and the progress the tribes were making in building schools and houses, concluding: "For that reason, because we are making such rapid progress, we ask the commission not to push us ahead too fast on the road we are to take."[14]

But the Indians had serious reasons for questioning the benefits to be obtained by accepting the commissioner's offer. Two Kiowas, Big Tree and Iseeo, spoke about the experience of the nearby Cheyenne-Arapahoe after allotment. Big Tree stated that

> A year ago this commission came to the Cheyenne and Arapahoe Indians; they talked to those Indians very good. These Indians came to the Kiowa and Comanche Reservation; we saw tears in their eyes; we saw they had nothing to their name.
>
> They are poor; they will be poor in the future; they had made a mistake in selling their country; that money was given to them but it was all gone.[15]

Iseeo, a young Kiowa sergeant in the U.S. Cavalry, rose to speak to the commissioners at the request of the chiefs. He apologized for his short hair and uniform, for not being a chief or a wise man, and for belonging both to the United States and the Kiowa tribe, but he spoke eloquently about the Cheyenne's experience.

> [I]t is only a few months ago that the Cheyennes came to this military reservation and brought their wagons and fancy shawls, velvet blankets, and carriages, and told us that the money that the Great Father had given them was all gone—that the money they got was invested in these things. Now the wagons are old, being used very hard, and the velvet shawls will be worn out. . . .
>
> In a few years these Cheyenne Indians will be the poorest Indians, and they will be coming all the time for ponies. Look at them today, surrounded by white men; they will get the Indians drunk and get his money; they will make him sign a contract to get anything that the Cheyenne has got, and the Cheyenne's life in the next three years will be worse than when he was an Indian; so that is why we say wait three years till we get some place picked out and some better way to get along in life. . . .

> Mother earth is something that we Indians love. The Great
> Father in Washington told us that this reservation was ours; that
> we would not be disturbed; that this place was for our use, and
> when you told us the purpose of the Government it made us
> uneasy. We do not know what to do about selling our mother to
> the Government. That makes us scared.[16]

Quanah Parker, who had grown rich from his own farm and from
dealings with Texas cattlemen, asked pointed questions about the
business aspects of the deal: "How much will be paid for one acre,
what the terms will be, and when it will be paid." He also noted that
Congress had not appropriated any money for the settlement, and
accused the commissioners of wanting to buy the land with "mouth
shoot." Quanah pointed out that the prices paid other tribes had
ranged from 50 cents to $1.25 per acre, and later in the council he
objected that the tribes would not be paid for the two sections in every
township reserved for schoolhouses, saying "I do not see where it is
any benefit to us." Quanah also commented that the Commission had
described the part of the reservation with rocks and hills as "worth-
less," and asked who would own any iron, silver, gold or coal which
might be found there.[17]

One of the Kiowas, named Komalty or Big Head, indicated that
the tribes were not fooled by the rosy picture Jerome had painted.

> We have listened to all the talk that the commission has made, and
> it will make a man rich to listen to it. It is deceiving. If we should
> agree to sign the contract, and each one take 160 acres, you must
> remember that we have horses and cattle; these will in a few years
> die of starvation. We have no machines to put up hay. Your talk is
> good, but that will be the case.[18]

Given the tribes' overwhelming opposition to the selling of the
reservation, it is surprising how quickly the Cherokee Commission
completed its task. In his study of the reservation during this period,
William T. Hagan attributes the Commission's success to smooth
dealing and the influence of Quanah Parker. By the time the commissioners reached this reservation, they had already struck similar agreements with numerous other tribes; they had learned to manipulate
local politics to build support for the government's deal. Hagan credits
Quanah with having been "architect of the Comanche surrender to the
Cherokee Commission," and asserts that without his support "there is
no way enough signatures could have been obtained."[19]

Throughout the proceedings, Quanah was the most frequent

speaker and most aggressive negotiator. On the fourth day of the meetings, Quanah broke the impasse with an announcement that he had sent for a lawyer and proposed that a representative of each tribe meet with the lawyer and the commissioners to examine the proposed agreement. Quanah also requested that once the tribes understood the agreement the commissioners adjourn for two months to let the tribes consider.[20]

Without agreeing to Quanah's plan, Jerome set a time the following morning to meet with the representatives and the lawyer. Several days later, the council reconvened; it was announced that the lawyer was unable to help the tribes at this point, and Quanah offered a compromise proposal: that the differences between the tribes and the Commission be resolved directly with Congress by a delegation from the tribes. Quanah thought the tribes should be paid a half million dollars more than the commissioners had offered, and asked the Commission to present both figures to Congress.[21]

Quanah got Lone Wolf and White Man to support his proposal, and the three commissioners announced the following day that they would accept Quanah's proposal. Despite this assurance, the document Jerome prepared for signatures was little different than the terms he had originally offered. The agreement as drafted and signed included the original $2 million figure, and gave the tribes only "an opportunity to be heard" in Congress for the balance. There was no provision included to delay implementation; Jerome and Sayre had argued that no such clause was necessary because it would take a few years for Congress to ratify the agreement.[22]

After reviewing the terms of his new draft, Jerome made it clear that he would no longer tolerate opposition. The commissioners raised a final question: which non-Indian people should be "adopted" into tribes as beneficiaries of the agreement? The commissioner's request for a list of non-Indian allotees was a useful device to generate more support for the agreement. The final list totalled twenty-five and included white "squaw men" as well as two of the interpreters for the Commission, and the wife of a third; Quanah's sharecropper; his son-in-law; Agent George Day; Lieutenant Hugh Scott, commander of the Indian cavalry at Fort Sill; and a Methodist minister who had lived five years on the reservation. Not all the Indians agreed that including non-Indians was a good idea; Tohauson, a Kiowa, said that all of "these white men here that are married into the tribe, are bad characters, and for that reason I am opposed to adopting them."[23]

With the support of three principal chiefs and the important non-Indians on the reservation, the commissioners were able to secure most of the signatures they needed. For two reasons the signers were primarily Comanches: Quanah Parker's considerable influence among the Comanches,[24] and the fact that the council at Fort Sill lay in the Comanche section of the reservation. There were many more Comanches at the meetings, most of the Kiowas remaining further north near Anadarko.

Lone Wolf, Big Tree, Komalty, and Iseeo, all Kiowas, had each signed the agreement, based apparently on their understanding that the commissioners had incorporated Quanah's proposals. When Jerome pressed the Kiowa members of the Fort Sill calvary troop to sign, however, they told him politely that they would wait for the rest of the Kiowas to act. Following an invitation from the headmen, the commissioners decided to move the talks to the agency at Anadarko to try to convince the Kiowas to sign.[25]

Before the commissioners left Fort Sill, they were already fighting rumors of foul play. Jerome denied that the commission had tried to coerce and "bull-doze" Indians into signing, or that the interpreters had been promised special favors or benefits and were therefore not translating properly. Lieutenant Scott said he had heard that threats were being made, and disclaiming his own interest in the agreement, promised that if any Indians took action against those who had signed, "they would feel the power of the law."[26]

At Anadarko, the commissioners heard the same arguments again: the Kiowas overwhelmingly chose to travel on the "old road" of the Medicine Lodge Treaty. A whole series of Kiowa speakers tried in vain to explain the Indians' position to the commission: Apiatan, Satakeah, Qualo, Amotah, Chatlekaungky, Flying Crow, Big Bow, and Little Robe.[27] The rumors that had spread at Fort Sill persisted in Anadarko, and although Jerome made several efforts to dispel them, the situation quickly grew tense.

At the start of the second session, the commission acknowledged the Kiowas' demand for a new interpreter. Jerome insisted that Joshua Givens, himself a Kiowa, remain at his post, but agreed to swear in additional interpreters "to sit by and listen and see that Joshua does right." Next, Big Tree, who had signed the document at Fort Sill, demanded to see the written contract, but Jerome refused.[28]

Another confrontation between Jerome and Big Tree virtually ended the discussion at the final session in Anadarko. Big Tree insisted that the Indians understood the proposal and wanted to respond, but Jerome had evidently lost patience.

Now I want to tell Big Tree also that the Government is the Great Father of the Indians and the white men also, and when the government wants to do anything it sends its commissioners out to tell the Indians or white men what it wants done. It is the Government that must regulate these things; nobody else can.

For his part, Big Tree was equally adamant:

I understood all that you have to say to the Indians. I listened and listened time and again until the words go through the other ear, and still you talk and talk and talk. Now you sit down and let us talk a little time.

The argument continued, Big Tree insisting:

I told you to sit down. You told the Indians on Saturday that Monday would be the day to talk, and now my ears are stuffed with the words of the commission.

A few moments later, Apiatan voiced the persisting suspicions of the Kiowas:

When the President of the United States sent you here did he instruct you to talk to these Indians about the sale of the surplus lands alone and the allotment business, and did he tell you also, outside the general council, to get signers in a dishonest way?

Jerome was outraged, and responded: "Let the council stop right here; I will not be talked to that way. . . . You can go home, all of you, and do not come back here."[29]

Except for a handful of Comanches, the Indians left in an uproar, and the last session closed with some moralizing by Jerome and Agent Day. Although Jerome had collected 456 signatures on his "agreement," he left the reservation deeply divided and mistrustful. During the debacle at Anadarko, the Indians were already meeting in council to find a way to stop the agreement. Gathered at the Methodist Church, the tribes drafted a memorial protesting the procedures and interpreters used by the commission and charging fraud and misrepresentation.[30]

Although Lone Wolf was among the Kiowas who had initially agreed to sign, he reverted to opposition almost immediately. Before the commissioners left the reservation, Lone Wolf paid them a visit with a group of other signers. The Indians suspected that they had been deceived by incorrect translation of the terms of the agreement. Their request to see the document was denied, as was their request to have their names erased.[31]

When they left the reservation, Jerome and his colleagues had collected 456 signatures. This was well over three-fourths of the adult male population as certified by Agent George Day. Day's count, totalling 562 eligible signers, accompanied the text of the Jerome agreement to Congress, but it was later refuted by evidence from the Interior Department that the correct number of adult Indian men was between 631 and 725.[32]

During the decade after the Jerome negotiations, the Kiowa, Comanche, and Apache reservation was tangled in factional disputes that involved the agents, cattlemen, and a series of other outsiders. The tribes were divided as well, the Comanches split between Quanah and Eschiti, and the Kiowas between Apiatan and Chatlekaungky, Lone Wolf's brother.[33] But despite the political maneuverings and tribal factionalism, the tribes were substantially united on one front: opposition to the Jerome agreement. At every council after the commissioners left the reservation the subject was raised and debated, and the three tribes sent frequent petitions and memorials to Congress expressing their opposition to the proposal. By the time the agreement reached Congress, however, the primary concern was not the consent or even the welfare of the Indians. A clamor to "open" the Kiowa, Comanche, and Apache reservation had brought increasing pressure on Congress to "ratify" any "agreement," regardless of the tribes' view.

RATIFYING ALLOTMENTS: THE ACT OF JUNE 6, 1900

Congress received the Jerome agreement in January 1893, three months after the commissioners had finished collecting signatures. Transmitted by President Benjamin Harrison, the text of the agreement was accompanied by a letter from Commissioner Atkins as well as Agent Day's certification that 456 of 562 eligible Indians had signed the document. The report did acknowledge the tribes' position on the price of the land, but made no effort to urge Congress to consider it.

> The Indians upon this reservation seem to believe (but whether from exercise of their own judgment or the advice of others the commission cannot determine) that their surplus land is worth two

and one half million dollars, and Congress may be induced to give them that much of it. Therefore, in compliance with their request, we report that they desire to be heard through an attorney and a delegation to Washington upon that question, the agreement signed, however, to be effective upon ratification no matter what Congress may do with their appeal for the extra half million dollars.[34]

Although it was more than seven years before the agreement was ratified, the debate began quickly. The first bill was introduced in September 1893, by Delegate Dennis Flynn from the Oklahoma Territory. In October, anthropologist James Mooney of the Bureau of American Ethnology wrote to the Indian Rights Association to enlist their support in the fight to prevent ratification. Mooney noted that "the need is urgent and immediate, as boomer organizations are already made up in all the important border towns of Texas, Oklahoma, and Kansas, and resolutions calling for immediate ratification are already before Congress."[35]

The three tribes held a general council in the same month and sent another memorial to Congress, this one drafted by a Washington, D.C. attorney, W.C. Shelley. Signed by 323 members of the tribe, the memorial set forth the history of "mendacity, fraud and coercion" in the dealings of the Cherokee Commission, and repudiated the agreement. The memorialists attacked the validity of the signatures, noting particularly that the list included at least seven of the non-Indian "squaw men" who stood to gain their own allotments under the agreement and who were clearly ineligible as signers.[36] The tribes also argued that, contrary to the assertions of the commissioners, allotments under the Dawes Act would have to conform to the Medicine Lodge Treaty, which provided for allotments of 320 acres, not 160. They also protested that their annual income from the current leases was much greater than the interest that would be generated from the funds involved in the sale, and complained that their demand for an additional half million dollars had not been recommended by the commissioners as promised.

After Herbert Welsh of the Indian Rights Association had checked with the references Mooney offered, Charles Painter, the IRA Washington agent, went to work lobbying against the bill. Despite the opposition of Commissioner Browning, Lone Wolf, Quanah, and a delegation representing the tribes arrived in Washington in March 1894 to meet with congressional committees about the bill.

Lone Wolf and Quanah testified before a subcommittee of the House Indian Affairs Committee.[37]

The legislation was blocked in Congress, but new bills were introduced in each succeeding session. Five years after Delegate Flynn's bill failed, a new campaign to ratify the agreement began to gain momentum. With increasing pressure from the western delegations to open more reservation land, two bills reached the House floor during the Fifty-fifth Congress in 1898.

The committee reports for both bills recommended an amended version of the bill for passage. The amendments to the agreement proposed in the House provided for an additional 480,000 tract—larger than the total area of the Indian allotments—to be retained by the tribes. They also removed Agent Day and Lieutenant Scott from the list of beneficiaries. Although the reports acknowledged the strong Indian opposition to the bills, the committee's sentiment seemed closer to the views expressed by the governor of the Oklahoma Territory, with which the reports ended: "I cannot refrain from urging . . . that these reservations be at once opened to settlement. They embrace some of the finest land in Oklahoma and would be capable of supporting a large population."[38]

The House bill to ratify the agreement with amendments passed in May 1898, and the debate shifted to the Senate, where the Kiowas had more aggressive political allies. Two Senate resolutions in January 1899 requested more information about the matter from the Secretary of Interior, and resulted in important documents being introduced into the Senate record. In response to the Senate request, Secretary C. N. Bliss and Indian Affairs Commissioner W. A. Jones sent letters expressing their view that the agreement should not be ratified because of the tribes' persistent opposition and because the allotments as proposed were too small to support families by livestock grazing and the land too poor to be suitable for agriculture. Bliss recommended that a new agreement be negotiated through an Indian inspector, and suggested that in any event the size of the allotments be doubled.[39]

Secretary Bliss also enclosed reports received from the Kiowa and Comanche reservation during the past five years which illustrated the depth of the tribes' opposition. A report dated August 1893 by Captain Hugh G. Brown, who was then acting agent on the reservation, described the aftermath of the Jerome Commission's visit very simply: "The Kiowas, Comanches and Apaches are almost without exception, now that they understand it, uniformly opposed to the agreement."[40]

Two days later Secretary Bliss reported the census figures that indicated that less than three-fourths of the adult Indian men had signed the agreement. A tribal roll, prepared less than three months after Agent Day's count of 562 adult men, listed 725 Indian men over age 18 and 639 men over 21.[41]

The material Bliss delivered to the Senate included a series of letters collected by the Indian Rights Association from federal geologists and hydrographers attesting to the region's poor soils and uncertain climate. When the Senate Committee on Indian Affairs reported favorably on the House bill in February, the Association responded within a week by issuing "An Appeal on Behalf of the Apaches, Kiowas, and Comanches" aimed at stopping the bill. The pamphlet, which included the same series of letters Bliss had sent to the Senate, argued that "no less than four hundred and eighty (480) acres should be alloted to each member of the tribes,"—three times what the Jerome agreement provided.[42]

The Association pamphlet was accompanied by a letter from Herbert Welsh, founder of the Indian Rights Association, to newspaper editors asking that the matter be publicized. Welsh argued that the question had a broad significance to a nation "upon the very verge of a colonial policy" in Cuba, the Philippines and Puerto Rico. He argued that if justice were not done the Indians, "we shall increase the chances that our management of outside dependent peoples will be conducted in the same unhappy way."

No bill passed in the Senate that term, but the exchange of volleys put both Indians and the Oklahoma boomers on notice that the Senate fight would be crucial. The tribes held another council in October, and drafted another petition to Congress, signed this time by 571 Indian men, 25 percent more than the original number of signatures on the Jerome document.[43]

The tribes' final memorial was transmitted to the House and Senate when the Fifty-Sixth Congress convened in January 1900. Accompanied by letters from Commissioner Jones and Ethan A. Hitchcock, the new Interior Secretary, the petition was a clear and simple statement of the Indians' repudiation.

> [E]ach and every one of us who signed that treaty do solemnly declare that if we had not been deceived we would never have signed it. . . .
>   We now realize that if this treaty is ratified we are doomed to destruction as a people and brought to the same impoverished

condition to which the Cheyenne and Arapahoe and other Indian tribes have been brought from the effects of prematurely opening their reservations for the settlement of white men among them.[44]

The tribes proposed an alternative to the Jerome agreement, asking that if they could not "be granted the privilege of keeping our reservation," that a new treaty be made which would provide sufficient land to graze cattle. The memorial also pointed out that the tribes were making a good-faith effort to conform to the demands of the new order.

> [W]e are not drunkards, nor do we molest the property of the whites who have located on lands adjoining ours. We have placed our children in schools provided by the Government and Christian societies . . . these several schools, having a capacity for 700 pupils, are kept filled with our children . . . [W]e point to these facts as evidence that we are striving in the right ways to fit our people for the day we realize must come, when their children will be dependent upon their own intelligence and physical strength for the support of themselves and their kindred.[45]

At the same time the Kiowas, Comanches, and Apaches were drafting their petition to Congress, the whites located around the reservation borders began collecting affidavits to submit to the Senate. The testimony compiled from hundred of eager boomers sought primarily to rebut the argument that the land was unfit for farming.[46]

The legislative debate had by this point shifted from the issue of allotment and opening the reservation to a battle over acreage. Under the original Jerome agreement, the tribes would have been permitted to keep only 453,000 acres, or about 15 percent of their reservation land. The IRA and Interior Department proposals to grant larger allotments meant there would be less land available for non-Indian settlement; these revisions were stridently opposed by the "boomers."

In February 1900, the House proponents of ratification tried a new approach, and added their two-year-old bill as a rider to another Senate Indian bill that concerned the Fort Hall Reservation in Idaho.[47] After the amended Fort Hall bill passed the House, it returned to the Senate, where Senator O. H. Platt of Connecticut, a loyal sympathizer of the Indian Rights Association, requested a conference on the amendment. Platt lost his bid to stop the legislation, however, and the bill passed the Senate without debate at the end of the session.[48] No words in the title of the Act of June 6, 1900 indicated that Section VI was a ratification of the long-disputed Jerome agreement. The ratification legislation amended the original Jerome agreement in several critical ways, but the amendments were never submitted to the three tribes for their approval.[49]

The legislative history of the ratification demonstrates that the interests of the tribes were sacrificed for a politically expedient result. Congress had been clearly informed that the tribes did not consent to the terms of the agreement: even if the number of initial signatures were sufficient, the "agreement" was repudiated time and again by the members of the tribes, eventually by a greater number than had originally signed.

For almost seven years the Indian Rights Association, architects and firm supporters of allotment, had worked to block ratification because it was against the interests of the tribes. The Association's opposition came both from a practical assessment—that the allotments were too small to be successful—and from the principle that the tribes' treaty required their consent before federal legislation could modify the Indians' property rights.

Proponents of the bill were hardly without influential friends; the "boomers" in Kansas and the Oklahoma Territory found a powerful ally in the railroads. For decades, the railroad lobby had posed a serious threat to tribal rights and interests, and different Indian nations had already suffered substantial legislative defeats at their hands.[50] For the Kiowas, Comanches, and Apaches, the story was no different. After losing the Senate fight, Samuel Brosius, Washington agent for the Indian Rights Association, commented that the bill had been railroaded through Congress, adding: "The word 'railroad' is used advisedly, since it is chiefly by reason of the efforts of the Chicago, Rock Island and Pacific railroad officers that the legislation was secured."[51]

THE END OF THE ROAD:
LONE WOLF V. HITCHCOCK

A month after Congress ratified the revised Jerome agreement, a delegation from the three tribes visited Washington to argue for a better bill. The group met briefly with President McKinley, but were informed that the matter would not be reconsidered. Once convinced that the bill would not be repealed, the tribes split again into factions. Lone Wolf and Eschiti were aligned with a group of Kiowas and Comanches unwilling to concede defeat, while Quanah Parker, Apiatan, and Apache John resigned themselves to allotment and fell in line as the officially recognized "principal chiefs" of the three tribes.[52]

It is hardly surprising that a leader like Quanah chose to acquiesce once allotment had been ratified. Much of his power and prestige was based on his ability to exploit the essentially colonial system of the reservation. From the Texas cattlemen through a whole string of Indian agents, Quanah's cooperation and his ability to bring his many followers around had been richly rewarded.[53]

It is less clear why Lone Wolf and Eschiti chose to risk their status as tribal leaders by continuing to oppose allotment. Cooperation with the federal bureaucracy had already become a sort of litmus test for tribal leadership, with the federal government in a strong position to select and support the "chiefs" among the tribes. One common method was to appoint some tribal leaders to special positions: Lone Wolf, Quanah, and White Man sat as judges on the reservation's Indian Court from 1886 to 1901, and were paid a salary of $10 per month.[54]

Perhaps because they had no leader like Quanah Parker, the Kiowas had not been as cooperative as the Comanches. Or perhaps stronger feelings among the Kiowas led Lone Wolf to become a different sort of leader. In any event, his efforts to block allotment earned Lone Wolf the enormous hostility of the agent, James Randlett, and before long he lost his status as a principal chief of the Kiowas.[55]

When Lone Wolf arrived with a delegation in Washington in June 1901, after retaining former congressman and federal judge William Springer as an attorney, his reception was none too warm. Springer wrote on June 23 to the Indian Rights Association requesting funds to pay the Indians' way home. Springer wrote, "Secretary Hitchcock will not recognize the delegates who have come to Washington to avert this outrage, and nine full blood Kiowas and Comanches are now here without money or means to return to their reservation."[56]

Matthew K. Sniffen quickly responded that the Association would be glad to send a committee member to see Hitchcock and President McKinley. The next day, however, Sniffen received a letter from Francis E. Leupp, a journalist who had served as the Association's Washington agent. Leupp wrote in confidence, urging that the Association act cautiously so far as Springer was concerned; he suggested that the lawyer was down on his luck and short of funds.[57]

Later the same week, N. Dubois Miller of the Association wrote to Secretary Hitchcock to ask for a clarification of the situation. The Secretary's prompt response reflected both Leupp's skepticisms and Lone Wolf's fading status. Hitchcock stated that he had twice received the delegation, but only unofficially. "This so-called delegation," wrote Hitchcock, "was wholly unauthorized to come here by his tribe." Hitchcock also commented that Springer had afterward attempted to collect a substantial fee for representing the Indians.[58]

Springer had filed a complaint for Lone Wolf in the equity division of the Supreme Court of the District of Columbia on June 6, naming Hitchcock a defendant. The suit sought to restrain the Interior Department from carrying out the provisions of the allotment act, arguing that the acts of Congress were "unconstitutional and void" and a violation of "solemn treaty provisions." On June 17, Springer amended the bill of complaint to include seven additional Indians as plaintiffs, and stated that the eight had been authorized to act as delegates of the three tribes at a general council held at Anadarko from June 3 to June 7.[59]

In a ruling handed down on June 20, the court denied a preliminary injunction and rejected Springer's contention that the acts deprived the tribes of their property without due process of law. The opinion by Justice A. C. Bradley in *Lone Wolf v. Hitchcock* described the history of the allotment legislation as "the usual process," and held that misunderstanding, deception, and lack of tribal consent were not relevant to the court's determination, the matter being one for exclusive consideration by Congress. As for the process due the tribes in Congress, "It is to be assumed that they [the tribes' objections] were carefully considered and determined with due regard to the public interests of and the rights of the Indian."[60]

On June 26, Springer appealed the court's final decree, but by the time the Court of Appeals heard the case the opening of the Kiowa, Comanche, and Apache reservation was an accomplished fact. By proclamation of President McKinley on July 4, 1901, the date of opening was set for August 6, 1901.[61]

The three tribes' reservation was one of the last to be opened in the "twin territories," and generated enormous interest. Registration of land-hungry whites began on July 10, and after two weeks more than

150,000 people had registered for the 13,000 allotments available. Before the date of opening, a lottery was held to select those who would be allowed to claim 160-acre homesteads at a price of $1.75 per acre.[62]

The *fait accompli* of 13,000 non-Indian homesteads cannot have helped Lone Wolf and Springer in their uphill legal battle. On December 4, 1901, the Court of Appeals of the District of Columbia rejected their appeal, with a broad holding about the legal effect of treaties and the status of Indian property rights. Chief Justice Alvey agreed with the lower court that Indian treaties were beyond the authority of the courts and found "question of mere policy in the treatment of Indians . . . the function alone of the legislative branch."[63]

Alvey considered this sufficient ground to reject the tribes' suit, but went on to consider the property rights of tribes to their treaty land: "Such lands and reservations are held by the Indians subject to the control and dominion of the United States, and such Indian tribes . . . have no title in the lands they occupy . . . their right is simply to occupy, at the will of the Government and under its protection."[64]

Samuel Brosius discussed the significance of the court's decision in his report from the Washington office for February 1902: "This is a sweeping decision, and under it no tribe of Indians have any title to land excepting such as hold in fee simple. The only tribes holding by fee simple, or patent from the United States, are Osages and the Five Civilized Tribes."[65] Brosius recommended that the Association finance an appeal to the Supreme Court because of the broad ramifications the decision would have on "all the other cases pending which affect the rights of Indians."

The Association's Executive Committee approved Brosius' suggestion and allocated an initial $400 for the project.[66]

In March, the Association retained Hampton L. Carson, a professor at the University of Pennsylvania Law School, to assist Springer in arguing the case. Carson was well known to the members of the Court, having just completed a history commissioned for the its centennial that included biographies of each Justice. The Association counted on his stature and skill, and Springer was grateful for Carson's help. Shortly after being retained, Carson gave the Association this evaluation: "The case is much more serious and difficult than I had imagined for the legal obstacles standing in the way are formidable. The chief question is whether the case is one within the power of the courts to relieve."[67]

In June 1902, the Indian Rights Association published a pamphlet in the hope of "arousing the public conscience to the danger that threatens." Written by Washington agent Samuel Brosius, the pamphlet charged that the legislative and executive branches "are seeking to enter upon a new policy in the treatment of our Indian wards. . . . The tendency seems to favor the abrogation and violation of solemn treaty obligations." Brosius identified the central issue as "whether Congress can divest an Indian tribe of its right of occupancy without tribal sanction," and found one answer to the question: "The bulwark of our liberties is based upon the theory of consent of the governed. This applies with equal force to the Indians to-day, and emphasizes the need of the red man wielding the ballot for his own protection."[68]

Brosius visited the Kiowa, Comanche, and Apache reservation during his summer 1902 field trip while the case was before the Supreme Court. During his visit, Agent Randlett told him that Lone Wolf and about 200 others had turned down the first per capita payment for their land. Randlett was "very bitter against Judge Springer for taking up Lone Wolf's cause."[69] Brosius explained to Randlett that the Association had become involved at the final stages because "so broad a question was now involved, threatening the property rights of all tribes."

Brosius reported that he had "found to my surprise that Lone Wolf is not the conservative and backward Indian that he has been reported to be by the Indian Agent and others. . . . Randlett gives Lone Wolf a very bad record: That he tries to keep up the old Indian customs, etc. I find the opposite to be the fact."[70] Brosius learned from a missionary family that the Kiowa leader and his followers were members of the Baptist Church, and "a hundred years ahead of his people in the matter of education and religion."[71] Brosius' report becomes still more surprising when one compares Randlett's complaints about Lone Wolf with his apparent toleration of Quanah Parker. Hagan reports that although Quanah had acquired a wide reputation as a model "progressive" tribal leader, his lifestyle was somewhat inconsistent, including several wives, long hair worn in braids, and participation in the peyote religion.[72] Lone Wolf's resistance to the agreement apparently overshadowed all other considerations when judging his behavior.

Agent Randlett, however, had not been appeased by Brosius' explanation that the Association was supporting Lone Wolf because of the national implications of the court decision. In September the agent wrote angrily to the commissioner of Indian Affairs charging that the Indian Rights Association and the Board of Indian Commissioners had "developed as allies of grafting attorneys who seem bent upon robbing the Indians of the magnanimous provisions made for them by the Act of Congress of June 6, 1900." With perhaps greater accuracy, Randlett described the effects of the controversy as "engendering a want of confidence and distrust which is disturbing the minds of Indians that has raised the question *What* calamity have we to expect next?"[73] The answer would come within four months, with the Supreme Court's calamitous ruling.

The challenge that confronted Carson and Springer in the Supreme Court was to distinguish Lone Wolf's case from a string of recent Supreme Court decisions that had denied the obligation to enforce Indian treaty rights. For the government, the task was easier; Assistant Attorney General Willis Van Devanter, who would himself be named to the Supreme Court bench in 1910, argued simply that the exercise of legislative authority in question was no different than others the Court had already upheld in previous cases.

The legal momentum was on the government's side. Beginning with *United States v. Kagama* in 1886,[74] which upheld the extension of federal criminal jurisdiction to crimes committed by Indians on Indian land, the Supreme Court had developed a doctrine that transformed Indian nations from independent sovereigns into dependent wards. The Court in *Kagama* acknowledged that the tribes' increasing helplessness was due largely to the federal government's dealings with them, yet the *Kagama* decision became the basis for attributing Congress even greater power to act on behalf of the tribes as a trustee or guardian.

In some of the cases following *Kagama*, the Court acquiesced to federal legislation which went far beyond the "duty of protection" invoked in *Kagama*. The post-*Kagama* cases interpreted the federal trust power as a blanket authority to preempt tribal government powers and functions as the national interests of the United States might dictate. Before *Lone Wolf*, the Court had not addressed treaty-recognized property rights, but allowed Congress to grant railroad companies unauthorized rights-of-way across tribal land,[75] to lease tribal resources for development without the tribe's consent,[76] and to fix the rolls of tribal membership.[77]

In many of these decisions the Court optimistically noted the government's moral obligation to act in the tribes' best interests, but found nothing inconsistent with applying a presumption of good faith and ignoring any indications to the contrary. One case, subsequently quoted by the Court in *Lone Wolf*, described a presumption that "the United States would be governed by such considerations of justice as would control a Christian people in their treatment of an ignorant and dependent race."[78]

The cumulative effect of the high court decisions was to reinterpret tribal property rights and political authority as a commodity granted to the tribes by the federal government. This interpretation was a complete shift from the early decisions of the Supreme Court under John Marshall, which recognized inherent sovereignty in the Indian tribes and viewed treaties as narrow delegations from the tribe to the United States of specific and limited powers.[79]

That Indian treaties—or those with any foreign nations—were not a subject for judicial interference had long been established in federal law as a corollary to the "political question" rule.[80] The Court's innovations in the wake of *Kagama* extended the political question rule to Congress' newly-discovered trustee "power" in Indian affairs, creating in effect a trust with no fiduciary obligations or limits on the trustee's power.

Before Lone Wolf's appeal reached the Supreme Court, the trap was set and ready to spring shut. Carson and Springer attempted both in their brief and in their oral argument to draw a line between political matters and property rights, urging that Congress had plenary power only where political questions were concerned.[81]

Springer and Carson argued in their brief in *Lone Wolf* that tribal consent was required by the treaties and the Dawes Act,[82] and called the taking of land from the Indians without their consent "an act without a precedent." To explain why the tribes' property rights should be respected when other tribal rights had been held abrogable, the lawyers argued that the Indians' treaty-recognized title was a vested property right, bringing it under the rule that legislative acts impairing vested rights are unconstitutional.[83]

The formalist argument was in the tradition of nineteenth-century property law, where the protection accorded any interest was capsulized in the legal label used to characterize it. Springer and Carson disputed the appeals court's labeling of the tribes as "tenants at will" of the United States; rather, they insisted that Supreme Court decisions had identified the tribes as "life tenants," the latter being a freehold estate, one of the magic words which brought it to the level of vested property right.[84]

Van Devanter's brief relied on the recent precedent and a straightforward argument: that Indians were wards of the government, that treaty-making was a political function, and that the Court had already upheld congressional "administration" of Indian property by direct legislative enactment. For good measure, the government brief pointed out that whether Congress had ever taken tribal land without tribal consent did not answer the question of its power to do so, and argued that the Indians had consented to the act as passed by accepting their allotments. Van Devanter also disputed the characterization of the Indian right of occupancy that the appellants developed, and argued further that the three tribes had not been deprived of their property; rather, there had been merely a change in the form of the assets, from land to money.[85]

Oral argument was held on October 23, 1902, with Springer and Carson sharing the duties. Springer wrote to Matthew Sniffen of the Association two weeks later with glowing praise for Carson's "clear and eloquent" closing argument and an optimistic assessment of the result.[86] Samuel Brosius wrote to Sniffen with the same enthusiasm, relating the account of an attorney who had heard Carson's argument and called it "the finest he had ever heard" before the Supreme Court, with the Court "a unit in paying Carson the closest attention." Brosius' acquaintance reported that the justices were "listless even to rudeness" during Van Devanter's argument, and "kept propounding questions to show they did not agree."[87]

Brosius' optimism proved unfounded, however; when the Supreme Court issued its opinion on January 5, 1903, the decision fit squarely in line with the preceding cases.

> We must presume that Congress acted in perfect good faith in dealing with the Indians of which complaint is made . . . In any event, as Congress possessed full power in the matter, the judiciary cannot question or inquire into the motives which prompted enactment of this legislation. If injury was occasioned, which we do not wish to be understood as implying, by the use made of Congress of its power, relief must be sought by an appeal to that party for redress and not to the courts.[88]

This ingenuous suggestion that the tribes appeal to Congress for relief shields the harsher truth evident in the facts before the Court in Lone Wolf's case. Since the tribes had used every possible means over a period of almost eight years to prevent passage of a ratification bill, their hope of "relief" from Congress was clearly meaningless.

In this context, the full import of *Lone Wolf v. Hitchcock* was immediately clear: all aspects of tribal political and property rights were now subject to radical changes at the whim of the legislative branch. At best, tribes might retain rights only so long as more powerful political pressure-groups had no interest in their Indian resources and no objection to their continued existence.

The final defeat of Indian rights in the courts was assessed by the Indian Rights Association at an executive committee meeting two days after the decision. The minutes of the meeting report that "Mr. Welsh suggested that in view of the uniformly unfavorable decision rendered on the Indian cases—which have cost a great deal of money—the Association ought to be very cautious about further appeals to the courts.[89]

The denial of judicial remedies created urgent new business in Washington for groups like the Association. In the next session of Congress, Senators and Representatives from western states moved to implement the broad power accorded them by the Court, and the "Friends of the Indian" scrambled to convince Congress of its "moral obligation." The Association was particularly active in fighting measures to allot the Rosebud Sioux reservation and to appropriate Chippewa timber resources.[90]

Both of these bills were eventually defeated, but the hectic round of lobbying set the pattern for the future. With no possibility of judicial reversal, every legislative battle to fend off treaty abrogation became crucially important. Without representation as tribes in Congress, and without the wealth required to support massive lobbies on their behalf, Indians have no assurance even today that their fundamental interests in property and political autonomy will be respected or even considered in Congress.

Lone Wolf's legacy lies not so much in the legal doctrine that bears his name, but in the dogged refusal to admit defeat that still characterizes native advocates who must deal with the federal government. The cast of characters has changed—today's uphill legislative battles are fought each term by Indian lobbyists, such as the representatives of the National Congress of American Indians or the Native American Rights Fund—but the problem remains the same.

Three-quarters of a century after *Lone Wolf*, the contours of the plenary power doctrine remain largely intact. Recent developments in federal Indian law have blunted some of the sharper outrages of the plenary power rule; several Supreme Court opinions have undermined the theory that Indian affairs are unreviewable as a type of "political question," and the Court has in a few cases scrutinized federal Indian legislation on constitutional grounds.[91] Ironically, although the plenary power rule of *Lone Wolf* continues to stand,[92] the argument made by Carson and Springer has been vindicated: treaty-recognized property rights are now legally distinguished from the "right of occupancy" of aboriginal title, and in a limited range of cases treaty title to property is now considered sufficiently vested to be protected by the Fifth Amendment.[93]

Despite these modest doctrinal advances, the courts continue to accord Congress the authority to regulate the internal affairs of Indian tribes and the power to abrogate venerable treaty obligations. New bills are introduced in each Congress seeking to legislate away Indian treaty provisions,[94] and despite occasional successes in the courts, Indian tribes still cannot rely on judicial review for protection against congressional assaults on their tribal property and governments.

N   O   T   E   S

1. Angie Debo, *A History of the Indians of the United States* (Norman, Okla.: University of Oklahoma Press, 1970), p. 253.
2. 24 Stat. 388, Feb. 8, 1887.
3. Indian Rights Association, *Twenty-First Annual Report*, (Philadelphia: Indian Rights Association, 1903), p. 24.
4. Medicine Lodge Treaty, ratified Aug. 25, 1868, 15 Stat. 581.
5. Proceedings of the Councils held by the Cherokee Commission at Fort Sill and Anadarko, Indian Territory, beginning Sept. 28, 1892; Senate Executive Doc. no. 77, 55th Cong., 3d. sess. (1899),p. 9.
6. See generally William T. Hagan, *United States—Comanche Relations: The Reservation Years* (New Haven, Connecticut: Yale University Press, 1976).
7. Kiowa author N. Scott Momaday comments in his memoir, *The Names* (New York: Harper Colophon Books, 1976), p. 26, on his great-grandfather, who was the younger Lone Wolf, and on his grand-

father, Mammedaty: "Mammedaty was the son of Guipagho the Younger and of Keahdinekeah, one of the wives of Pohdlohk. His grandfather Guipagho the Elder was a famous chief, for whom the town of Lone Wolf, Oklahoma, is named, and like his father, Mammedaty lived in the reflected glory of a large reputation." The elder Lone Wolf was imprisoned at Fort Sill and at Fort Marion, Florida, from 1875 to 1879, following the Kiowas' last military resistance. He died in a malaria epidemic in 1879, a year after his return to the reservation. See W. S. Nye, *Carbine and Lance* (Norman, Okla.: University of Oklahoma Press, 1943), pp. 188, 193, 231, and 235.

8. *Ibid.*
9. Senate Executive Doc. no. 17, 52d Cong., 2d sess. (1893).
10. Proceedings, p. 18.
11. Proceedings, p. 10.
12. Proceedings, p. 19–20.
13. Proceedings, p. 19–20.
14. Proceedings, p. 19–20.
15. Proceedings, p. 14.
16. Proceedings, p. 22–23.
17. Proceedings, p. 11–12, 18, 34.
18. Proceedings, p. 33. Hagan points out that the average annual rainfall in the region was less than 20 inches and the amount of land required to graze one cow was at least 15 acres—factors that demonstrated what a slim chance of self sufficiency the Commission's proposal offered. Hagan, *The Reservation Years*, p. 207.
19. Hagan, *The Reservation Years*, pp. 203–204, 210, 214.
20. Proceedings, p. 30.
21. Proceedings, pp. 34, 37.
22. Proceedings, pp. 17, 42.
23. Proceedings, pp. 38–39.
24. Hagan, *The Reservation Years*, p. 210.
25. Proceedings, pp. 40–43.
26. Proceedings, pp. 41–42.
27. Proceedings, pp. 43–47.
28. Proceedings, p. 48.
29. Proceedings, p. 48.
30. Hagan, *The Reservation Years*, p. 251.
31. Letter from Captain H. Brown, Aug. 28, 1893, reprinted in Senate Doc. no. 77, 55th Cong., 3d sess. (1899), p. 6; see also the Transcript of Record for *Lone Wolf V. Hitchcock*, Supreme Court of the United States, October Term 1901, Docket no. 601 (Bill of Complaint filed in the Supreme Court for the District of Columbia).
32. Senate Doc. no. 84, 55th Cong., 3d sess. (1899).
33. Hagan, *The Reservation Years*, pp. 216–249.

34. Senate Executive Doc. no. 17, 52nd Cong., 2d sess. (1893). This provision was read to the council at Fort Sill by Commissioner Jerome; Proceedings, p. 32.

35. Letter from James Mooney to Herbert Welsh, Indian Rights Association Papers, Oct. 17, 1893, Microfilm reel 133; reprinted in Senate Doc. no. 77, 55th Cong., 3d sess. (1899), pp. 7–8.

36. Senate Miscellaneous Doc. no. 102, 53d Cong., 2d sess. (1894).

37. Hagan, *The Reservation Years*, pp. 253–54.

38. House Report no. 1281 and House Report no. 431, 53d Cong., 2d sess. (1898).

39. Senate Doc. no. 77, 55th Cong., 3d sess. (1899).

40. *Ibid.*

41. Senate Doc. no. 84, 55th Cong. 3d sess. (1899).

42. *An Appeal on Behalf of the Apaches, Kiowas, and Comanches*, Indian Rights Association Papers: pamphlet no. 51; Microfilm reel 102, Feb. 1899.

43. Senate Doc. no. 76, 56th Cong., 1st sess. (1900).

44. *Ibid.*

45. *Ibid.*

46. Senate Doc. no. 170, 56th Cong., 1st sess. (1900).

47. House Report no. 419, 56th Cong., 1st sess. (1900).

48. 1900 Senate Journal at 450, Act of 6 June 1900, 31 Stat. 672.

49. The amendments are detailed in Lone Wolf's complaint, Transcript of Record, pp. 9–11.

50. See, for example, the discussion in Ira C. Clarke, *Then Came the Railroads* (Norman, Okla.: University of Oklahoma Press, 1958), pp. 119–130.

51. Indian Rights Association, *Twentieth Annual Report* (1902), p. 38.

52. Hagan, *The Reservation Years*, pp. 262–263.

53. *Id.* p. 181, 208, 236–237. Quanah's own spread included 100 acres farmed by sharecroppers and hired hands and enough grazing land to support 400 to 500 head of cattle. The Cherokee Commissioners visited Quanah's home during the negotiations at Fort Sill, and were highly impressed by his two-story home, ten-room house and its comfortable furnishings. Proceedings, p. 32.

54. Nye, *Carbine and Lance*, p. 260.

55. Compare James Mooney, *The Ghost Dance Religion and the Sioux Outbreak of 1890* (Washington, D.C.: Bureau of American Ethnology, 1896; Chicago & London: University of Chicago Press, 1965), p. 311 ("Sketch of the Kiowa" in 1893 notes that "their present chief is Gu'i-pa'go, Lone Wolf"), with James Mooney, *Bulletin of the Bureau of American Ethnology* (1907), pp. 699–700 (Entry for "Kiowa" tribe states that "their present chief is Gui-pa'go, 'Lone

Wolf,' but his title is disputed by Apiatan"). Quanah, on the other hand, was still a wealthy and much-remarked chief in 1905, when he was invited to ride in Teddy Roosevelt's inaugural parade. Hagan, *The Reservation Years*.

56. Letter from William Springer to Herbert Welsh, June 23, 1901; Indian Rights Association Papers, Microfilm reel 134.

57. Letter from Francis Leupp to Matthew K. Sniffen, June 25, 1901; Indian Rights Association Papers, Microfilm reel 134.

58. Letters from Ethan Hitchcock to N. Dubois Miller, July 3, 1901; Indian Rights Association Papers, Microfilm reel 134.

59. Transcript of Record for *Lone Wolf*, pp. 13–14, 20.

60. Transcript of Record for *Lone Wolf*, p. 30.

61. 32 Stat. *Appx. Proc.* 11, July 4, 1901.

62. Grant Foreman, *A History of Oklahoma* (Norman, Okla.: University of Oklahoma Press, 1942), pp. 248–250.

63. Transcript of Record for *Lone Wolf*, p. 42.

64. Transcript of Record for *Lone Wolf*, p. 43.

65. Report of the Washington Agent, March 4, 1902; Indian Rights Association Papers, Office Reports, Microfilm reel 101.

66. Executive Committee Meeting Minutes, Mar. 5, 1902, Indian Rights Association Papers, Microfilm reel 99.

67. Quoted in letter from Samuel Brosius to Matthew Sniffen, March 18, 1902; Indian Rights Association Papers, Letterpress Book, vol. 16, pp. 496–497, Microfilm reel 75.

68. Samuel Brosius, *A New Indian Policy—The Red Man's Rights in Jeopardy*, Indian Rights Association Papers, pamphlet no. 62, Microfilm reel 102, June 1902.

69. Quoted in letter from Matthew Sniffen to William Springer, Sept. 25, 1902, Indian Rights Association Papers, Letterpress Book, vol. 16, p. 696, Microfilm reel 75.

70. Sniffen, Sept. 25, 1902 letter, IRA Papers.

71. Samuel Brosius, March 18, 1902 letter, IRA Papers.

72. Hagan, *The Reservation Years*, 279.

73. Letter from Agent Randlett to Commissioner of Indian Affairs, Sept. 1, 1902 (copy in the Indian Rights Association Papers with a letter from Brosius, Oct. 20, 1902, Microfilm reel 16).

74. *United States v. Kagama*, 118 U.S. 375 (1886).

75. *Cherokee Nation v. Southern Kansas Railway Co., 135 U.S. 641 (1890)*.

76. *Cherokee Nation v. Hitchcock*, 187 U.S. 294 (1902).

77. *Stephens v. Cherokee Nation*, 174 U.S. 445 (1899).

78. *Beecher v. Wetherby*, 95 U.S. 517, 525 (1877).

79. See *Cherokee Nation v. Georgia*, 30 U.S. (5 Pet.) 1 (1831) and *Worcester v. Georgia*, 31 U.S. (6 Pet.) 515 (1832). The shift in legal doctrine is

discussed in Russel L. Barsh & James Y. Henderson, *The Road: Indian Tribes and Political Liberty* (Berkeley: University of California Press, 1980), pp. 85–95.

80. *The Cherokee Tobacco*, 78 U.S. (11 Wall) 616 (1870).

81. Transcript of Record, Brief and Argument of Appellants, Oct. 13, 1902.

82. The Dawes Act provides that tribal consent to allotment will be secured "in conformity with the statute or treaty under which the reservation is held." General Allotment Act, 24 Stat. 388 (1887), codified at 25 U.S.C. §. 331 *et seq.* (1976). This is pointed out in the appellants' Brief p. 59.

83. Appellants' Brief, p. 30.

84. The debate can be traced to Chief Justice John Marshall's opinion in *Johnson v. McIntosh*, 21 U.S. (8 Wheat) 543 (1823), which labeled aboriginal Indian title a "right of occupancy," defeasible only by the sovereign. The phrase Marshall thus invented to rationalize two systems of land tenure became a source of confusion in cases such as *Lone Wolf*, and in more recent times has been the source of a legal distinction between aboriginal and treaty-recognized title. See Newton, "At the Whim of the Sovereign: Aboriginal Title Reconsidered," *Hastings Law Journal* vol. 31, p. 1215 (1980). In *Lone Wolf*, however, the court makes no distinction between the "right of occupancy" rule of the aboriginal title cases and the situation where tribes hold title under agreements with the United States.

85. Transcript of Record, Brief for Appellees, Oct. 18, 1902.

86. Letter from William Springer to Matthew K. Sniffen, Nov. 10, 1902, Indian Rights Association Papers, Microfilm reel 16.

87. Letter from Samuel Brosius to Matthew K. Sniffen, Nov. 17, 1902, Indian Rights Association Papers, Microfilm reel 16.

88. *Lone Wolf v. Hitchcock*, 187 U.S. 535 (1903).

89. Executive Committee Meeting Minutes, Jan. 7, 1903, Indian Rights Association Papers, Microfilm reel 99.

90. Indian Rights Association, *Twenty-Second Annual Report* (1904), p. 21. See also Philip C. Garrett, *Another "Century of Dishonor"?* Indian Rights Association Papers, pamphlet no. 68, Microfilm reel 102, Feb. 1904.

91. See generally the modern formulation of the political question doctrine in *Baker v. Carr*, 369 U.S. 186 (1962), and the rejection of the old rule in Indian cases announced in *United States v. Sioux Nation*, 448 U.S. 371 (1980) and *Delaware Tribal Business Committee v. Weeks*, 430 U.S. 73 (1977).

92. *United States v. Sioux Nation* carefully distinguished the facts in that dispute from the situation in *Lone Wolf*, which it characterized as involving " a mere change in the form of investment of tribal prop-

erty" pursuant to the federal trusteeship, and therefore not an unconstitutional taking. *Sioux Nation* at 413. See generally Comment, Federal Plenary Power in Indian Affairs after *Weeks* and *Sioux Nation*, *University of Pennsylvania Law Review*, vol. 131, p. 235 (1982).

93.   *Tee-Hit-Ton Indians v. United States*, 348 U.S. 272 (1955).
      See generally, Newton, "At the Whim of the Sovereign."
94.   See, for example, the Ancient Indian Land Claims Settlement Act, S. 2084 and H.R. 5494, 97th Cong., 2d sess. (1982), and the Steelhead Trout Protection Act, S. 874, 97th Cong., 1st sess. (1981).

I N D E X

A

A Century of Dishonor (Jackson), 4, 20, 47

Aboriginal title, 195–197; Marshall's definition of, 244 n.84

Abourezk, James (Senator), 95

Abourezk Commission. *See* American Indian Policy Review Commission

Act of August 15, 1894, 116

Act of February 15, 1929, 125

Act of February 16, 1889, 120

Act of July 14, 1956, 127

Act of July 31, 1882, 124

Act of June 6, 1900, 230–231, 236

Act of March 2, 1906, 116

Act of March 3, 1927, 121

Act of May 18, 1916, 120

Act of May 29, 1924, 121

AIPRC. *See* American Indian Policy Review Commission

Alaska Native Land Claims Settlement Act (1971), 89; provisions of, 50, 114, 207

Alaska Natives, 111; claims of, resolved, 114

Aleuts, 50

All Pueblo Council, 30, 135

Allotment Act. *See* Dawes Act; General Allotment Act

Allotment policy; effects of, 80–81, 201; implementation of, 63, 67–68, 120; provisions for individual choice, 116; reformers' beliefs about, 22; supporters and opponents of, 47–48; trust provisions of, 116; urged upon Kiowas, Comanches, and Apaches,

217–226. *See also* Assimilation policy; General Allotment Act

A Month Among the Sioux (Welsh), 21–22

American Indian Capitol Conference on Poverty, 15

American Indian Defense Association, 28, 33, 35, 135, 142

American Indian Life, 72

American Indian Movement, 87, 89, 90

American Indian Policy Review Commission, 93, 128; composition and staff of, 93–94; criticizes Indian Reorganization Act, 132–133; final report of, 94

American Indian Religious Freedom Act (1978), 52, 53, 95

American Red Cross, 14

Ancient Indian Land Claims Settlement Bill of 1982, 188

Andrus, Cecil D. (Secretary of the Interior), 94–95

Another "Century of Dishonor"?, 14

Apache, John, 232

Apaches, Jicarilla, 177

Apiatan, 225, 232

Appropriation Act of June 7, 1897, 124

Area Redevelopment Act, 81

Assimilation policy: contradictory implementation of, 119–120; as implemented by allotment, 22; as outgrowth of social Darwinism, 6; recommended by Hoover Commission, 111; reformers' debate over, 20–39. *See also* Allotment policy; General Allotment Act

Assimilative Crimes Act (1898), 109

247